Sociological Lives and Ideas
An Introduction to the Classical Theorists
Second Edition

Fred C. Pampel
University of Colorado, Boulder

Worth Publishers

Publisher: Catherine Woods
Acquisitions Editor: Erik Gilg
Marketing Manager: Scott Guile
Photo Editor: Cecilia Varas
Art Director: Babara Reingold
Cover Designer: Kevin Kall
Text Designer: Paul Lacy
Project Editor: Dana Kasowitz
Illustrations: TSI Graphics
Production Manager: Barbara Anne Seixas
Composition: TSI Graphics
Printing and Binding: RR Donnelley

Illustration credits: Karl Marx (facing p. 1), © Archive Photos; Émile Durkheim (p. 42), Corbis/Bettmann; Max Weber (p. 86), akg-images/Archiv für Kunst und Geschichte; Georg Simmel (p. 128), The Granger Collection; George Herbert Mead (p. 168), The Granger Collection; W. E. B. Du Bois (p. 210), © Corbis.

Library of Congress Control Number: 2006931434

ISBN-13: 978-0-7167-7915-5
ISBN-10: 0-7167-7915-3

© 2007 by Worth Publishers

Printed in the United States of America

First printing

Worth Publishers
41 Madison Avenue
New York, NY 10010
www.worthpublishers.com

To Jane

Contents

Preface

The second edition of this book has the same aim as the first: to explain classical sociological theory in a way that undergraduate students can understand and appreciate. It does so by emphasizing the biographies of the classical theorists and founders of sociology along with their ideas. The lives of the theorists reveal that sociology involves real people concerned about the issues and problems of their times and countries. Further, as I try to illustrate throughout the book, the issues and problems addressed by the classical theorists still have relevance today.

Following the lives of the theorists as they ask questions, devise answers, and grow as persons and scholars should make it easier for students to relate to possibly difficult ideas. Given the fascinating lives of the theorists, this biographical approach can help make otherwise dull material interesting and abstract ideas more concrete and memorable. More importantly, it provides a helpful learning device. Students often enjoy and remember biographical events and experiences. Once grasped, the biographical framework helps students organize and remember the abstract details of the theorists' concepts. Along with a list of ideas to master, many students benefit from a logically ordered scheme to organize those ideas. The lives and backgrounds of the theorists offer such a scheme.

For the same reasons, I present basic historical facts about the political and intellectual times of the theorists along with the biographical details. Basic facts about the misery of workers in England during the early stages of the Industrial Revolution, the instability of French political regimes after the Revolution of 1789, and the dictatorial political leadership of Germany before and after Bismarck help illuminate the lives and works of Marx, Durkheim, and Weber. The elementary discussions of English, French, and German history for this period of disruptive change should help students understand and remember the closely related sociological material.

While emphasizing biography and history, however, I avoid reducing the theories and ideas to mere expressions of psychological traits or personal experiences. The theories have validity and importance regardless of the motives and personalities of the theorists, and shed light on social life in a wide variety of times and places, regardless of the historical location of the theorists. Rather than attribute the content of the theories to biography, I use the personal and historical background to help explain the problems and issues the theorists selected for study and the logical progression of their thought. Background information can clarify the theorists' choices of topics and help organize the sequence of ideas without making the theories any less general or the content any less important.

I concentrate largely on five theorists—Marx, Durkheim, Weber, Simmel, and Mead. The work of each helped transform the social philosophy of earlier centuries into the modern discipline of sociology and continues to directly influence researchers and scholars today. Each developed or contributed heavily to currently active schools or traditions of social theory. Undergraduate students who gain an understanding of these five theorists will have also gained a fundamental understanding of the field of sociology. They may also come to appreciate the attraction of sociology and sociological theory to many of us. In addition, I add a new chapter to the second edition on the African-American sociologist W. E. B. Du Bois. Although not held in the same esteem by sociologists as Marx, Durkheim, or Weber, the work of Du Bois raises issues about racial inequality that the others largely neglect. By presenting his arguments about the sources and persistence of discrimination and racism in America (and by extension to many other nations across the world), the chapter highlights theories of modern race relations. Beyond that, the chapter provides a fascinating story of the life and times of a great African American and an often neglected classical social theorist.

The chapters take the following form. After an overview of the theorists' work and the problems they addressed, the first section describes the youthful experiences that shaped their lives and interests. The second section describes the historical and intellectual backgrounds of the theorists. The remaining sections, by interspersing biography and theory, follow the adult lives and ideas of the theorists in roughly chronological order. The next-to-last section also includes contemporary examples of how scholars employ the concepts and address the questions raised by each theorist. And the last section summarizes the major points of the theorists' work.

I owe thanks to many friends and colleagues who read and commented on each of the chapters. Joyce Nielsen, Jane Hegstrom, Sandy Kail, and Carrie Foote-Ardah, who reviewed each chapter, helped me enormously with their suggestions. Others commented on individual chapters, including Dan Cress, Margie Zamudio, Tom Mayer, Martha Gimenez, Oto Bartos, Gary Marx, Paul Colomy, Mathieu Deflem, Robert Alun Jones, Norman Denzin, Dmitri Shalin, Lewis Coser, Seth

Pauley, Phil Zuckerman, and Leslie Irvine. I much appreciate their advice. Finally, I thank my wife, Jane, who has read the manuscript more often than she would have liked, but each time identified unnecessary jargon and complexity.

If you have any comments or suggestions about this book, feel free to write to me at fred.pampel@colorado.edu

Fred C. Pampel
January 2006

chapter 1

The Sources of Human Misery: Karl Marx and the Centrality of Social Class

We don't have to look far to notice social inequality. At one extreme, we recognize the plight of the homeless, immigrants, residents of city slums, and victims of discrimination; millions of people live in poverty even in the richest nations in the world. At the other extreme, we see the enormous wealth of investment bankers, sports stars, and Hollywood celebrities. Similarly, the owners and top executives of businesses do much better than the workers in the organizations, stores, and factories owned by the businesses.

One generally accepted explanation of this inequality focuses on differences among individuals in talent, effort, originality, and plain luck. Although citizens show sympathy for the disadvantaged and support government programs to help them, they tend to view the world in terms of individual competition. A certain degree of inequality necessarily results between the winners and losers in this competition. Of course, much political debate exists about public spending, tax rates, and government intervention to make the competition more even, but not about the necessity of inequality.

More than 150 years ago, Karl Marx saw problems of inequality even more starkly than we do today. He entered adulthood during the early stages of industrialization, a system of economic production that created entirely new forms of disparity. The misery of men, women, and children working 16 hours a day in filthy, cold, and dark factories for starvation wages contrasted with the new wealth of business owners. Marx and others moved by the injustice of this new form of inequality looked for explanations and solutions to the problem.

Marx personally experienced deprivation in his life. Born to a prosperous Jewish lawyer in western Germany, he obtained a Ph.D. in philosophy and married his childhood sweetheart. However, after running into political trouble with German, French, and Belgian authorities, he and his family settled in London, where they lived in destitution. During these years of bitter poverty, he wrote steadily, but he survived only through the generosity of friends.

In his writings, Marx presented an original and appealing sociological perspective on economic life, inequality, and the sources of social misery, developing a social theory that identified the economic and social bases of individual behavior. Economists at the time argued that laws of supply and demand resulted from individuals making free choices in their own self-interest. In contrast, Marx argued that membership in social classes made up of workers or owners limits the freedom of individuals to act as they would like: workers must take low-wage jobs to survive, and owners must pay low wages to keep their profit high.

Rather than attributing the problems of workers and the poor to the inevitable sorting of winners and losers in economic competition among individuals, Marx attributed them to flaws and contradictions in economic and social relationships based on class differences. A new, classless system of social and economic relationships would, according to Marx, correct the problems created by private property. Regardless of individual differences, inequality and misery would exist until socialism and the public ownership of property replaced capitalism.

Given its focus on these issues, Marx's work influenced the lives of ordinary people more than that of any other sociological theorist. At one time, more than a third of the world lived under communist governments that claimed to follow Marx's ideas, while other governments and their citizens ferociously opposed both communism and Marx's ideas. The conflict between communist and free-market nations nearly resulted in nuclear war between the Soviet Union and the United States. Neither supporters nor opponents can deny the importance of Marx's writings.

The conflict over communism has, however, distorted and oversimplified Marx's ideas. More than that of other sociological theorists, his work has become associated with political movements and labels that attract some and repel others. As a result, the term *Marxism* has been employed so widely as to lose nearly all meaning. We need to cut through the political use and misuse of Marx's ideas to highlight the central contribution he made to sociology. Even if socialism or communism had never existed, we would continue to study Marx's writing, thinking, and theory because he examined the characteristics of social relationships that produce injustice, inequality, and misery.

1. TOWARD PERMANENT EXILE

There seemed little reason for Karl Marx to stay in Germany. Although he had spent all of his 25 years there, he now saw few opportunities for a career, detested the government authorities who had been harassing him, and had little desire to be near his or his fiancée's family. Combative and stubborn even as a child, he became even more bitter and angry as a young adult because of the treatment he had received from the larger world. His occupational, political, and family problems combined to encourage him to leave.

Germany in 1843 did indeed seem a poor place for Marx, who had been born in 1818 in the small town of Trier, near the Dutch border in the western German province of Westphalia. Just before his birth, Westphalia and other parts of western Germany had come under the control of the powerful eastern German state of Prussia. Although centered hundreds of miles away in Berlin and extending eastward into modern-day Poland, Prussia tightly controlled its western territories. Marx, with strong opinions and a drive to express them, was bound to offend the Prussian authorities.

At first, however, Marx seemed unconcerned with either Prussia or politics. When he started college at the University of Bonn, he distinguished himself by spending more money than his father gave him, participating in a sword duel that left a scar on his face, and being cited for "nocturnal drunkenness and riot" by the dean (Walton 1986:52). He expressed little interest in the problems of the world and seemed happy devoting his time to writing poetry. Concerned that his intelligent son had no clear purpose in his studies, Marx's father convinced him to transfer to the University of Berlin—a more serious intellectual institution of ideas and scholarship.

At the University of Berlin, Marx revealed his intellectual capabilities. Although initially studying law, he soon became attracted to philosophy. In a letter to his father, he said that during his first year in Berlin he wrote, in addition to his poetry, "a complex classification of legal concepts 300 pages long, a new basic system of metaphysics, a comic novel, a tragic play ... [and] a philosophical dialogue" (McLellan 1971:4). He would often stay up for days and nights at a time, working so hard that he fell ill and had to stay in bed for weeks.

A Critic of Religion

Reflecting his newfound interest, Marx became involved with a group of other philosophy students at the University of Berlin who studied, debated, and revised the ideas of Germany's most famous philosopher, Georg Friedrich Hegel. These "young Hegelians" adopted the complex terminology and ideas of Hegel, whose writings stand as some of the most difficult and impenetrable texts in the field of philosophy.

The young Hegelians also drew out implications of Hegel's work to criticize traditional Christianity, the Prussian monarchy, and the lack of democratic freedom. At first, when cloaked as part of the widely respected philosophy of Hegel, these radical views garnered little attention from the government. Indeed, much of their criticism took the form of discussions in Berlin coffeehouses and beer cellars among typically rambunctious students.

Marx distinguished himself among these students. Already widely read, he used his knowledge and impressive verbal abilities to dissect and criticize the nuances of Hegelian philosophy. Always quick to respond to disagreement, he made his debate partners wary of his bitter and contemptuous retorts. Eventually, he abandoned his legal studies for philosophy.

One older student, Bruno Bauer, who highly respected Marx's brilliant philosophical mind and biting wit, received a position at the University of Bonn. Bauer in turn arranged for a position in Bonn for Marx, who needed first to complete his dissertation. Marx chose a specialized topic comparing two Greek philosophers, Democritus and Epicurus. Since those outside the field of philosophy would find the topic of little interest, Marx could plan a safe career teaching esoteric philosophy to German students.

Before this plan could begin, however, Bauer was fired for his criticism of Christianity: he had bluntly questioned the miracles attributed to Jesus by the Bible. Among students in private gatherings, such comments caused few problems, but publication of these views in Prussia was a different story. In a time of strong ties between church and state, when Prussian authorities treated criticisms of the church as treason, punishment for such bold and blasphemous statements was not surprising. Perhaps more surprising was that the Ministry of Education in Berlin also blacklisted Marx because of his association with Bauer and others. Marx finished his dissertation, but he could not find employment teaching at a university.

Despite his brilliance, Marx found his chances for a teaching career ended. Perhaps other routes would better allow him to express his views. Soon after he completed his dissertation, his reputation as an original and powerful thinker provided him with the opportunity to contribute articles to a journal. Considering his strongly prodemocratic views, distaste for religion of any type, and support for freedom of the press, he was well suited to write about politics.

A Critic of the German Government

The opportunity came from an older German radical, Moses Hess, who had persuaded some German businessmen to fund a journal supporting democratic freedom and opposing Prussian policies. Germany's first communist, Hess viewed private property as a source of evil and had recently converted a young Friedrich Engels to his philosophy. In meeting with Hess, Marx dominated the conversation with his own opinions about philosophy. At the time he knew little of communism and was not one to be converted by Hess or others. Still, his liberal, antigovernment beliefs suited him well for the journal and greatly impressed Hess.

Published in Cologne, the largest city in the Rhineland of western Germany, the journal advocated policies of democratic freedom and free trade that suited the goals of business owners. Over the next few months, Marx wrote articles that effectively criticized government censorship, laws that prevented the poor from using firewood available in the nearby forests during winter, and the poverty among winegrowers near the Mosel River (still today the source of popular German wines). Indeed, the owners of the journal found his articles so effective that they appointed Marx as editor in 1842 at the young age of 24.

As editor, Marx increased circulation from 400 to 3,400 by unceasing attacks on other newspapers, the government bureaucracy, legislators, censors, landowners, and the rich. Lively and scrappy, the journal became more radical than it had been before, thus gaining increased attention from the government. Censors reviewed proofs before every issue, deleting or forcing changes in material they thought the least bit critical of the government. The hounding and harassment from politicians, police, and opposition newspapers drove Marx to nervous exhaustion. Shortly after Marx became editor of the paper, his escalating criticism of the Prussian rulers led the authorities to close it down.

As if government efforts to prevent him from having a career as a professor or a journalist were not enough to lead Marx to consider leaving Germany, the recent loss of close family ties contributed further. Marx was close to his father, Heinrich, and to Ludwig von Westphalen, the father of his fiancée, Jenny. However, after both had died, Marx lacked warm family ties.

Heinrich Marx, with a personality just the opposite of that of his eldest and headstrong son Karl, had provided comforting support. Where Heinrich had been adaptable, moderate, agreeable, optimistic, cautious, and diplomatic, Karl was stubborn, pessimistic, fierce, angry, dominating, and combative. Recognizing early the unusually energetic, bright, and difficult nature of his son, he constantly urged Karl to moderate his extreme ideas and habits and avoid offending others. They remained close until Heinrich died in 1839, when Karl was 21 years old.

Ludwig von Westphalen had provided more of a role model for Marx. A high government official and perhaps the leading citizen in Marx's hometown of Trier, Westphalen had taken an interest in the bright son of his neighbor, Heinrich Marx. The two often went on walks in the nearby woods, talking about literature and poetry. Marx viewed him as a second father. Perhaps more importantly, Herr Westphalen gave his (grudging) permission for Marx to become engaged to his daughter, Jenny. She was considered Trier's most attractive and desirable young woman and was described as beautiful, well-educated, witty, charming, and filled with humor. Since Marx had few prospects for a stable and well-paying career, most members of the Marx and Westphalen families opposed the relationship.

Plans for Marriage and Leaving Germany

When Westphalen died in 1842, Marx and Jenny lost their only family support for their marriage. Jenny had to battle with her conservative and narrow-minded relatives, who revealed religious and class bigotry in their concerns with Marx's Jewish origins and lower social position. Despite his wealth when alive, Westphalen left little in the way of inheritance. Financial ties to the family would not keep Marx and Jenny in Germany.

Marx similarly received little personal or financial support from his mother, Henriette. In contrast to her son's intensity and impracticality, she was orderly, frugal, and careful. Moreover, she lacked the open-mindedness of her husband in regard to others in general and her oldest son in particular. She opposed Marx's engagement to Jenny, his interest in the high-flown ideas of poetry and philosophy, and his wasteful spending habits; in return, Marx viewed his mother as ignorant and stingy. After the death of his father, Marx demanded money from his father's estate, but Henriette was reluctant to give any of her modest resources to a son with no sense of a budget.

Withstanding family opposition after the deaths of Heinrich Marx and Ludwig von Westphalen, Marx and Jenny remained passionately in love and resolved to marry anyway. Concerned with the practical difficulties of how Karl would support her without a stable career and occupation, Jenny had delayed the marriage eight years from the time of their engagement, during which time she refused many other marriage offers from men with better career prospects.

Most agreed that the two made an unusual pair. Far from handsome, Marx had a swarthy complexion, a stocky build, and wild and wavy hair. Exaggerating, an acquaintance described Marx as "nearly the most unattractive man on whom the sun ever shown" (Padover 1978:46); one could more positively describe Marx's looks as exotic rather than ugly. In terms of personality, he was energetic and exuberant, but also intolerant and sarcastic. He hated criticism much more than most and reacted to it with biting anger and hostility. A friend described him as having "rages without compare, as if ten thousand devils had him by the hair" (Hawthorne 1987:51). Still, his romantic poetry, self-assurance, and devotion made it hard for Jenny to resist him.

Whatever the source of their attraction, both Marx and Jenny hoped that leaving Germany would give them a fresh start. After the years of waiting, he and Jenny made plans to marry and enjoy a relationship as husband and wife. They would then move to Paris, where Marx could freely pursue a career as a journalist, writer, and editor, leaving behind his disapproving family, his youthful days as a student, and the suffocating environment of a backward country.

By leaving Germany, however, Marx would complete a transformation in his views of politics and the world. Now a liberal advocate of democracy and a free press, he would become a revolutionary communist. Although Marx knew little of communism and did not have a reputation as a revolutionary, he would shortly change. His move from Germany also signaled another change: it represented the first step in permanent exile from his country. For the rest of his life, he would return to Germany for only months at a time.

2. RESPONSES TO INDUSTRIALISM

Marx was not the only one disillusioned by the problems of the early 1800s; for good reasons, the troubles of the first half of the nineteenth century concerned many. These troubles and the desire to rectify them would greatly influence Marx's ideas.

Some 50 years before Marx's birth, many thinkers of the French Enlightenment had optimistically expected the steady improvement of social life. They believed that the principles of rational thought, science, and personal freedom would, by replacing religious myths and eliminating the power of the aristocracy, produce greater individual happiness and better societies. If, in the past, tradition had corrupted men and women's natural goodness, new and more rational social institutions could improve and perhaps even perfect social life.

New Wealth, New Problems

Despite these hopes, rationality also contributed to the Industrial Revolution, which seemed at first to have created more misery than goodness. The Industrial Revolution, which first emerged in England during the mid-1700s, combined commerce and trade with recent scientific and technological advances. **Capitalism,** or private production for a market in pursuit of profit, combined with new forms of industrial organization to create enormous wealth, bringing remarkable changes in every facet of society.

On the positive side, industrial capitalism brought vast new products such as clothes, household goods, and food to the population at cheap prices. As a result, much of England enjoyed better diets, lower mortality rates, and a better standard of living. For example, the life expectancy of 33 years in the Middle Ages rose to 43 years by 1850 and would continue to increase even more quickly in the next century (Weeks 1989:176).

To some, the Industrial Revolution also brought wealth that in the past only kings and lords had enjoyed. By the 1800s, the middle-class beneficiaries of commerce and trade—those not born into wealth, but who gained it from the businesses and factories they came to own—could afford to display their good fortune. The newly rich purchased the latest fashions in expensive stores, displayed their horses and carriages in rides through city parks and wide boulevards, and attended operas and grand balls late into the night. While taking for granted the wealth of the aristocracy, many greeted the new riches of business owners with envy and anger. A startling and novel contrast arose between the conditions of the new middle classes and ordinary working people.

On the negative side, industrial capitalism brought new kinds of misery. First, changes in technology displaced huge numbers of people from rural areas. Improvements in agricultural production—such as new techniques of crop rotation, new strains of crops, and new seed-planting and harvesting machines—reduced the need for human labor. They also resulted in larger farms that pushed small farmers out of business. Combined with high rates of fertility in rural areas, these changes created large masses of people without any means of economic support.

Second, industrial capitalism created a system of factory work that, however efficient, undermined traditional family and community ties. At first, new machines increased the efficiency of individual workers but nonetheless allowed families to continue to work together at home. A new class of business middlemen emerged to provide supplies for these homeworkers and to sell the completed products to others for a substantial profit. However, as technology continued to advance and machines became too large to fit into the homes of workers, investors built factories to hold the new machines. Located near sources of power to run large machines, factories required workers to migrate to these locations, or at least leave home to go to work.

Third, besides weakening traditional bonds between people, the factory system created a variety of new social problems. With migration from rural areas to the location of factories, new cities became filled with persons unknown to one another. With poorly constructed housing, few sanitation facilities, and excessive crowding, these new cities contained highly visible and serious problems of poverty, crime, disease, and pollution. And with large numbers of people in need of jobs, factory owners found they could hire employees for miserly wages—especially women and children, who would work for even less money than men.

The Misery of Industrial Workers

In testimony before Parliament in 1832, a young boy named Peter Smart described the agony of his life as a factory worker (Lenski & Lenski 1987:253). Locked on the premises of a textile mill, he would begin work at 4:00 A.M. and continue until 11:00 P.M.—if he did not keel over from exhaustion before then. Those children who tried to escape often faced lashing with a whip. Even if he had escaped, there was little else he could do. His mother, who worked and lived in another nearby factory, could not support him; government agencies, which sent orphaned and destitute children back to work in factories, could not support him. Those not working in factories had to turn to the pickpocketing and petty theft described by Charles Dickens in *Oliver Twist*.

The government provided little help or protection to vulnerable factory workers. To the contrary, an English law passed in 1800 banned trade unions from representing workers. Not until 1833 did laws prevent employment altogether of children under age 9 and employment of older children for more than 12 hours a day (Viault 1990:236). Further, tariffs limited the import of cheap food from other nations and raised the cost of bread for the poor. Designed to protect large landowners, who desired to sell their grain at high prices without competition from grain grown in other countries, these laws contributed to starvation among the poor.

The misery and suffering of workers led to riots. Groups called Luddites (a name still used today to describe persons blindly opposed to technological advance) roamed industrial areas trying to destroy the machines that seemed to enslave them. Many workers idealized the past times of sunlight, fresh air, and the beauty of rural life, when family and community ties had helped give meaning to daily tasks. They hoped that, by destroying machines and the dirty, dangerous, and dark factories that contained them, they could return to dignified, secure, and rewarding work without constant supervision and abuse by foremen.

Even those who could avoid the degrading work in factories faced other traumas from industrial development: the lives of individuals became increasingly subject to large-scale market forces which they didn't understand and over which they had little control. Unknown financial speculators might create huge increases in the price of bread, unknown inventors might design new machines that would force workers out of their jobs, and unknown business owners might lay off large numbers of workers during periods of high unemployment. The growth of crime and pollution in cities also deeply affected people but was completely beyond their control.

Economic Explanations

How did thinkers respond to these changes? Two broad reactions to the Industrial Revolution emerged, one defending capitalism and the other one calling for its destruction.

The first reaction came from English economists, who argued that free markets, economic competition, and individual self-interest brought economic efficiency and national wealth. Dating back to Adam Smith's famous book *The Wealth of Nations,* many English economists opposed government intervention for purposes other than enforcing freely made contracts. Instead, they argued that, through the invisible hand of the market, free individuals pursuing their own interests would contribute to the economic well-being of all members of a society. Advocates of this view naturally focused on the improvements in the standard of living, nutrition, and health that came with the Industrial Revolution.

According to this perspective, the misery of workers resulted not so much from free markets as from high rates of fertility. In discussing problems of population growth in the early 1800s, at the time problems of the Industrial Revolution had begun to peak, Thomas Malthus noted the simple fact that populations grow faster than their food supply. Famine, war, disease, and poverty inevitably result. Industrial workers thus faced the same problem others had faced throughout human history: too many children and too many people resulted in too little food and too little income to purchase food.

David Ricardo, another English economist, developed this train of thought further. He claimed that wages would necessarily remain near the subsistence level. Following the logic of supply and demand, wages would rise if the need for workers exceeded the number of available workers. But with better wages, workers could afford to have more children and the prospects of survival for their children would improve. This would soon increase the supply of workers relative to demand and lower wages back to the subsistence level. Although Malthus and Ricardo both deplored the conditions of poverty in England, others used their arguments to justify inhuman working conditions.

Socialist Explanations

Another, more critical reaction came from French writers who advocated replacing an economy based on profit and private property with one based on public ownership and democracy. Loosely united under the label *socialism* or *communism,* these viewpoints emphasized the social or communal sharing of products of the Industrial Revolution and the desire to abolish private property. They quite obviously differed greatly from the views of English political economists.

Although industrial development did not occur as early and as quickly in France as in England, the workers there still suffered. In addition, improvements in working conditions came more slowly in France. When strikes and riots among workers occurred, the king used troops to end them forcibly. Through bribery of corrupt government officials, capitalist financiers obtained enormous power, preventing even the modest reforms regarding trade unions and worker protection that eventually emerged in England. As it had decades earlier during the French Revolution, Paris rather than London became the center of radical activity.

One early French socialist, Claude Saint-Simon, argued in the early 1800s that economic factors determined the course of history. He distinguished two basic social classes—a minority who owned the main economic resources of a community and a majority who owned little or nothing. Since the beginning of civilization, the advantaged and tyrannical minority had reduced the deprived majority to economic slavery and had tried to prevent any change that would correct such inequality. Class economic domination, along with class conflict and struggle, had existed throughout history.

Several later French writers, such as Charles Fourier and Pierre Proudhon, advocated the establishment of small communities of workers to rectify the unfairness described by Saint-Simon. They proposed dividing industrial society into small, self-governing communities that could share the resources and benefits of industrial development; they also hoped to replace private property and excessive governmental power with an economic system based on cooperation. Wanting the benefits of industrial capitalism without its evils, some of their followers established—seldom with any success—these types of settlements.

Other writers championed the overthrow of existing institutions rather than the establishment of separate communities. To reach these goals, some groups battled the ruling class with terrorism; other groups called for spontaneous uprisings among the urban poor as a step toward revolution; still others advocated gradual improvement in the position of workers through unions and government legislation. Although many variations in socialist and communist ideas existed, they were united in their criticism of capitalism and the changes it had brought.

If the British economists seemed excessively hard-hearted in their views, the French socialists seemed naive and impractical. Revolutions, such as in France in 1789, had occurred before without bringing a permanent change in the position of workers and the poor. Why wouldn't future revolutions fail as well? Socialists, seeming to think that their good intentions alone would bring about the needed change, failed to explain how a society based on equality could replace one based on greed. In the years to come, Marx would provide such an explanation by adapting the logic of the British economists to the goals of the French socialists.

In the meantime, however, industrialization and the debate over its consequences did not immediately affect Marx. Compared to England and France, Germany remained economically backward. As a result, the growth of the factory system, apparent in England and to a lesser extent in France, did not occur to the same degree in Germany, but neither did the high level of economic development. The economic and political backwardness of Germany meant that Marx had much to learn about industrial changes in other European countries.

3. THE MATERIAL BASIS OF SOCIAL LIFE

Marx's exit from Germany soon brought personal fulfillment. In June 1843, after their long and frustrating eight-year engagement, Marx and Jenny finally married in a church ceremony in the town of Jenny's grandmother, but none of Marx's still-resentful relatives attended, not even his mother and five sisters. After a honeymoon in Switzerland paid for by Jenny's mother, the newlyweds moved to Paris in October 1843. Now ages 25 and 29, the new husband and wife set up their own household.

These were blissful times for both. Marx took pride in the beauty and intelligence of his wife and in the birth of their first child, a daughter nicknamed Jennychen, in May 1844. Jenny took pride in her husband's writing, journalism, and devotion to radical change, and her letters during brief periods of separation show a jealous and passionate attachment to him. The next year, in September 1845, Jenny gave birth to their second daughter, Laura.

The two enjoyed the cultural and social life of Paris, spending their money recklessly; neither had a careful sense of financial discipline. The young couple found wonderful shops selling the latest fashions and a wide variety of tempting products difficult to resist. They sometimes bought elegant, costly, and unnecessary gifts for one another, such as a leather buggy whip for Karl—who had neither a horse nor a buggy (Peters 1986:46). Yet they could also see the more excessive and wasteful luxury of rich Parisians all around them. The unequal wealth apparent to Marx in Paris no doubt contributed to his hostility toward the rich and sympathy for the poor.

Intellectually, Marx found the freedom of discussion and the stimulation of new ideas exhilarating. Because the French king showed surprising tolerance for some types of dissent, especially compared to his Prussian counterpart, Marx had the opportunity to acquaint himself with new ideas discussed in Paris by exiles and revolutionaries from all over the world. He read widely; spent time in cafes with (sometimes quite famous) writers, thinkers, and radicals; and attended meetings of German workers living in Paris. The contact with others who shared similar views gave him a feeling of optimism and a sense of belonging.

Nearly all his life, Marx had enjoyed a tremendous appetite for learning. Arnold Ruge, his collaborator on a new journal in Paris, described Marx's activities at this time: "He reads much, works with uncommon intensity, does not go to bed for three, four nights in succession, and constantly plunges anew into an endless ocean of books" (Padover 1978:188). Because of his immense learning, doctorate in philosophy, and skill in verbal argument, Marx soon gained much respect in radical circles. Still in his 20s, he impressed people as a thinker with unlimited potential.

Marx did little to present his ideas in any systematic form during these years; rather, he criticized the ideas of others as a way to give shape to his own. "Marx proved a witty, relentlessly logical and devastatingly critical writer" (Walton 1986:53) who "was always happiest when he could work out his own views by attacking others" (McLellan 1971:69). However uncertain his own views, Marx found flaws in other approaches to understanding the sources of misery in society.

Ideas Versus Material Factors

German philosophy generally and Hegelian philosophy specifically became the first subject of his criticism. To Marx, the supremacy they gave to ideas seemed inadequate to explain the social and political problems he encountered. His background in philosophy had initially led to the naive expectation that rational ideas alone would steadily spread throughout society, create political freedom, and eliminate the constraints of government and religion. Yet his experience as an editor who involved himself in real-life struggles for freedom and equality showed that economic interests rather than ideas seemed most important in influencing political decisions.

Marx asked himself: Would leaders in Germany, France, or England voluntarily give up their power in response to rational arguments? Would businessmen share their profits with workers because of abstract philosophic principles? Marx's failure to effect changes in Germany through his writings indicated to him that they would not. He reasoned that the financial interests of the political and economic elite would lead them to reject any arguments that challenged their advantaged position. Disillusionment with the possibility of change in Prussia thus led Marx to a new thought—perhaps ideas and argument alone could not create meaningful social change.

In contrast to Hegel and the young Hegelians, Marx came to believe that he needed to understand concrete social and historical factors. Rather than contemplate reality through thought alone, Marx directed his attention to the **material factors** of life: the actions people take and the objects they use to produce what they need to support themselves. Agricultural societies relied on material factors such as land, animals, plows, farming traditions, grain mills, and human labor to grow food and exchange that food for shelter, clothing, and tools. As technology developed, production of goods became more efficient. In capitalist societies, material factors such as coal, machines, factories, railroads, and new forms of human labor could produce much more than could agricultural societies.

Given the importance of material factors for the survival of societies, social relations follow from the kind of material production that dominates. In agricultural societies, differences between lords and serfs, between those who own the land and those who work the land, define social relationships. In capitalist societies, production defines social relations based on differences between the owners of capital and the workers.

Both these systems of production are based on private property. Of the material factors of life, Marx distinguished between human labor and the **means of production**—the land, tools, and machines used to produce finished goods. With private property, some own the means of production, but most own only their own labor power. As a result, inequality characterizes social relations in most past and current societies.

Marx thus turned Hegel's philosophy upside down by making material factors rather than ideas central to social life, an idea that also suggested the need for action rather than thought alone. He became increasingly irritated by his former friends and allies in Berlin—the young Hegelians who continued their devotion to obscure philosophy, pure thought, and words without action (Berlin 1996:106). Their criticisms did nothing to bring about change in the material conditions of society. If problems do not lie in the mind, but in the organization of social life, then action rather than thought alone would be needed to change this organization.

About this time, Marx's former philosophical colleague and friend, Bruno Bauer, suggested a solution to the problem of anti-Semitism. He said that the prejudice and discrimination against Jews would end if, as a first step, Jews converted to Christianity and thereby gained the same civil rights as Christians. Consistent with his newfound materialism, Marx claimed instead that political freedom would only come from economic freedom: Jews, like all others in society, needed economic equality rather than religious conversion.

The Form of Social Change

Marx's materialism also gave new meaning to Hegel's philosophy of social change. For Hegel, all the world's events and ideas fit together into a unitary whole, with each part contributing to the movement of life toward the final goal of a completely rational world. Understanding one part thus requires understanding its relationship to other parts and to the larger whole. All of culture, morality, ethics, tradition, law, religion, and science create a unified, but constantly changing, system. Many found this grandiose claim attractive and exciting, offering as it did the hope that we can understand the logic behind the infinite complexity of the world.

Within this unified system, change occurs in the form of conflict and contradiction. Rather than smooth and steady forward progress, change occurs with sudden and huge movements as underlying forces burst through. "Every idea, every force, irrepressibly bred its opposite, and the two merged into a 'unity' that in turn produced its own contradictions"

(Heilbroner 1967:129). According to Hegel's **dialectic**, historical change results from opposing forces: something happens (called the *thesis*), a reaction occurs (called the *antithesis*), and an integration results from the conflict of the two opposing forces (called the *synthesis*).

Yet Hegel saw an end to this conflict and contradiction: each step moves the world closer to the ideals of freedom and reason. As history unfolds, people become increasingly aware of a force larger than themselves—the growth of reason. Since one part of life flows into its opposite, all parts blend together into a unitary whole and all parts contribute to the movement toward the final goal. Hegel could thus posit the existence of opposites—disunity and unity, conflict and progress, emotion and reason.

Marx gave new meaning to Hegel's perspective on unity and change. For Marx, change still occurs in the form of opposites, but it involves conflict between older and newer methods of production. In all but the simplest societies, struggle and conflict exist between those who own the means of production and those who do not. However, the nature of the struggle and conflict changes with the development of technology and new forms of ownership. Capitalist factory production, for example, develops in opposition to and comes to replace land-based crop production. Within capitalism, conflict then develops between the capitalists and the workers.

Contradictions still exist within a unified whole, as they do in Hegel's scheme, but now they involve conflict between economic groups rather than opposing ideas. Change still occurs in sudden bursts, but now it relates to material factors of production. Laws of change now move inevitably toward a goal involving a new form of production and collective ownership rather than toward the growth of reason.

Alienation

The attention to material factors also led Marx to consider the consequences of private property for the nature of work. Within a system of private property such as capitalism, work produces **alienation**—workers' separation from and loss of control over material production. Marx believed that humans have the potential to reach a state of closeness with what they produce and with other persons. Although the individual creatively strives toward self-fulfillment, relations of production based on private property and specialization hinder this goal.

Alienation among workers occurs in several ways:

1. Workers become alienated from their *labor*. Under systems of private property, work becomes a means to an end—earning wages—rather than a fulfilling end in itself. Work becomes something bought and sold like any other product rather than a spontaneous and creative activity.

2. Workers become alienated from the *products of their labor.* With specialization, workers contribute only a small part to the final product, see the product disappear into a vast sales market, and get little sense of accomplishment from their effort.

3. Workers become alienated from *other people.* Others become objects used to make exchanges of goods and money, or competitors in the market or workplace. Money and the commodities money represents come to dominate human relationships.

4. Workers become alienated from *themselves or their creative potential.* Although new forms of production create new potential for people to realize their abilities and capacities, the social relations of production based on private ownership frustrate that potential.

Marx envisioned another kind of society, one that eliminates private property and wage labor. Sharing rather than owning the means of production would make "it possible for me to do one thing today and another tomorrow, to hunt in the morning, fish in the afternoon, breed cattle in the evening, criticize after dinner, just as I like without ever becoming a hunter, a fisherman, a herdsman, or a critic" (McLellan 1971:36). However, none of this can come about through wishful thinking. The laws of economic change have to work themselves out—a topic to which Marx would devote much effort in the next several decades. In the meantime, Marx had taken initial steps in this direction with his rejection of German idealistic philosophy.

4. A REVOLUTIONARY SOCIALIST

While in Paris, Marx renewed his acquaintance with a fellow German, Friedrich Engels, whom he had met briefly some years earlier. This time, realizing their common interests, they spent ten days in near-constant conversation about their commitment to revolutionary socialism and their views of the future of capitalism. Their meeting began a lifelong collaboration and deep friendship.

Marx and Engels

The two young men nicely balanced each other. Where Marx was stubborn, bold, energetic, and arrogant, Engels was easygoing, loyal, patient, and flexible. Where Marx was wounded and enraged by criticism, Engels was supportive, dependable, and admiring of Marx's skills. Where Marx was brilliantly original but disorganized and complex in his thinking, Engels could quickly and efficiently organize, perhaps even oversimplify, the concepts of others. And where Marx was ponderously slow to publish because of the enormous time he spent reading, thinking, and taking notes, Engels could write quickly and effectively.

Marx had little personal experience with the plight of the working class, but Engels could describe to him in concrete detail the appalling conditions of workers in England. Marx's knowledge of workers came from his years in Germany, where industry remained relatively undeveloped and poverty prevailed among rural peasants. In contrast, Engels had seen firsthand the state of workers in a cotton mill in England owned by his father. Based on his experiences, Engels later published a book, *The Condition of the Working Class in England*, and brought Marx to England to view directly the consequences of industrial development under capitalism.

Engels differed from Marx in another, more practical way. He had the chance to pursue a financially rewarding business career because his father owned textile mills and wanted his son to join the business. However, he rejected this work for radical politics and revolutionary activity as a young man. Later in life, in part to help support Marx financially, Engels did join his father's business. Although successful and to all appearances a typical businessman, he maintained his socialist views and provided the kind of steady, reliable economic and personal support that Marx needed to continue writing.

Combined with what he learned from Engels, Marx's experiences with workers in Paris contributed to his thinking. Paris contained many small businesses rather than huge factories as in England, and workers in Paris did not experience the misery of English workers. Still, differences between workers and owners or the poor and the well-off in Paris were obvious for anyone to see. The intelligent and discontented French workers he met helped move Marx toward a more radical position about the need for social change.

In the meantime, Marx began to face the financial problems that would haunt him for decades to come. His only source of potential economic support in Paris—the editorship of a new journal—did not work out. One problem was his friction with Arnold Ruge, the publisher, on the direction of the journal. Marx's increasingly radical beliefs, involvement in communist organizations, and support for workers diverged from the more moderate views of Ruge. Further, as occurred throughout his life with nearly everyone except his wife and Engels, Marx's quarrelsome nature made cooperation difficult. Marx wanted to dominate all activities he became involved with, and any resistance by colleagues to that domination elicited bitter criticism. Ruge later wrote of Marx that "I have suffered a great deal of unpleasantness through his hatred of me ... he wants to destroy even the memory of our relationship" (Schwarzschild 1947:88). Even without this conflict, however, the journal would not have lasted long or produced any income; it ceased publication after only one issue and made no profit. To support himself, Marx had to appeal for funds from friends in Germany and later to sell some of his household goods.

Need for a Scientific Theory

Perhaps in part as a result of his money problems, Marx completed his transformation from a democratic critic of the Prussian monarchy to a socialist favoring armed revolution. In Paris, he came to identify with the suffering, poverty, and misery of workers and to predict that the struggle to improve their lives would result in a better world. He came to believe that capitalist society contained flaws that would bring about its downfall and replacement by communism. He came to support armed revolution rather than peaceful change to bring about that downfall and create a society ruled by workers.

As his beliefs changed, Marx realized the inadequacy of the naive and romantic ideas of the French socialists. He adopted their emphasis on class conflict and their criticisms of private property but wanted an explanation of the sources of misery based on scientific analysis. Rather than vague and unrealistic images of a socialist future in which people would willingly cooperate with one another, he sought to find laws that would lead to the downfall of capitalism.

Although he had not yet identified the precise mechanisms that would produce revolution, Marx came to believe that the laws of change would inevitably bring this result. When the conditions of the workers and poor became intolerable, they would unite to overthrow the government, replace capitalism with socialism, and end the oppression of workers. The unstoppable forces of history would require this result.

How could Marx claim to predict the future? Briefly, he saw that current events had historical parallels. When industry replaced agriculture as the major form of production, a kind of revolution occurred as landowners lost power to the new owners of factories and businesses. Violent revolts and civil wars often accompanied these changes. For example, the French Revolution in part involved small-business owners and workers in Paris overthrowing the landed aristocracy, while the American Civil War pitted the industrial North against the agricultural South. The same underlying logic and forces that had led to these revolutions would lead to a new revolution—only this time, workers would take control from those who enslaved them.

Marx wanted to convince others of these truths through analysis and logic rather than emotion. He thought that the enthusiasm of other revolutionary leaders might attract followers but would not bring lasting change. Emotional appeals would lead only to unplanned uprisings that the authorities would quickly crush or to the founding of socialist communities that would not survive in the capitalist market.

For both workers and leaders, facts would eliminate the illusions and mistakes common among those who desired social change. The scientific perspective also melded nicely with Marx's desire to study and understand work, production, and social relationships. Rejecting German philosophy's focus on pure thought, Marx believed that the scientific perspective must observe, describe, and explain the concrete material conditions of human life. He would later write that economic change could be studied "with the precision of natural science" (Padover 1978:320).

Indeed, in years to come Marx would battle with those who advocated the overthrow of capitalism without a doctrine. He opposed the use of terrorism and secret conspiracies, since the isolated action of a few could do little to bring about lasting change until social and economic conditions were ripe for the combined action of all workers. He opposed those who wanted to return to an idealized past of villages, small businesses, and craftworkers, since this goal denies the reality of social classes and large-scale capitalist production. The social and economic laws of historical change should guide the workers' movement and revolutionary strategy.

In the meantime, Marx hoped that his work could help the process of revolution along. Few people understood the workings of the system, the flaws of capitalism, and the logic of change. Although intellectuals like Marx could not change the material conditions that produced the misery of workers, they could help organize and inspire the revolution. Their efforts and writings might bring material conditions to the stage of crisis more quickly than would occur otherwise and thereby help speed up the laws of social change.

Need for a Sociological Theory

If Marx rejected the methods of socialists even while agreeing with their goals, he had even more problems with the intellectual alternative offered by British economists. Although Smith, Malthus, and Ricardo studied economics with scientific methods, their work failed to consider the importance of social relationships to economic behavior and capitalism. Marx's attention to the means of obtaining material resources for survival required equal attention to social relationships.

In all but the simplest societies, production involves social relationships between those who own the economic means of production and those who do not. The social organization of owners and nonowners makes human work the property of others. Rather than being the voluntary choices of free individuals, however, these relationships involve social domination of one group by another, a domination that constrains the choices of individuals.

This view is inherently sociological—it recognizes that society is created by active individuals producing for their survival, but it also holds that these social forces, once they have been created, come to limit individual action. Individuals create forms of production, such as capitalism, that produce unequal class relations. These structures in turn become external and coercive, affecting the thoughts, needs, and behaviors of inviduals. The actions of business owners and workers differ substantially because of their class positions and material interests.

The individualism of the British political economists treated people as isolated and separate units that cooperate in order to fulfill personal needs and wants. Social life thus came from individuals acting in their own self-interest, maximizing their happiness, and contributing to the functioning of the larger economy. Humans naturally pursued profit, made free choices, and exchanged goods in the market to improve their lives. In contrast, Marx viewed individuals' pursuit of profit in the market as part of a particular form of social organization. The social ties between owners and workers, buyers and sellers, and rulers and the ruled meant that isolated individuals making free choices do not exist.

The British economists aggravated their flawed thinking by identifying general laws that they claimed applied to all people, places, and times. Marx thought such views foolish—the behavior of people under capitalism followed certain laws, but these laws differed from those that guided people under the feudalism of the Middle Ages or the slave-owning society of the Roman Empire. Laws of economics, private property, and political rule varied across historical periods and thus required the study of history and social life.

Marx's claims that social institutions and social behavior are shaped by relations of production rather than by the human mind or by individual choices meant that poverty and misery resulted not from human nature but from the social organization of society. Rather than being the inevitable consequence of excess population growth, human suffering came from particular social relations organized around the ownership of property and domination of one class by another. Just as private property had existed in most societies throughout history, so did poverty and misery.

However, compared to slave- and land-based societies, capitalist societies made the poverty and misery seem worse. Capitalism had produced wealth that was unimaginable centuries earlier, but the potential of this new productive capacity to improve the lives of everyone would not be realized as long as private property remained the basis of social organization. Improvement would come with the elimination of class domination.

5. *THE COMMUNIST MANIFESTO*

Eventually, Marx's emerging beliefs led to his expulsion from Paris. Prussian agents noticed an article by Marx stating that the overthrow of the political and social order was necessary for socialism to emerge. Viewing this as treason, the Prussian ambassador to France requested that Marx not be allowed to stay in Paris. The French king complied, and again, only 16 months after he had left Germany, Marx found himself a political exile.

While other scholars could advocate reform and cooperation with the government from privileged positions in universities, Marx would have to spread his ideas through action as a member of underground groups. Freed of respectability, he could criticize without concern for what he could lose and he could identify with a revolutionary future rather than with the present. Indeed, the isolation and marginality that followed his expulsion from Paris allowed him to see beneath the day-to-day activities of capitalism and discern the underlying patterns not apparent to those actively involved in commercial activities (Coser 1977:85).

Having chosen the course of his life—devotion to understanding capitalism through scientific study and to ending capitalism through revolution—Marx began his involuntary political exile in 1845 at age 26 by moving to Brussels, Belgium. Given his past trouble with the Prussian government, he had to petition the Belgian king to stay in Brussels, receiving permission only by agreeing to abstain from political activities. Although Marx in no way intended to abide fully by that promise, it did prevent him from earning a steady income as a journalist or editor.

The promise brought immediate problems. Soon after arriving in Brussels, Marx, with the help of Engels, began to build and lead a communist organization made up mostly of German radicals living throughout Europe. Prussian spies, still watching Marx, reported on his activities to the Belgian king, trying (but failing) to get him expelled from Brussels as they had from Paris. In anger at these efforts, Marx renounced his Prussian citizenship. He became a stateless person who could enter Prussia only with special permission from the authorities. He would come to regret this decision in later years.

Financially, the high cost of living in Brussels made the lack of a steady source of income especially trying. Marx again would turn to Engels and other friends to take up collections for him. He also would go to his mother to draw on his future inheritance and to a rich uncle for a loan. Borrowing hurt Marx's pride, resulting in health problems and frequent rages against a society that put him in this position (Padover 1978:204). Yet, devoted as he was to the coming worker revolution and hounded by creditors during his three years in Brussels, he had to get money however he could.

Despite the problems they faced, Jenny and Karl remained hopeful and deeply in love. Karl appeared personally self-assured, physically broad-shouldered and vigorous, and intellectually superior to all he met. Jenny believed with her husband that their deprivation would not last long. The worker revolution would come soon, and with it Marx would become a powerful leader and could enjoy the benefits of a communist society.

The Key Concept: Social Class

During this time, Marx first presented his arguments in a readable and inspiring form. The London-based central committee of the Communist League asked Marx and Engels to write a statement of the group's aims and beliefs. The resulting *Communist Manifesto* appeared in early 1848. The relatively brief statement "defined the main lines of his views that future work would refine" (Coser 1977:63). Although not immediately influential, the power and eloquence of the arguments in the manifesto made Marx and Engels confident about the future.

The Communist Manifesto threatened, explained, and prophesied. It threatened enemies of the workers with a movement that would destroy capitalism and unite those it exploited. It explained how social conflict would inevitably bring this result. And it prophesied a new communist society that would eliminate social inequality. In the last sentences of the manifesto, Marx and Engels wrote, "The communists disdain to conceal their views and aims. They openly declare that their ends can be obtained only by the forcible overthrow of all existing social conditions. Let the ruling classes tremble at a communist revolution. The proletarians have nothing to lose but their chains. They have a world to win. Working men of all countries, unite."

Building on his early work, Marx argued that class struggle held the key to understanding the problems of modern society. Others had identified the existence of social classes, but Marx improved on their work by defining more precisely the boundaries and relationships between them. According to Marx, **classes** consist of persons who have the same position and perform the same function in the organization of production. Dominant classes derive their privilege from ownership of the means of production (e.g., land, capital), whereas subordinate classes own nothing but their own labor power. Although dominant classes have higher income and wealth than subordinate classes, income or wealth does not define classes; social relations that arise from ownership and nonownership of the means of production do.

Class differences in position and function vary with the type of production that dominates a society or historical period. In ancient Roman society, slave owners and slaves comprised the two central classes. In the feudal society of the Middle Ages, landowners and serfs comprised the two central classes. In capitalist society, owners of capital (or the **bourgeoisie**) and workers (or the **proletariat**) make up the two central classes. As the reigning form of economic production changes from slavery to land to capital, so does the nature of the ownership of the dominant class and the nature of the work of the subordinate class.

Although other classes and divisions also exist under capitalism, they do not play a historically decisive role in the struggle between classes. Classes comprising landowners and peasants persist. Shopkeepers, craftworkers and artisans, and owners of small businesses, called the *petty bourgeoisie,* do not have to work for others like the proletariat but do not employ large numbers of workers like the bourgeoisie. Those without jobs or family to support them, called by Marx the *lumpenproletariat* (or, translated literally, the ragamuffin or riff-raff proletariat), have to depend on petty crime or charity. However, these groups lack clear connections to the means of production, do not have conflicting interests with one another, and eventually become absorbed into the working class.

Class Struggle

As in the past, the two classes central to capitalist societies have competing interests that produce conflict. The working class produces wealth through its labor but gets only a small share of the wealth in the form of modest wages. The capitalist class does not produce wealth but owns the capital needed for the workers to produce wealth. As owners of banks, buildings, machines, natural resources, and transportation networks, they have control over the ability of workers to use their labor to produce. To gain the fruits of their labor, workers would benefit from ending private property and sharing the means of production.

Although many utopian socialists hoped that class differences might disappear thanks to the understanding and goodwill of people, Marx saw conflict and struggle as inevitable because of the existence of social classes. Because of their opposing interests, classes cannot cooperate for a better world. Change must come from protests, strikes, or the armed revolution of the working class against the bourgeoisie. Similarly, classes with less distinct positions in the production process cannot participate in the struggle to the same extent as the bourgeoisie and proletariat. Conflict is central to Marx's view of class and society.

During the early stages of industrial capitalism, Marx argued, the bourgeoisie have the advantage in class struggle. As owners of the means of production, members of the business class also own newspapers to publicize their views, can finance politicians to pass laws they desire, and can support thinkers to help justify their dominant position. Given their general control of democratic governments, the propertied class can use the state to define property rights in its favor and enforce them. According to Marx, capitalists favor the political freedom of democratic governments because it reinforces the power they already have in the market.

The working class begins only with an advantage in numbers but eventually benefits from increased solidarity, cooperation, and communication. During economic recessions, capitalists, shopkeepers, small landowners, and craftworkers lose what they own and enter the proletariat. The size of the proletariat increases, while the size of the bourgeoisie and intermediate classes declines. Unlike other thinkers who foresaw society breaking apart as it became more specialized, Marx foresaw that members of the same social class would become increasingly similar and united.

At the same time, members of the two different social classes become increasingly less alike. Within classes, differences based on national citizenship, region of residence, religious affiliation, or family background decline relative to the bond of having a common position as owners or workers. Among the bourgeoisie, differences between finance capitalists and industrial capitalists, or between large manufacturers and small manufacturers, decline in importance. Across classes, inequalities in income, wealth, and well-being steadily increase, thereby intensifying conflict.

As the working class gets larger and more deprived, its members come to recognize their common interest in ending a system based on private property. The large numbers of deprived workers concentrated together in pockets of poverty can more easily communicate about their plight. With the help of intellectual leaders like Marx, they also come to understand the source of the problems and the solution in the overthrow of capitalism. Despite efforts of the bourgeoisie to convince them otherwise, workers come to see the true nature of reality.

The Failed Revolution of 1848

Marx's hope for the future contrasted with the views of other thinkers. Where others expected current problems to grow worse in the future, Marx predicted something altogether different and better than existed at the present. Class inequality would end with the collective control of property and with the growth in the size and power of the working class. The use of the state to brutalize workers would end with the disappearance of the state. The genius of Marx's reading of the future comes from his ability to understand the complex workings of the forces below the surface rather than merely project current trends forward.

After completion of *The Communist Manifesto,* events foreshadowing a worker revolution gave Marx even more confidence in his predictions. Beginning in 1847, an economic depression, a slowdown in world trade, and poor harvests contributed to rising unemployment and food prices. The resulting discontent boiled over first in Paris, where French rebels succeeded in overthrowing the king in February 1848. Demonstrations in Berlin followed, which frightened the Prussian king into promising democratic reforms. In Brussels, German workers began to arm themselves (Marx used an advance on his inheritance from his mother to buy arms for these rebels). Marx and many others believed the time of revolution had come.

A government reaction to the riots and protests soon dashed the hopes of the revolutionaries. Belgian troops crushed the small numbers of armed workers, forcing Marx and other Germans to leave the country. After a brief stay in Paris, where he came as a guest of the leaders of the new French Republic, Marx then returned to Germany (without permission from authorities). To aid in the struggle, he began to publish a new journal in Cologne. His efforts accomplished little, however. The king reneged on his promised reforms, imposed marital law, and closed down hostile newspapers.

No longer a citizen of Prussia, Marx was forced by the government to leave for Paris. Worse, in France a national election had removed the more radical leaders from power. In a four-day battle over the outcome, the new government of moderates used French troops to put down a demonstration by workers. No longer welcome in Paris, Marx would have to move again. The Revolution of 1848 in Europe had brought little change after all.

How could Marx explain the failure? He reasoned that before the workers could take power from the bourgeoisie, the bourgeoisie had to consolidate the power they had seized from the landed aristocracy. According to the laws of social and economic change, newly emerging classes had to struggle against dominant, but declining, classes. Once they succeeded, other new classes would emerge to struggle with the currently dominant class. However, until conditions were ripe, until the logic of material production had worked itself out, efforts by a disadvantaged minority to bring about change would fail. At this stage, economic conditions had not yet reached the low point necessary for widespread action of workers against owners.

6. CAPITAL AND SURPLUS LABOR

The failed Revolution of 1848 left Marx disappointed. He still recognized the struggle between classes as the central fact of social life and predicted the eventual victory of workers in this struggle. Yet the forces of economic change that would bring about this victory would take longer than he had originally thought. In the meantime, he would have to provide proof of the laws of change he had described in order to convince those discouraged by the events of the last year or two that his predictions would come to pass. He would have to struggle to advance his ideas and remain confident and persistent in the face of criticism.

Although Marx's reasoning made sense intellectually, it brought little solace to his personal life. Both he and Jenny had been arrested and temporarily jailed in Brussels, and he had faced arrest and several trials in Germany before being expelled. All this time he had little money to support himself and his family; he had to pawn family goods to survive.

With few other places to go, Marx moved to London, which, as a place to live, had some advantages. In contrast to the harassment he had faced in Germany, France, and Belgium, his presence was treated with mild indifference and tolerance by the English authorities. Without censorship, he could freely write and publish. With many other foreign refugees living there, he had the chance to socialize and discuss affairs with those from similar backgrounds. With beautiful parks, free lectures, and cheap seating in theaters, he could enjoy his leisure time.

Despite these advantages, Marx did not expect to stay long. He thought that the coming worker revolution would allow him to return to the Continent shortly. It became apparent, however, that the revolution would not come soon. After the problems of the late 1840s, all of Europe experienced an economic boom; the prosperity convinced him that an insurrection now would again fail. Unable to predict with precision when the proper moment for a revolution would come, he began to realize he might have to stay in London for some time. In fact, he would live the rest of his life there. Worse, if he felt that he and his family had already made considerable sacrifices for his cause, the sacrifices to come would seem many times greater.

Poverty and Sorrow

Again, financial problems made life miserable for Marx and his family. Despite living in the cheapest quarters he could find, he and his family seldom had sufficient food. They bought what they could on credit but then faced the unpleasant experience of having creditors pursue them. The landlord of one of their early apartments evicted the family into the street, forcing them to sell their beds to pay debts. They eventually found lodging in two small rooms in Soho—then a slum filled with immigrants, now a lively, if slightly seedy, area filled with restaurants, nightclubs, and tourists.

Their fourth child, born seven weeks after Jenny had arrived in London, faced the same misery as the rest of the family. Jenny wrote in a letter that "since he came into the world he has not slept a single night, at most two or three hours, [has] violent cramps, [and] always hovered between death and a miserable life" (McLellan 1974:227). The child died within the year, but Jenny found herself pregnant again. Once born, that child died as well, as did their only remaining son at age 7. Marx wrote later that "the death of my child has profoundly shaken my heart and my brain, and I feel the loss with the same intensity as on the first day. My wife is completely broken" (McLellan 1971:65). Of the seven children born to Marx and Jenny, only three survived.

A report of a Prussian spy, who had presented himself to Marx as a sympathetic follower, described the Marx's home: "[In] one of the worst, and thus cheapest, quarters in London ... everything is broken, ragged, tattered; everything is covered with finger-thick dust; everywhere the greatest disorder ... everything is piled helter-skelter on the [single] table [in the room]" (McLellan 1974:268–69). The fumes from fireplace coals and Marx's cigars and pipes made it hard to see. Yet the two adults and three to four children lived in these two rooms.

Naturally, the strain took a toll. Marx suffered from liver problems, boils, headaches, hemorrhoids, and rheumatism, often having to spend days and even weeks in bed. Jenny suffered "hysterical outbreaks," with wailing, complaining, and tears.

The spy further described Marx's personal habits at that time (Padover 1978:291–92): "In private life he is a highly disorderly person. Washing, grooming, and changing underwear are rarities with him. ... Often he loafs all day long, but if he has work to do, he works day and night tirelessly. He does not have a fixed time for sleeping and staying up; very often he stays up all night, and at noon he lies down on the sofa fully dressed and sleeps until evening, unconcerned about the comings and goings around him." More generously, the spy said of Marx: "One sees in him a man of genius and energy; his intellectual superiority exerts irresistible power on his surroundings." With his children, "who are very good looking and have the intelligent eyes of their father ... he is the most tender and docile of men."

Writing His Masterpiece

Marx's attitude toward revolution led him to withdraw from most political activity for many years. Until the workers understood their historical revolutionary role, they would be powerless against the armed forces of the government. He would need to contribute instead to the slow process of education, which would lead to a permanent revolution. He broke with other exiled radicals, who were too passionate, too willing to compromise, or too lacking in principle for him.

Combined with his poverty and sickness, Marx's isolation from political activities brought out the worst in his personality. His natural suspiciousness, aggressiveness, and quarrelsomeness separated him from many radicals. Although the humiliations of poverty and the lack of respect he thought he deserved harmed his personality, they contributed to his work. "Acute misery of isolation and marginality, in its turn fueled and refueled the sense of outrage and indignation that informs his work" (Coser 1977:85). Anger and hate helped give him the strength and desire to become such an insightful and unyielding critic.

Given the trials Marx faced, other men might have questioned or discarded their views. Yet Marx never questioned his own ideas, instead blaming the outside world for his problems and viewing self-pity as a frivolous personal weakness. He continued to believe in the importance of his work, never seriously considering taking a job that would obstruct his writing and research. Moreover, he remained close to those who continued to support his work and ideas.

Marx spent much of his time—typically from 10:00 A.M. to 7:00 P.M.—in the reading room of the British Museum. The library there contained seldom-read reports of the British government on factory conditions, business facts, and economic trends. His massive notes taken from these reports would provide the evidence needed to prove his theory. Although his review of the evidence was selective, his attention to social and economic data represented a first step in empirical social science.

He spent 18 years working on his masterpiece, *Capital.* In 1851 he said he would finish in five weeks, in 1859 he said he would finish in six weeks, and in 1865 he provided his publisher with a bundle of illegible papers that took two years to edit and publish. In 1867, Volume 1 came out. He never finished other volumes himself; but after his death, Engels reworked and edited Marx's rough drafts and notes to produce Volume 2 in 1885 and Volume 3 in 1894. Volume 4, little more than notes on other writers, appeared in 1910.

Marx wrote that to produce this book he had "sacrificed health, happiness, and family. ... I laugh at so-called 'practical men' and their wisdom. If one were willing to be an ox, one could naturally turn one's back on human suffering and look after one's own skin. But I would have really considered myself 'unpractical' if I caved in before making my book, or at least my manuscript, quite ready" (McLellan 1971:83).

Why the delay and struggle in finishing the book? Financial and health problems often prevented Marx from working, and he spent time on smaller projects during those years. Perhaps the major explanation, however, is that he was a notoriously slow writer who spent most of his time reading and taking notes. Engels constantly encouraged him to stop reading and start writing, but Marx could not accelerate the slow process of organizing all the information he had accumulated and putting on paper all the complex ideas he had.

The Source of Value

Marx began *Capital* with a discussion of commodities. Like other economists at the time, he accepted the premise that the value of a commodity or product came from the amount of labor used to produce it. The more labor contributed by workers, the greater the value. In precapitalist societies, a tanner and a carpenter exchanging leather for furniture could in rough terms decide on the equivalency between, say, a leather coat and a wooden chair based on how much labor it took to produce each product. The trade would fairly meet the living needs of both.

However, industrial capitalism changes the nature of exchange. Workers can produce more than they need to survive, and one class can benefit from this new productive capacity. Laws of private ownership give capitalists ownership of the final product, even though the labor of the worker gives the product its value. The capitalist can make a profit simply by selling the product while paying workers less than the amount of value they contributed to it. At minimum, workers need wages to meet basic needs for food, clothing, and shelter. By paying subsistence wages, capitalists can keep the remaining value for profit.

In Marx's view, profit equals unpaid labor that workers involuntarily contribute. Workers spend part of their workday contributing value in exchange for their wages, but they spend the remaining part of the day contributing value that goes only to the capitalist. Marx called the extra or unpaid work contributed by workers **surplus value**. By virtue of their ownership of the means of production, capitalists are in the position to take from workers this surplus value as profit. The capitalist does little to deserve what rightfully belongs to the worker, but the system of social relations under capitalism—a system in which some own the means of production and others own only their own labor—creates this exploitation of one class by another.

Behind the activities of production and exchange lie unequal social relations. This conception of value portrays a system of stolen work that warrants moral indignation but, more to Marx's purpose, also has implications for processes of change. A contradiction exists between (1) the advancing technology of production that requires organization and cooperation and (2) the unequal social relations based on private property that require individualistic competition.

Given the constraints faced by workers (and by Marx himself in his financial difficulties), the claim that individuals have rights and freedoms in modern societies makes little sense; those rights guarantee most people the chance to become slaves to wage labor. Rather than isolated individuals making choices, the social world consists of unequal social relationships based on the nature of economic production. Property ownership and the sale of work for pay may seem natural and necessary, but they actually stem from a particular form of social organization. True rights and freedom would come with the end of classes, when the worker's labor is no longer a commodity to be sold for wages.

The Sources of Revolution

In *Capital*, Marx aimed to prove his claim that the end of capitalism was not only desirable but inevitable. He needed to demonstrate, rather than merely assert, that the pursuit of profit under a system of private ownership of the means of production resulted in the downfall of that system. His reasoning went as follows.

Over time, the contradictions contained in the system worsen. Better than any other previous system, capitalism produces goods and products to sell. However, the supply of products soon exceeds the demand of buyers and the money available to buy them. To compete in the market and maintain profits, capitalists try to cut costs by forcing workers to work longer and harder. Eventually, they try to cut costs by replacing workers with machines. Yet, since value comes from workers, machines increase only short-term profit—fewer workers means lower profits in the longer run.

In turn, lower wages and fewer workers result in periods of economic crisis. Sales and profits drop, while business bankruptcies and unemployment increase. Only a small number of the largest companies can survive. Many capitalists lose their businesses, and teachers, shopkeepers, and others who depend on larger businesses for their livelihood lose their jobs during these depressions. Many from the capitalist class are forced to join the working class. With their growing numbers, workers develop a sense of unity with one another and feelings of class solidarity. The growing power and solidarity of workers in the class struggle eventually result in revolution and communism.

The first volume of *Capital* was not an immediate success. The massive book received little attention at first and earned few royalties. Workers could not understand it, and intellectuals ignored it. Slowly, as its message came to be known in Europe and Russia, it began to have some influence. Young revolutionaries would come to London to visit Marx and share their hopes for coming change. Yet compared to the effort put into the book, the response was disheartening. Marx now worked less hard on his writing, still reading and taking notes but failing to organize them for additional volumes. Not until after his death, in 1883, would Engels and others organize these writings and notes into additional volumes of *Capital*.

7. THE POWER OF IDEOLOGY

Financial help came in 1863 and 1864 from the death of an admirer and friend in England and of Marx's mother in Germany, both of whom left modest inheritances. Still lacking any sense of budgetary discipline, Marx used the new funds to move to a much nicer home in a less congested part of London. As these funds ran out, Engels came to the rescue. Tiring of his dual role as revolutionary and successful capitalist, he managed in 1869 to sell his share of his dead father's business for a substantial profit, which he used to retire to London and set up an annuity for his friend and colleague. The annuity provided Marx with a substantial yearly income that well exceeded the average in London. The torture of poverty ended for the last 15 to 20 years of Marx's life.

Marx continued to suffer from health problems, especially from boils and skin irritations that made both sitting and moving uncomfortable. When not bothered by illness, however, he appeared to his family

and close friends as kind, generous, and even jovial. With his three sur-
viving daughters, he played games, read stories, and went on picnics. As
they grew older, he treated them as intellectual equals, insisting on good
schooling and music lessons. Throughout his life, Marx's daughters were
devoted to him.

The International

During these years, Marx sometimes presented his views less rigidly
than he had in the past. Although he supported armed revolution all his
life, he also began to admit the possibility of change through other
means. If rulers responded to social and economic changes with violence, so would the workers. In France, for example, a worker's revolt in
1870 resulted in violence (and, alas, the defeat of the workers). Perhaps
in England or Holland, however, the rulers would allow workers to gain
political power and make needed changes without violence.

A willingness to wait patiently for the proper conditions to emerge
guided his activities as the leader of a new organization of workers from
across the world called the International. More an organization that publicized views advocating on behalf of workers than a trade union itself,
the International nonetheless gained a large following of union members
and affiliates. Marx used the International to help spread his views outside England, and *Capital* became an influential guide for the organization. He thought that the International could prepare workers for a communist society by educating them about the laws of change and the need
to organize and cooperate.

As a result of these views, he had to battle more impatient radicals
on the Continent who conspired to advocate immediate violence. Anar-
chists, who opposed all form of government and authority—even that of
the proletariat—challenged the goals of the International and Marx's
strategy of waiting for economic conditions to worsen. At the other pole,
social democrats favored the establishment of a worker's political party
to bring about change. Although the International dissolved from the internal conflict, Marx gained much influence and helped secure his reputation through his activities on behalf of this organization.

Religion, Law, and Politics

Marx realized that the dominance of the capitalist class would limit the
effectiveness of his organizational and intellectual efforts. Capitalists
had the advantage in the class struggle of controlling the noneconomic
as well as economic institutions of society. He defined **ideology** as a
system of ideas, attitudes, and beliefs that stem from the social relations within a particular system of production. Ideology justifies the
material interests of the dominant class. Since ideology favors one class
over another and hides the conflict that really underlies social relations,

Marx's work in opposition to capitalism would for now have only limited influence.

Consider some of the ideological forces that favor bourgeois values and beliefs. According to Marx, religion, which guides the thoughts and behaviors of huge numbers of people, does little to question the nature of existing social relationships. Religion functions to moderate the pain of life on earth. It directs attention to a better life in the afterworld rather than to improvements in material conditions in this world and advocates individual efforts to follow social rules rather than group efforts to bring about social change. An atheist and critic of religion since a young man, Marx called religion the opiate of the people—something that gives temporary relief and a sense of well-being without changing the situation that causes the pain in the first place.

Like religious institutions, legal and political institutions favor the interests of the dominant class. In blunt terms, Marx wrote, "The ruling ideas are nothing more than the ideal expression of the dominant material relationships." The state or government serves as an instrument of the ruling class to oppress subordinate classes. After all, how can the state act otherwise? Its power depends on taxes generated by commerce, sales, and wealth—all factors controlled by the bourgeoisie in capitalist societies. In the long run, the interests of government leaders are the same as the interests of the dominant class.

Rather than changing society, the state helps maintain unequal social relations. The only institution given legitimate control over the military and police, the state can use violence to defend capitalists against worker protests and rebellions. If capitalists themselves cannot control the larger number of workers, they can rely on government police and military (paid with taxes from the bourgeoisie) to restrain them. The leaders of France, Belgium, Austria, Italy, and Prussia thus used their troops to end the rebellions of 1848.

The government also establishes the legal code that maintains private property and justifies government acts of violence. Laws guaranteeing the sanctity of private property favor dominant classes over subordinate ones, reinforcing existing inequality and injustice rather than bringing about cooperation and justice. Marx of course favored legal changes that supported workers—and many statutes helping to protect workers emerged during his lifetime—but he did not expect that laws would change significantly until the form of material production changed.

One can exaggerate the independent influence of material factors on ideal factors in Marx's work. In contrast to some of his blunter statements about the dominance of the ruling class, his studies of history reveal that political factors can operate separately from class interests. Indeed, Marx's ideas and ideals have themselves became remarkably influential in guiding the behavior of millions of the world's people. In this sense, culture, language, and beliefs can influence material conditions as well as result from them. Yet, in the long run, class determines ideology, values, and beliefs.

Continuing Class Conflict

In 1881 Jenny died of cancer, and Engels remarked at the time that Marx would die with her. Indeed, his health problems forced him to travel to North Africa and other parts of England seeking warmer and drier weather. When at home, he continued to read and work in his study, but without concrete goals for publication. One night, his daughters heard him move from his bed to his study. Knowing their father to be quite sick, they soon checked the study and found that he had died at his desk (Wilson 1940:333). In 1883, Marx was buried in Highgate Cemetery, London, near his home.

Despite limited influence during his life, Marx's ideas came to dominate the twentieth century. With the Russian Revolution in 1917, the control of Eastern Europe under communism after World War II, the Chinese Revolution in 1949, and the Cuban Revolution in 1959, large parts of the world's population adopted various forms of Marxism. These developments associated Marx with totalitarian control of society and an economy controlled by state bureaucracies—results at odds with Marx's goal of human freedom. The end of communism in the Soviet Union and Eastern Europe as well as the movement toward free markets and democratic governments almost everywhere else reflect a near-unanimous rejection of Soviet-style Marxism.

Still, within the high-income democracies of Western Europe, class struggle remains an important part of political conflict. In attempting to understand the sources of political divisions, political sociologists in recent decades have extended and revised Marx's concepts. Class conflict exists in North America and Western Europe in the form of competition between political parties. Socialist or social democratic parties representing workers desire to use taxes and public spending to reduce the role of the market in workers' lives, while conservative parties representing business and the middle classes desire the opposite.

Recall that Marx saw the treatment of workers' labor as a commodity to be sold for wages on the market as an essential component of capitalism. Accordingly, socialist or social democratic parties desire to reduce the dependence of workers on earnings and the labor market. They want government programs to provide for essential services—such as health care, pensions, and assistance when unemployed—on the basis of need rather than private income. These programs favor the interests of workers by lessening the importance of wages for social well-being and making labor less of a commodity.

Peaceful Class Conflict

Scholars today identify three changes since Marx's time that warrant a shift in worker strategy from armed conflict to peaceful competition in the political arena. First, the extension of the right to vote to most adults during the twentieth century gave the working class a new tool. Democratic elections give each person one vote, which favors the larger working class; the private market gives each dollar one vote, which favors richer business owners. Although money certainly influences elections, workers have a better chance to realize their interests democratically than economically.

Second, the growth of labor unions has provided the basis for organized action. Electoral victory requires organizing diverse and geographically separated workers into a cohesive group that recognizes and acts in its own interests. Where unions are centralized and large, they can mobilize workers to support socialist parties and policies that reduce the commodity status of workers. In Sweden, for example, more than 90 percent of workers belong to unions, and the Social Democratic party there has remained in power for much of the last 50 years.

Third, the growth of the welfare state provides workers with alternate means of support. In Sweden, more than 50 percent of national income is taxed by the government for redistribution in the form of public programs. All citizens, regardless of their income or work history, can receive generous benefits for health care, retirement, and other services. The welfare state has grown in the twentieth century in part because of the pressure of labor unions and socialist parties, but the acceptance of state intervention in the economy makes worker goals easier to realize.

The end result could be described as socialism through democratic means. One recent scholar argues that "Marx contended that once capitalism had created the material conditions for socialism the growth of working class organization would be the critical development for the transition to socialism. Many have viewed this as an argument in favor of union organization and participation in the political arena. Socialism has come to a large extent in many countries from the organization of the proletariat and the development of the welfare state" (Stephens 1979:2). Although incorrect in many of his predictions, Marx's claim for the importance of class relations for both capitalism and socialism remains valid.

Unlike Marx, however, scholars today do not view this outcome as inevitable. In many nations, organizing labor unions has been difficult. Less than 20 percent of workers belong to unions in the United States, and these workers are split into numerous unions with different interests and goals. When in power, the Democratic party, although more liberal than Republicans, has not always responded with programs favoring workers. As a result, government policies for pensions, unemployment, and health care do less to protect workers in the United States than in most European nations.

With adaptation, scholars still find Marx's work insightful and valuable in understanding modern society. Although not inevitable, the organization of workers into a powerful economic and political force has emerged with industrial growth in some nations. Although more complex than Marx had predicted, the struggle between classes remains basic to political parties in most nations. Although not rapid and violent, important changes have occurred in public policies that support workers and those in need. Capitalism in its pure form has indeed adapted and changed for many of the reasons Marx said it would.

SUMMARY

Along with enormous new wealth, industrial capitalism brought misery to workers and created new forms of poverty during the late 1700s and early 1800s. Marx rejected two dominant views about industrial capitalism and its consequences. He rejected the views of English economists, who focused on the laws of supply and demand and attributed the problems of workers to high fertility as much as to low wages. He also rejected the views of French socialist writers, who ignored laws of social change and naively hoped that good intentions alone could end private property and social misery.

Instead, Marx argued that economic well-being depends on social relations and that social relations depend on class position. In basic terms, Marx defined social classes as persons who have the same position and perform the same role in the production of food, machines, and goods. Upper classes derive their privilege from ownership of the means of production, and lower classes own nothing but their own labor power. In capitalism, owners of capital control such things as factories, banks, and railroads, while workers must depend on wage earnings for survival. Classes define the central division in society.

The attention to classes emphasizes the importance of work and economic arrangements. In contrast to philosophers who gave primacy to the world of ideas, Marx realized that humans, in order to survive, must first develop ways to produce food, shelter, and clothing. The mode of production of a society—how people produce what they need to support them in life—determines the kind of class relations that exist in a society. Marx attributed the sources of human misery—poverty, inequality, injustice—to unequal class relations. Only by changing the nature of production could society rectify the sources of human misery.

According to Marx, unequal class relations result in the exploitation of workers by capitalists. The value of products that people make, sell, and buy comes from the amount of labor workers exert to produce them. However, laws of private property give capitalists ownership of the products, and capitalists can make a profit simply by selling the product, while paying workers less than the amount of value they contribute to it. By paying miserly wages, capitalists can keep the remaining value for profit—value that rightfully belongs to the worker. Workers and owners under capitalism come to have competing interests.

Competing class interests highlight the central importance of social conflict and domination in social life. To continue to maximize profit in competitive markets, business owners must reduce the wages and increase the hours of workers. To improve their lives, workers desire to share in the profits. The effort of both classes to realize their clashing interests creates conflict and struggle, which cannot be wished away or settled by reasonable people discussing their differences.

Dominant classes have advantages in this social conflict. Although workers have the advantage of large numbers, capitalists own the sources of information: governments use police violence against striking workers in support of capitalists, newspapers and universities advocate political views favoring capitalists, and religion focuses on the rewards after life rather than on changing the world now. In the short run, therefore, workers face enormous obstacles in improving their lives.

Social conflict, however, produces pressures for social change that eventually come to favor workers over capitalists. Unequal social relations ultimately produce cycles of economic depression and unemployment and each cycle worsens the conditions of workers, who will come to act as a class in advocating revolution. Eventually, these pressures toward change will burst open, bringing about a revolution and a classless society. These laws of social change made Marx's theory scientific and realistic rather than utopian and romantic.

In addition to describing the material bases of society, the nature of social conflict, and the inevitability of social change, Marx emphasized action. He described the unjust treatment of workers with indignity and bitterness, hoping he could help improve their lives. His emotional criticism of capitalism and stirring calls for action continue to influence many readers. In this way, Marx's approach differs from those who advocate objective and unemotional scholarship.

Despite the attention it gives to economics, Marx's work is inherently sociological. Economists often treat people as isolated and separate units that cooperate to fulfill personal needs and wants. In contrast, Marx viewed pursuit of profit in the market by individuals as part of a particular form of social organization: the social ties between owners and workers, buyers and sellers, and rulers and the ruled mean that isolated individuals making free choices do not exist. Understanding class relations is the key to understanding social life. Although the conditions and nature of class conflict have changed, Marx's ideas still have relevance today in the competition between classes, political parties, and advantaged and disadvantaged groups.

DISCUSSION QUESTIONS

1. What consequences did Marx's political and religious views have for his professional opportunities in Germany? How might his treatment by German authorities have contributed to the later transformation of his liberal and democratic views to revolutionary and socialist views?

2. Describe the costs and benefits of industrial capitalism and the divergent reaction of English economists and French socialists to those costs and benefits. Do these views correspond to different economic and political beliefs about capitalism today?

3. Explain what Marx meant by material factors and means of production. How did Marx apply Hegel's concept of dialectic change to understand changes in material factors?

4. Define alienation and the forms it takes among workers in capitalism. Does the concept apply as much today as in the past?

5. What criticisms did Marx make of the work of the French socialists? How did his view of the importance of domination and inequality in social relationships contradict the assumptions made by British economists about individual free choice?

6. During the struggle between classes in capitalism, what changes occur in the size and power of the working class that eventually produce revolution? Why, according to Marx, did the events of 1848 fail to lead to a successful revolution?

7. How did financial problems in London affect Marx's family, living conditions, and personality? Did Marx's problems supporting himself contribute more generally to his perspective on capitalism?

8. What gives value to a commodity? What is surplus labor? What contradiction stems from unequal social relations in industrial capitalism, and how does it produce economic crises?

9. How do religious, legal, and government institutions in capitalist society favor capitalists? Give examples of capital's ideological power in modern society.

10. What form does class conflict often take in high-income political democracies today? What changes since Marx's time have contributed to the form of modern class conflict?

REFERENCES

PRIMARY SOURCES

Marx, Karl. 1963 [1852]. *The Eighteenth Brumaire of Louis Bonaparte.* New York: International Publishers.

Marx, Karl. 1964. *Karl Marx: Early Writings* (edited & translated by T. B. Bottomore). New York: McGraw-Hill.

Marx, Karl. 1992 [1867]. *Capital* (Vol. 1; translated by Ben Fowkes). New York: Viking Penguin.

Marx, Karl, & Friedrich Engels. 1970 [1846]. *The German Ideology* (edited by C. J. Arthur). New York: International Publishers.

Marx, Karl, & Friedrich Engels. 1992 [1848]. *The Communist Manifesto.* New York: Bantam Books.

SECONDARY SOURCES

Aron, Raymond. 1965. *Main Currents in Sociological Thought* (Vol. 1). Garden City, NY: Doubleday.

Ashley, David, & David Michael Orenstein. 1995. *Sociological Theory: Classic Statements* (3rd ed.). Boston: Allyn & Bacon.

Berger, Peter. 1986. *The Capitalist Revolution.* New York: Basic Books.

Berlin, Isaiah. 1996. *Karl Marx* (4th ed.). New York: Oxford University Press.

Collins, Randall. 1985. *Three Sociological Traditions.* New York: Oxford University Press.

Collins, Randall, & Michael Makowsky. 1989. *The Discovery of Society* (4th ed.). New York: Random House.

Coser, Lewis A. 1977. *Masters of Sociological Thought* (2nd ed.). San Diego: Harcourt Brace Jovanovich.

Dahrendorf, Ralf. 1959. *Class and Class Conflict in Industrial Society.* Stanford, CA: Stanford University.

Esping-Andersen, Gsta. 1990. *The Three Worlds of Welfare Capitalism.* Princeton, NJ: Princeton University Press.

Giddens, Anthony. 1971. *Capitalism and Modern Social Theory.* London: Cambridge University Press.

Gouldner, Alvin. 1970. *The Coming Crisis of Western Sociology.* New York: Basic Books.

Hawthorne, Geoffrey. 1987. *Enlightenment and Despair: A History of Sociological Theory* (2nd ed.). Cambridge, UK: Cambridge University Press.

Heilbroner, Robert L. 1967. *The Worldly Philosophers.* New York: Simon & Schuster.

Korpi, Walter. 1983. *The Democratic Class Struggle.* London: Routledge & Kegan Paul.

Lenski, Gerhard, & Jean Lenski. 1987. *Human Societies: An Introduction to Macrosociology* (5th ed.). New York: McGraw-Hill.

Lipset, Seymour Martin. 1964. *Political Man: The Social Bases of Politics.* Garden City, NY: Anchor.

McLellan, David. 1971. *The Thought of Karl Marx: An Introduction.* New York: Harper & Row.

McLellan, David. 1974. *Karl Marx: His Life and Thought.* New York: Harper & Row.

Morrison, Ken. 1995. *Marx, Durkheim, Weber: The Formation of Modern Social Thought.* Thousands Oaks, CA: Sage.

Myles, John. 1984. *Old Age in the Welfare State: The Political Economy of Public Pensions.* Boston: Little, Brown.

Nisbet, Robert A. 1966. *The Sociological Tradition.* New York: Basic Books.

Padover, Saul K. 1978. *Karl Marx: An Intimate Biography.* New York: McGraw-Hill.

Peters, H. F. 1986. *Red Jenny: A Life with Karl Marx.* London: Allen & Unwin.

Ritzer, George. 1996. *Sociological Theory* (4th ed.). New York: McGraw-Hill.

Rubel, Maximilien. 1965. *Marx: Life and Works* (translated by Mary Bottomore). New York: Facts on File.

Schwarzschild, Leopold. 1947. *Karl Marx: The Red Prussian.* New York: Grosset & Dunlap.

Stephens, John D. 1979. *The Transition from Capitalism to Socialism.* London: Macmillan.

Viault, Birdsall S. 1990. *Modern European History.* New York: McGraw-Hill.

Walton, John. 1986. *Sociology and Critical Inquiry.* Chicago: Dorsey.

Weeks, John R. 1989. *Population: Introduction to Concepts and Issues* (4th ed.). Belmont, CA: Wadsworth.

Wilson, Edmund. 1940. *To the Finland Station.* New York: Harcourt Brace Jovanovich.

Worsley, Peter. 1982. *Marx and Marxism.* London: Tavistock.

REFERENCE NOTES

Citations for quotations and special points of interest are given in the text. Listed here are citations to sources for major topics covered in each section of the chapter.

1. **Toward Permanent Exile:** Marx's youth (Coser 1977:58–60; Walton 1986:52–53); Bauer and Marx (Padover 1978:124; McLellan 1974:43; Ashley & Orenstein 1995:224); Marx and Hess (Berlin 1996:55; McLellan 1971:4); Journalism experience (Coser 1977:60; Padover 1978:145–146; Berlin 1996:55); Relationship with father (Padover 1978:7; Berlin 1996:21); Ludwig von Westphalen (Berlin 1996:23; Coser 1977:79); Jenny (Padover 1978:48); Marx's mother (Berlin 1996:23; Padover 1978:11); Family opposition (McLellan 1974:65; Padover 1978:53); Marx's looks and personality (Padover 1978:46–47; Hawthorne 1987:51); Marx and communism (Berlin 1996:60; Coser 1977:62).

2. **Responses to Industrialism:** Industrial transformation (Berger 1986:3, 17, 34, 42; Viault 1990:236, 258; Lenski & Lenski 1987:235, 252; Nisbet 1966:23); Adam Smith (Heilbroner 1967:38–67); Malthus (Heilbroner 1967:68–75); Ricardo (Heilbroner 1967:75–95); French writers (Berlin 1996:62, 66–69; Ashley & Orenstein 1995:227); Saint-Simon (Berlin 1996:66); Fourier (Heilbroner 1967:96–122); Proudhon (Berlin 1996:69–70, 82); Germany (Coser 1977:77).

3. **The Material Basis of Social Life:** In Paris (Padover 1978; 159–160; Peters 1986:46–50; Berlin 1996:61); Marx's intellectual activities (Padover 1978:188–192; Walton 1986:53; McLellan 1971:69); Materialism (Berlin 1996:106–107; Giddens 1971:xiii, 7; Morrison 1995:319; Berlin 1996:53); Hegel (Heilbroner 1967:129; Coser 1977:70–72; Ashley & Orenstein 1995:236); Alienation (McLellan 1971:36).

4. **A Revolutionary Socialist:** Engels (McLellan 1974:131; Ritzer 1996:47; Berlin 1996:75; Worsley 1982:29; Padover 1978:186–187); Arnold Ruge (McLellan 1971:16; Schwarzschild 1947:88; Padover 1978:176, 199); Marx's transformation (Collins 1985:54); Scientific theory (Coser 1977:82; Worsley 1982:32; Ashley & Orenstein 1995:242; Berlin 1996:64; Coser 1977:81; Padover 1978:320); Sociological theory (Ritzer 1996:62; Giddens 1971:10, 23; Aron 1965:161).

5. ***The Communist Manifesto:*** Exile (Padover 1978:197–199; Gouldner 1970:20; Collins & Makowsky 1989:32; Coser 1977:85; McLellan 1971:29); In Brussels (Padover 1978: 204, 208, 244–245); *Manifesto* (Marx & Engels 1992[1867]); Coser 1977:63; Giddens 1971:37; Aron 1965:152; Nisbet 1966: 285); Revolution of 1848 (Berlin 1996: 180; Ashley & Orenstein 1995:228; Viault 1990:284–285; McLellan 1974:190, 224).

6. **Capital and Surplus Labor:** Life in London (Berlin 1996:129–130; McLellan 1974:224–228, 268–269; Padover 1978:287–292; Coser 1977:63; Ashley & Orenstein 1995:225; McLellan 1971:65); Prussian spy (McLellan 1974:268–269); Attitude toward revolution (Berlin 1996:137–139); Personality (Berlin 1996:134, 143, 206–207; Coser 1977:64, 85; Wilson 1940:151); Writing *Capital* (Berlin 1996:183; Heilbroner 1967:140; McLellan 1971:83; Rubel 1965:25); On *Capital* (Worsley 1982:20; Heilbroner 1967:113; Nisbet 1966:136; Giddens 1971:35); Reaction (McLellan 1974:353; Padover 1978:370).

7. **The Power of Ideology:** Finances (Coser 1977:67; McLellan 1974:329; Padover 1978:338; Coser 1977:67); Family (Padover 1978:472–473); Less rigid views (Padover 1978:381; Berlin 1996:189; McLellan 1971:201); International (Padover 1978:392; Berlin 1996:169); Ideology (Morrison 1995:317; Worsley 1982:27; Giddens 1971:40, 209; Berlin 1996:208; Nisbet 1966:206); Death (McLellan 1974:425; Wilson 1940:333); Scholars today (Lipset 1964; Korpi 1983; Dahrendorf 1959; Esping-Andersen 1990; Myles 1984; Stephens 1979).

chapter 2

The Problem of Social Order: Émile Durkheim and Morality in Modern Societies

With a population of more than 260 million and citizens set apart by their race, ethnic group, religious beliefs, immigration status, region of residence, political views, income, and values, the United States contains enormous diversity. Some even wonder how we manage to co-exist with such diversity. How does a democracy based on civility, compromise, and understanding work as well as it does in the face of the potential for hostility, extremism, and self-interest? Forces of division in democratic societies show in conflicts over war, immigration, racial discrimination, abortion, economic inequality, and innumerable other issues.

The potential for disorder and conflict shows in other ways. Modern societies exhibit high rates of violence in both suicide and homicide. Compared to other nations, the United States has especially high rates of murder, and parts of the country, particularly rural western states, have suicide rates as high as any place in the world. The United States also has higher rates of divorce than most nations. All these indicators may reflect weakened bonds among members of modern society.

That our society nonetheless manages to function in the face of potential disorder reflects the need to balance individual interests with public interests. Yet sometimes the proper balance is hard to find. While some worry about the power of society to control our lives, others worry about the lack of social ties in an increasingly self-centered world.

In the late 1800s, the French sociologist Émile Durkheim considered the same issues. After a century of political violence, rule by monarchs, and a disastrous defeat in war with Germany, France had recently established a democracy. Yet many groups still opposed democracy, and the threat of revolution remained strong. Durkheim worried about the ability of France specifically and modern societies more generally to withstand the forces of violence, breakdown, division, and individualism. He further worried about rising rates of suicide and divorce in France and throughout Europe—symptoms of the lack of ties of individuals to larger groups.

Durkheim did more than worry. Possessed of a coolly rational personality and a keen ability to grasp complex issues, he advocated the use of logical thinking and scientific methods to understand the social sources of these problems. In so doing, he defined a new field of study that emphasized the decisive influence of group membership on individual behavior.

Threats to democracy and peace seem less severe today than in Durkheim's time, but many of the insights Durkheim offered about the problems of his time still are relevant today. His work stressed the basic needs of societies for social order and moral behavior and described the problems created by trends toward individualism. In studying crime, suicide, morality, loss of community ties, and the sources of religious meaning, he linked individual behavior to the ties people have to their social groups.

Compared to Karl Marx, Émile Durkheim has had little influence on world politics and social movements. Other than social scientists in the United States and intellectuals in France, few know Durkheim's name well. Students new to sociology, however, learn early about Durkheim. More than any other theorist, he defined sociology as a separate field with its own goals, methods, and objects of study. His ideas helped establish sociology as a new discipline at French universities, and his classic works offered fine examples of theories and research methods to sociologists in the United States.

During his lifetime, Durkheim faced heated criticism for his advocacy of sociology. Today, most sociologists accept his attention to social forces, even if they disagree with more specific details of his approach. The problem of social order that he addressed and his attack on unrestrained individualism remain essential to the field. Even today, sociologists and concerned citizens still debate the same problem Durkheim did: How can we balance the need to belong to and find moral guidance from the larger community with the need to express our individuality and enjoy our personal freedom?

1. FROM SMALL-TOWN FRANCE TO PARIS

In 1879, Émile Durkheim entered France's most prestigious college, the École Normale Supérieure. He found that it required an astounding amount of work: every day except Sunday, students rose at 6:30 A.M. (6:00 in the summer), ate a quick breakfast, and proceeded to attend classes and study for the next 11 hours (Clark 1973:38–39). Although stimulating, the work was also exhausting, and students looked forward to sleep at the end of the day.

Sleep often came with difficulty, however. The college lodgings were bare, dark, and unhealthy. Too cold at times and stuffy and hot at other times, the rooms made sleep uncomfortable and rest difficult. For Durkheim, problems during his first year in college made sleep all the more difficult. Things had not worked out as he had expected. He had always wanted to come to Paris to study at the École Normale, but now, at age 21, he felt immensely disappointed.

Not many years earlier, Durkheim's teachers, family, and friends had viewed him as destined for greatness as a scholar. In the small French town of Épinal, with a population of only a few thousand, he had shown such brilliance in school that he had skipped two grades. His serious personality and studious nature suited him well for a career as a scholar and teacher. Even his rabbi father, who at one time might have wanted his son also to become a rabbi, came to agree that Émile should go to Paris to prepare for entrance into a prestigious college.

Having done exactly that, Durkheim realized he had opportunities that few if any of his friends and acquaintances would have. For one, he could live in Paris. Even in 1879, Paris was perceived by many as the world's greatest city. London might have had more industry and commerce, Rome might have had a longer history as the center of an empire, and Vienna might have had an exceptional tradition in music and the arts, but Paris had it all—beauty, art, wealth, tradition, power, prestige, and confidence.

During the 1600s and 1700s, Paris had been home to some of the world's richest and most powerful kings, the center of the philosophical Enlightenment and rationalism in Europe, and the source of stirrings for democracy that had culminated in the French Revolution. More recently, Paris had seen the artistic revolution of Impressionism emerge, the immensely popular and powerful writing of Victor Hugo in Les Misérables, and the scientific discovery of bacteria by Louis Pasteur. Even if some outside of France failed to recognize the greatness of this wonderful city, those inside France, spread around the country in rural areas and smaller cities, viewed Paris as the spiritual center of the country and perhaps the world (Braudel 1988).

Durkheim also had the opportunity to enjoy the intellectual stimulation at the École Normale. Not surprisingly, given its central role in French life, Paris contained France's best schools, and exceptional students from all over the country came to attend several elite lycées (an advanced version of high school), colleges, and universities in Paris. Particularly intense competition existed to attend two colleges: the École Normale Supérieure for training in arts and sciences—needed to teach at the lycées—and the École Polytechnique for training in engineering and the applied sciences. If accepted at these schools, students received free room, board, and tuition. Thus, with work and intelligence, even students from modest backgrounds like Durkheim's could afford to attend the nation's best colleges.

So intense was the competition to attend the École Normale that only 50 of 500 applicants were accepted each year, often after several attempts (Clark 1973:38). Students often had to attend a lycée for extra years to prepare for entrance exams that lasted four days. But after much effort, Durkheim reached his goal: he had enrolled in the École Normale to prepare for a career in teaching.

Competition and Isolation

Still, the delights of Paris and the intellectual stimulation of college could not make up for other difficulties. No longer the school's best student, as he had been in Épinal, he found his classmates equally or more intelligent and knowledgeable. In fact, having come to Paris several years earlier to prepare for the entrance exam at one of the superb Parisian lycées, Durkheim had the rude shock of failing twice to receive scores high enough for admittance. Only on the third try did he pass. Once at the École Normale, he faced academic competition with a brilliant group of young scholars that would have made almost anyone insecure about his abilities. And Durkheim, less sophisticated and poorer than many students from Paris and larger towns, felt the fear of failure even more strongly: given the high expectations for him of his family and others in Épinal, doing badly would result in special humiliation.

Perhaps even worse than the fear of failure, Durkheim felt lonely and isolated (Lukes 1985:42). He missed his close-knit family. His father had fallen ill in recent years, and Durkheim did all he could to act as head of the family, but the distance of Paris from his hometown, as well as the rigid demands of school, made contact difficult. In addition, he found to his regret that the academic world required individual competition more than cooperation. Rather than intense individualism, he would have preferred something more like his family life: to work more closely with a cohesive group of students and colleagues who shared his goals, ideas, and values.

Durkheim had made friends, of course, and he and his fellow students would spend the limited free time they had discussing controversial issues of the day. Debates over philosophy, politics, religion, morals, and ethics could keep them busy for hours. From these discussions grew friendships that would last the rest of his life. Even so, he felt as if he did not quite belong. In truth, many viewed him as remote and unfriendly— he just couldn't relax and have fun.

Nearly every day, Durkheim had to get up early in the morning for another grueling cycle of work and study. He had classes in Latin and Greek that each met for three hours a week, while the more interesting classes in literature, philosophy, and history each met for only two hours a week. The emphasis on memorizing ancient languages that no one spoke hardly seemed good preparation for entering an increasingly modern, technologically advanced, and fast-changing world. Still, he had to do well even in those classes he disliked.

What frustrated Durkheim about the study of ancient philosophies and languages was that they had little relevance to the real problems facing France at the time. After a century of political conflict with failed revolutions, three kings, and two emperors, France had recently established a Republic that vested power in the citizens and democratically elected representatives. Yet conflict still continued, and the Republic could topple. Fervently devoted to a democratic Republic, Durkheim wanted to do whatever he could to protect it.

Little of what he learned seemed relevant to his democratic goals, nor did the classics have much to say about the growing social problems of crime, suicide, and alcoholism. People seemed less devoted than in the past to religion and traditional moral beliefs of right and wrong. Industrialization had changed the nature of work, and the growth of cities had moved people away from their farmland, relatives, neighbors, and small communities. Although the personal freedom that came with these changes brought pleasure, it also reduced social unity and increased social problems. Modern French society needed moral guidance and social order—but that would not come from Greek and Latin philosophy.

Shallowness and Showiness

Durkheim might have looked forward more to classes in literature, philosophy, and history but for another problem: although the topics had more relevance to modern life than Latin or Greek, the teachers and curriculum lacked substance. Teachers seemed showy, trying to impress students with flowery language, appeals to emotion, and poetic analogies. Rather than knowing a lot about a few specialized subjects, the teachers knew a little about many topics; Durkheim thought they could move smoothly from one topic to another but, on being pressed to delve deeper into a topic, could offer little of value.

The curriculum aggravated this tendency toward shallowness and superficiality by grouping all courses under the category of arts and letters rather than dividing them into specialized subjects. As a result, students could not specialize in one particular field. The broad literary and humanistic emphasis of the curriculum seemed to Durkheim to contradict the trends toward scientific specialization in the outside world.

Given his dedicated and disciplined approach to life, Durkheim intensely wanted the opportunity for systematic learning. He still wanted to study philosophy, but he wanted to learn a more scientific approach to philosophical, political, and social topics. Although he scored well on his exams, he could not bring himself to imitate the phony showiness of many of his teachers and fellow students in his papers and discussions. And although he knew he appeared to be serious and distant to others, he could not help himself. His personality, modest background, and values contradicted the teaching philosophy of most French schools.

One fellow student personified what Durkheim disliked about the style of learning at the École Normale. Henri Bergson, who had grown up in Paris and been educated in the best schools there, used the kind of high-flown and superficial reasoning that irritated Durkheim. Critics subsequently would claim that Bergson relied on clever images and comparisons rather than on careful and logical reasoning to make his arguments. He claimed competence in mathematics and science, but could easily misuse precise terms to fit his own more mystical viewpoints.

With a creative imagination and literary skill that many found stimulating and charming, Bergson would eventually become a renowned philosopher and win the Nobel Prize in literature. Hundreds would come to his lectures and read his books for their poetic language and remarkable style. Durkheim, however, viewed him at school (and would continue to view him later in life) as a rival advocate of a shallow and unscientific philosophy.

No doubt Bergson likewise cared little for Durkheim. Later in life Bergson made fun of Durkheim's intensity and seriousness. As Bergson and his friends would leave a discussion, Durkheim would continue trying to convince listeners with complex arguments: "On the steps of the staircase or even at lunchtime, he would immobilize us with four-forked dilemmas" (Lukes 1985:52). Durkheim's friends found the arguments insightful and impressive, but others found them boring and impossible to follow. Bergson and his friends had as much contempt for Durkheim's style as Durkheim had for Bergson's.

Even so, Durkheim resolved to apply his careful and complex logic to philosophical questions even if others more devoted to literature, art, and performance ridiculed his efforts. He wanted to study crucial moral and philosophical questions but to do so scientifically and systematically. He also wanted to apply his skills and methods to topics of importance to France and its citizens—crime and suicide, integration and unity, morality and social order. Perhaps his own studies would at some point provide the knowledge to guide social reforms that would make for a better life for everyone.

2. POLITICAL AND SOCIAL PROBLEMS IN FRANCE

Durkheim had good reason to worry about France's future. Since the French Revolution nearly a century earlier, France had gone through numerous violent changes in government that warned of more problems in Durkheim's time. The brief period of democracy after the French Revolution in 1789 was a time of terrifying persecution of all those who disagreed with the leaders. During the Reign of Terror, revolutionaries executed 16,000 persons. In 1799, Napoleon seized power and in 1804 declared himself emperor. Three kings followed Napoleon's defeat at Waterloo, but none received widespread support from the population. Another revolution in 1848 replaced the monarchy with a Republic.

Unfortunately, voters in the newly instituted democracy proceeded to elect Napoleon's nephew as president. A few years later, he overthrew the democratic government and declared himself emperor. During the 20-year rule of Napoleon III, France remained deeply divided over the coup and discontented over the failure of democracy. Fortunately for Napoleon III, economic prosperity moderated the potential for conflict. Yet eventually things turned out badly, much as for his uncle before him. Napoleon III lost his empire in a war with Prussia and fled to England in 1871.

The military loss in the Franco-Prussian War of 1871 represented a low point in French history, demoralizing France for decades to come. Before the war, most of the French had believed that their army was Europe's most powerful. Hadn't Napoleon nearly conquered all of Europe earlier in the century? Hadn't French soldiers proven themselves to be brave and skilled fighters in combat? Many had thought it was time to reassert French military power in a war with the arrogant Prussians. Napoleon III, hoping to relive the glory of Napoleon I and regain France's honor, had declared war on Prussia. He, other leaders, and the French population had expected certain victory.

In fact, things turned out just the opposite. Prussia invaded with unexpected suddenness, routing the unprepared French army in days and surrounding Paris soon after. In the eyes of the world, Prussia and the newly emerging nation of Germany had humiliated France.

An Unstable Democracy

In the wake of this defeat, conflicts among the French intensified. Under the eye of Prussian premier Otto von Bismarck, elections established a democratic government whose leaders hoped eventually to install another king. More radical residents of Paris, however, set up their own government and national army in opposition to the new government. After failure to come to terms, a French army invaded Paris and massacred more than 20,000 defenders of Paris. As if defeat by a foreign enemy had not been humiliating enough, a brief but bloody civil war made things all the worse.

Many wondered how a democracy could last after such experiences. One faction desired a return to monarchy and to a prominent role for the Catholic Church. In their view, a return to traditional rulers and values would bring the stability needed to return France to its former strength;

they blamed the loss to Prussia on the unpatriotic actions of republicans, workers, and radicals. In the decades to come, conservative supporters of royalty and the church stood behind any general who promised to restore the lost power and military glory of France by overthrowing the democratic government.

Another faction consisted of a growing, but still relatively small, class of urban workers demanding political rights that traditional regimes had denied them. These radicals wanted a secular rather than a religious nation and advocated equality rather than inherited differences in status, power, and wealth. They believed that only a democracy that gave each person an equal say in government could fairly represent the needs of workers. In the economic realm, workers favored higher wages, government support for labor unions, and public welfare programs to protect those in need. More extreme socialists wanted to abolish private property altogether.

A third faction of urban business owners supported individual rights and free markets. These capitalists wanted freedom from the economic restrictions imposed by the aristocracy and landowners as well as freedom from the political restrictions imposed by kings and emperors. They also wanted to contain the economic threat of radical socialists and workers who demanded high wages, greater taxes, and economic equality.

Compromise among these groups and other smaller groups with more specialized goals seemed impossible. Each aimed for total victory rather than compromise. If on the losing side of a decision, each group wanted to avenge that loss rather than move forward. As a result, little trust existed among the factions and agreements seldom lasted. Under the republican system of government in France, leaders came from coalitions formed among elected representatives. In 39 years, the French Republic saw its legislators create and disband 49 governments, with each one lasting on average nine months (Bernstein 1990:235).

These conflicts in public life cost France much of its greatness. Although Germany, England, and the United States also experienced political struggles, the politicians in these nations seemed willing to cooperate when necessary. In contrast, the French were contentious, passionate, and unwilling to compromise. They were proud, vain, and desiring of individual glory, unable to put aside their differences to achieve long-term goals. They still viewed France as a great and powerful nation but could not unite in order to realize that potential greatness. Slowly but steadily, generation after generation, France's military strength and international pride shrank during the 1800s. Although still the cultural and intellectual center of Europe, France had to face its decline as a world power.

The conflicts also revealed a troubling potential for abuse of power by political leaders, the military, and popular mobs. Although violence had occurred throughout the history of France and the rest of Europe, the traditional authority of the family, church, and king had managed to maintain some stability in the face of conflict. With the French Revolution, Napoleon's wars against Europe, and the Paris revolt after the war with Prussia, lethal violence directed by government leaders had increased. Freedom in some ways aggravated rather than moderated violence.

Concern with Social Problems

France's troubles went beyond the loss of military prestige and the excesses of government-sponsored violence. The growth in the 1800s of divorce, suicide, and anti-Semitism presented problems as well. Although divorce was outlawed from 1816 to 1884, the rate of formal separations increased steadily. After eventual legalization in 1884, the divorce rate rose quickly (Gillis 1996). Divorce represented one further step, according to many, in the continuing breakdown of the family and Catholic morality; it reflected excessive concern with self-interest rather than the stability of the family, community, and society.

Along with divorce and family breakdown, many in France worried about the declining birth rate. Fertility declined in France earlier than in most other European countries for reasons we still do not fully understand. But observers at the time pointed to rising divorce, declining religion, and growing selfishness as the causes. Too few people, they declared, willingly sacrificed their own pleasure for the good of children and the future of French society.

Rather than producing happiness, the increased freedom of individuals from the family and the church produced the opposite. A review of suicide statistics around 1860 showed that the highest rates were in France and Germany—the nations most advanced economically. Within nations, the review showed that the highest rates were in large industrial cities. When Durkheim later reported such patterns, he suggested that unhappiness increased in the richest nations. Freedom and greater wealth seemed to expand desires for even more wealth and pleasure that often could not be fulfilled.

The problems led to rising hostility and discrimination against Jewish citizens. Anti-Semitism grew with the military losses, economic dissatisfaction, and loss of traditional values. In the 1890s, anti-Semitism would result in the conviction and imprisonment of a Jewish army colonel, Alfred Dreyfus, on bogus charges of spying for Germany. The efforts of many to right the unjust punishment of Dreyfus clashed with the rabid hatred of Jews exhibited by many others during this disgraceful episode. The resulting political crisis nearly threatened the survival of the French Republic.

Both military and social problems stemmed from the increasing complexity of society and the growing differences among its members. Whereas strong families, religions, and communities had given coherence to life in the past, modern industrial society was much more impersonal. People worked for a company and owner whom they rarely knew, had few ties to other residents of large cities, and were subject to technological forces beyond their control and understanding. Most importantly, differences in social position meant people no longer shared a common set of ideas about right and wrong.

Intellectuals and politicians looked for explanations for France's political and social troubles. The answers people gave depended on their political beliefs, but a theme began to emerge: industrial development, the growth of cities, and the decline of traditional ties to the family, community, and church had weakened the bonds people had to other members of society. Values emphasizing individual freedom and self-interest had undermined traditional authority. Religious ideas of right and wrong no longer united people as they had in the past.

The problems of society become most visible when change occurs, and recent decades had brought immense social and economic changes. It seemed futile to fight the changes brought about by industrialization, science, rationalism, and freedom. If such changes also encouraged excessive individualism, the solution could not come from returning to the past. As a result, French intellectuals remained pessimistic about the ability of French democracy to survive and resist the power of surrounding nations.

Loss of Religion in Modern Society

Modern sociology emerged in France in part as an attempt to improve French society in the face of political disorder, military weakness, and moral decay. Its advocates hoped to identify principles of social order and suggest ways of applying these principles in social reforms. Auguste Comte, the first to use the term *sociology,* argued that a systematic understanding of how society works could provide a guide for political and social reforms and a more orderly society.

Sociologists often considered how to replace the loss of religious faith with some other moral force to unify society. They asked: How can society enforce ideas of right and wrong without God and the threat of punishment in the afterlife? How can society exist without a king to enforce the laws? For some, the answer would come from a new religion. Comte proposed a religion of humanity based on science to replace a weakened Catholicism. Still others sought a secular religion based on equality and the abolition of private property. Yet these proposals failed to gain widespread acceptance among the French.

Following Comte, many began to view the conflict and problems in France as part of the larger conflict between tradition and modernism (Lukes 1985:196). Without individual desires for freedom from traditions, the higher standard of living brought about by industrialism and modernization would not have occurred. But without the control imposed by the traditional authority of king, church, community, and family, individualism led to a lack of restraint, social conflict, and deviance. To deal with this dilemma, society had to restrain individualism in a way consistent with the nature of modern society. Society could not return to the old ways, nor could it continue on in the direction of excessive individualism and social disorder. How could modern society reconcile the need for stability with the desire for freedom, the need for a shared morality with the growing differences in society?

Such was the social and intellectual environment that shaped Durkheim's ideas as a young student. Having come from a close-knit family and community, he found the conflict and lack of cooperation in Paris troubling. Having experienced the invasion of the German army while a child, he found the loss of the war with Prussia personally hurtful. The victorious Germans forced the French government to give them two states near the border, Alsace and Lorraine, territory that contained Durkheim's hometown of Épinal. He had grown up under German occupation, and his family continued to live in the now-German territories.

Durkheim saw the problems brought about by modernism as representing a moral rather than an economic crisis and its solution as requiring the study of ethics and philosophy rather than economics or engineering (Nisbet 1966:18). A new system of values and morality could best deal with the problems of suicide, conflict, and family breakdown. A purely technical solution, like correcting a malfunctioning machine in one of the growing number of factories, would not be enough.

Durkheim also knew that a return to the religious beliefs of traditional communities would not be possible; in fact, he had come to reject the Jewish religion of his family. France needed a secular rather than a religious solution to the moral problems of a modern industrial society. Even as a young man, he resisted the efforts of conservatives to strengthen the power of Catholicism and supported the efforts of those who sought to limit the power of the church in education and politics.

Still, he had only the vaguest notion of how to reconcile the growing individualism of modern societies with the continuing need for social solidarity. How could the freedom of modern French democracy survive without the common values and morality that connect members of a society? How could a society find the proper balance of order and disorder to maximize the well-being of its members? Such questions would occupy Durkheim for the rest of his life.

3. THE MORAL BASIS OF SOCIAL LIFE

Over the years, Durkheim's dislike of the classical form of education in France began to take a toll. He performed well in his first year at the École Normale, receiving honors in return for his hard work. But by his third year, when all students prepared for a national test, he had lost enthusiasm for what he saw as irrelevant learning. Combined with some health problems, his negative attitude led to a poor performance on the national test; of all the students from his school taking the exam that year, his score fell second from the bottom.

All had not been wasted, however. Durkheim did find several professors whose ideas and methods he admired, who offered insights into the social sources of France's problems and suggested ways that leaders might address these problems. He came to respect and admire those few professors whose ideas seemed especially relevant to problems of social life. In turn, these professors admired Durkheim's brightness and devotion to scientific learning. Despite poor performance in some classes, he was able to obtain their support.

After graduation, Durkheim found teaching jobs at lycées in towns surrounding Paris. Although such work would keep him busy, it could not satisfy his enormous ambitions—he wanted national recognition as a writer, scholar, and professor and to become part of France's intellectual elite. Given his intense and studious nature, he would not imitate the frivolous dabbling of most scholars but would dedicate himself to the in-depth study of his concerns.

A Sociology of Morality

Sometime during his last year at the École Normale, Durkheim decided to devote himself to the field of sociology. First used in the 1830s, the term *sociology* had more recently fallen into disuse. The early practitioners of sociology in France, such as Comte, had reputations as eccentric and self-promoting rather than as serious scholars. Durkheim, however, saw that the field could help him understand pressing social concerns about individualism and contribute to the improvement of French society. He also saw that the new field could provide him an opportunity to advance his own image of scholarship, one that differed from the outdated approaches he had learned in school.

As a first step, completing a dissertation would allow him to join the faculty of a university. It seemed reasonable to start with the study of the relationship between the individual and society. Durkheim reasoned that social order and unity related closely to **morality**—a system of rules of right and wrong that determine social and individual conduct. If he could understand the sources of morality in society, he could suggest ways to put new moral principles into practice. Further, if he could understand how morality comes to control individual behavior, he could suggest ways to better connect individuals to social groups and society.

Durkheim had read of philosophical approaches to morality or ethics. He knew that throughout history, philosophers had attempted to deduce rules of conduct from general principles of right and wrong, rules that came from abstract reasoning rather than from observations of actual social behavior. Moral philosophies often assumed that all humans had certain characteristics and that rules of right and wrong should be consistent with those characteristics. According to this view-point, morality based on a common human nature should apply to all times, places, and societies.

In Durkheim's view, such general principles made little sense. After all, since societies change, shouldn't morality change as well? Durkheim had begun to read some works in the newly emerging field of sociology that described how societies changed from having a small and simple or-ganization to having a large and complex organization. How could a single principle of right and wrong or a single set of laws apply to such different societies and different social conditions? Without studying morality in relation to the types of societies that existed, philosophical approaches would be flawed.

Can Self-Interest Produce Cooperation?

Durkheim turned elsewhere to try to understand the sources of morality. In the previous decade, the English philosopher Herbert Spencer had published three volumes entitled *Principles of Sociology*. A bit eccentric, Spencer had no training in philosophy or sociology and refused to read the works of other philosophers and sociologists lest they disturb the purity of his own thought. Instead, he adapted and applied work on bi-ological evolution to social life. He saw evolution from the simple to complex as a universal principle of social change and suggested that so-ciety could be viewed as an organism whose parts contribute to the func-tioning of the whole.

Although Durkheim would rely on some of Spencer's insights, he was bothered by an underlying assumption about social life contained in the work of Spencer and most other English philosophers and econo-mists at the time. A long English intellectual tradition treated the indi-vidual as central to understanding social cooperation and morality. Dating back to the 1600s, English thinkers had asked how society could exist when it consisted of hundreds of thousands of different individuals, all with their own selfish desires. By the 1800s, Spencer and many others were offering a startling and paradoxical answer: cooperative social be-havior comes from rational individuals acting in their own self-interest.

On the surface, acting on self-interest would appear to prevent rather than aid social cooperation. Individuals have desires for pleasure, power, and a long life. If humans act in their self-interest only by trying to obtain power over others, this would lead to conflict, murder, and chaos as people try to impose their will on others. Force and fraud would become the dominant form of social interaction.

In the larger picture, however, the use of force and fraud does not fall within the bounds of an individual's self-interest. Since cheating and stealing from others means others may also cheat and steal, people come to realize that they would gain in the long run by cooperating with one another. This realization leads people to make informal and unwritten social contracts (or agreements) with others, agreeing to exchange valued goods and services so that everyone comes out better off than when they started. As the basis of social cooperation, social contracts maximize the personal well-being of members of a society. People can act to further the interests of others as a means to further their own goals. Social life thus follows from individual desires and self-interest.

These arguments matched English desires for individual freedom (and had proven crucial in the founding of American democracy). In the past, powerful leaders and groups had imposed their will on others, preventing individuals from acting freely in their own self-interest. In premodern societies, for example, slavery, monarchy, and religion had limited the freedom and happiness of individuals. Fortunately, societies had evolved toward greater freedom and happiness. In modern democratic societies, individuals striving to maximize their liberty and individual well-being indirectly contributed to morality and social cooperation.

The Importance of Trust

Durkheim realized that there was a problem in this reasoning. Treating each individual as self-interested and separate from others produced a logical contradiction: quite simply, rational individuals would not form social contracts without the existence of a larger group or society that specified and enforced the rules for such a contract. In Durkheim's view, Spencer could not explain how solidarity among diverse individuals in society emerged.

To illustrate how individual self-interest and cooperation relies on social values, consider an example. When two individuals make an exchange, they have to share the rewards. They each get something they want but have to give up something they like. For example, one person gives up free time to work and the other gives up money for the work. Although better than making no exchange, the exchange contains a risk that the other person might cheat by taking something and not giving anything in return. Given that risk, rational persons would not enter into a social contract unless they had confidence that the other person would live up to the bargain. Trust that the other person will not cheat comes from widespread acceptance of rules of right and wrong.

Durkheim reasoned that the willingness of individuals to enter into a social contract relies on the preexisting acceptance of morality. Strong ties of individuals to larger groups that specify rules of right and wrong make cooperation possible. In short, rational action depends on a nonrational foundation. More than being the result of sheer self-interest, social exchanges depend on the duty people have to the larger groups to which they belong.

This insight, one of the most original and important in the history of sociology, offered a framework for a sociological understanding of individual behavior. The idea that shared social values, rather than individual self-interest, makes social cooperation possible directed attention to the study of society in its own right rather than as a by-product of individual action. The group rather than the individual would become the unit of analysis. Groups could not exist without individuals, but once individuals formed larger groups, the groups persist after the exit of the original members. The same holds true for a society: once it emerged, social life took on a life of its own by outlasting the death of old members and the entrance of new members.

The Reality of Social Groups

Durkheim's reasoning emphasized the importance of the group and society, reflecting the common saying that the whole is greater than the sum of its parts. The combined actions of individual members of an orchestra or football team produce something special; the beauty of a symphony or a well-executed pass play comes from the merging of individuals into a larger group. People talk about the Chicago Symphony or the Denver Broncos as groups that represent something more than the individuals who belong to them. Because society works in much the same way, it deserves to be studied separately from the individuals who comprise it. Durkheim believed sociology should focus on the patterns of interaction among people and the moral values and beliefs these interactions produced.

Durkheim's **social realism** (a name that was initially attributed to Durkheim's work by his opponents) posits that the shared values and social relationships within society exist separately from and strongly influence the behavior of individual members. In this sense, society acts as an external constraint on the behavior of individuals: it imposes moral obligations on them to act in certain ways rather than others and to conform to ideas of right and wrong. Rather than being caused by biological or psychological impulses, the behavior of individuals results in part from forces outside themselves.

These forces appear in the pressures we face from our families, friends, neighbors, employers, and governments. For example, millions of college students, all with different personalities, biological characteristics, and personal preferences, nonetheless act in much the same way. Parents, teachers, administrators, and fellow students expect them to study, behave in class, and act decently toward others. If they do not, they face formal expulsion from college or informal isolation from others. Even if people are not aware of them, external forces exert an immense influence on their behaviors.

Social realism views these external constraints on individuals as sufficiently real for social scientists to treat them as "things" (or what Durkheim called **social facts**). Social constraints come from morality—values about good and bad, religious beliefs, bonds among group members, formal laws, and informal norms of right and wrong behavior. We typically cannot "see" morality itself or the social constraints it imposes on our behavior; we can only see the people who conform or do not conform to morality. Even so, we know social morality exists because it has real and observable consequences for the behavior of individuals.

In terms of their observable consequences, social forces are as real as physical forces. Like electricity, morality typically cannot be seen, but we can feel its effects. For example, finding ourselves in a situation in which we do not know the rules of acceptable behavior leaves us feeling uncomfortable—and we can tell by the stares and disapproving looks of others that we have done something wrong. At the extreme, violation of morality can result in prison, violence, or even death. These consequences are quite real.

The Implications of Social Realism

The perspective of social realism dealt with several problems Durkheim faced in his thinking. First, social realism could explain differences in morality across societies. If the structures of groups and societies differ, so would the morality and the actions of individuals within those groups and societies. Rather than identifying a single principle of morality that should apply to all societies, Durkheim could understand morality in relation to the nature of a particular society. Further, he could try to understand why changes from small and simply organized societies to large and complex ones resulted in different moralities.

Second, Durkheim could use social realism as an approach to understanding individualism. Rather than an inevitable consequence of freedom or personal desires, individualism developed as a product of society. In relatively simple tribal societies and small villages, few social differences existed and shared morality enforced similarity in thoughts and behavior. In contrast, the social organization of larger, richer, and more modern societies promotes social differences and individualism. And even within modern societies, some areas have advanced further economically and value individualism more than others. If he could understand the complex relationship between social organization and morality, Durkheim could suggest ways to encourage less individualistic moralities in modern societies. Social realism thus provided a way to address the social problems of modern French society.

Finally, and perhaps most importantly, social realism justified the existence of sociology as an independent field of study. Since society cannot be reduced to the characteristics of individuals, sociology or the study of society cannot be reduced to psychology or biology. Psychologists can study individuals in isolation from others, and sociologists can study the properties of groups and societies made up of individuals. Since society is distinct from its individual parts, we cannot reduce society to individuals any more than we can reduce biology to chemistry.

4. THE SCIENTIFIC COMPARISON OF SOCIETIES

Although Durkheim knew what he wanted to study—social morality and its influence on individuals—he did not know how to study them. Fortunately, an opportunity came along that proved crucial to developing a sociological method. He received a grant to travel to Germany, where he could study intellectual developments outside of France. What he discovered there stimulated Durkheim's thinking about sociology: German psychologists had begun to develop scientific laboratories for the study of human behavior similar to scientific laboratories for the study of chemistry or physics.

German Social Science

The first key to social science in Germany was the careful and systematic observation of social behavior. We take it for granted today that social scientists should observe behavior, but in France in Durkheim's time, where traditional philosophical methods emphasized individual reasoning and deduction, they rarely used observational methods. They aimed for clarity in thought but did not actually observe the way the world works. In contrast, German social scientists tried to rely on established facts to reach conclusions about social life.

The second key to social science in Germany, which derived from the belief that systematic observation of behavior could proceed best by comparison, was the application of the experimental method to social behavior. The **experimental method** compared behavior under two conditions: one included a treatment that the researcher would expect to affect an outcome behavior, and the other did not include that treatment. Therefore, differences in outcomes likely stemmed from the experimental treatment. In a lab, for example, one could compare the performance of subjects on a test when some receive money for a good score and others do not. The differences in scores would reveal the impact of financial motivation on performance. Such methods might also be applied to other social behaviors.

The experimental study of social behavior contrasted with another approach to studying society common in France: the use of literary description to understand social life. Novels in the tradition of literary realism provided detailed and fascinating descriptions of social life, but they also included poetic exaggerations, emphasized feeling and emotion, and made generalizations based on limited and biased experiences. In contrast to literary methods, the experimental method offered a way to understand—not just describe—the causes of behavior.

Durkheim was receptive to these German ideas. In less developed form, the application of the scientific method to social behavior had emerged in France in the work of Auguste Comte, who had treated science as a guide to social thought and action that would make traditional philosophy unnecessary. Similarly, several of Durkheim's teachers had advocated careful observation of historical records and use of rigorous methods. In the physical sciences, many famous French scientists had made valuable contributions to our understanding of the physical world.

Still, the scientific method had not had the same impact in France as it had in Germany. Consistent with the type of education Durkheim himself had received, French science stressed individual brilliance and originality rather than systemic observation and carefulness. Where German science emphasized cooperation among scholars in complex and large projects, French science relied on the efforts of the isolated individual scholar. Where German science emphasized precise measurement and careful observation, French science emphasized innovative theories.

In Durkheim's view, the German model of science would deal with two other problems that he believed hindered French scholarship. First, a scientific approach would avoid to some degree the political biases that entered into debates over social issues. Conservatives advocated a return to tradition, and socialists advocated abolishing private property. Rather than being merely a means to justify preexisting political beliefs, science would, according to Durkheim, rely on unbiased evaluation of the facts.

Second, the scientific method would preclude the shallowness of the intellectual dilettantes he had encountered in school. A ruthless attention to facts and details would require researchers to specialize in their studies. Broad but superficial statements about social life, such as those Durkheim had heard so often from his fellow students and professors, could not stand up to careful scientific observation. At the same time, the scientific approach would provide laws that generalized from the specific events that historians described (but often failed to explain).

A Comparative Science of Morality

One problem remained. How could one make scientific observations of morality? After all, morality consists of ideas about right and wrong that we cannot directly observe. We can see people who belong to groups and societies, but we cannot see the values and beliefs that guide their behavior. If the scientific method worked for studying behaviors in a lab, how would it work in the real world for something like morality?

German social science had no answer to this, but Durkheim did. He reasoned that scholars could study the *outcomes* of morality even if they could not study morality directly. For example, he could treat written legal codes and the specified punishments for violation of laws as concrete indicators of morality. Since laws represented values of right and wrong, the scientific study of laws in societies could say much about morality.

Similarly, scholars could study the reactions of members of a society or group to the violation of informal or unwritten rules. The stronger the reaction of others to a certain behavior, and the greater the anger aroused by an action, the more important that rule was to the moral code. Thus, without observing the values themselves, Durkheim could use systematic observation of the behavioral consequences of them in laws, rules, and punishments to indirectly understand the nature of morality.

Further, in studying the influence of morality, researchers could employ a variation on the experimental method. Rather than manipulate conditions in a lab, the method would compare the behaviors of different groups and societies. If the reaction to violation of rules differed across societies, the nature of morality would differ as well. Scholars could not create experiments but could compare naturally existing societies. By means of comparative social observation, Durkheim hoped to identify social laws. Societies are governed by laws, just as other parts of nature are governed by laws. However, laws will vary with types of society.

One dimension of comparison involved differences across societies at different stages of social and economic development. Comte and Spencer, for example, had classified societies by their evolution from relatively simple social organization to more complex and differentiated social organization. Special insight into morality in modern society could come from contrasting it with morality in traditional societies.

Here at last was an outlet for Durkheim's logical and systematic mind and an object for his attraction to specialized and in-depth knowledge. He could continue to study important social issues related to morality, individualism, and conflict, but he could do so scientifically. He could move past the study of classic, but outdated, literature and philosophy to develop a modern approach to France's problems. He could advocate the development of the field of sociology as a legitimate scientific enterprise comparable to physics or chemistry.

Durkheim returned from Germany filled with ideas about how to create a scientific field for the study of morality and social problems. Despite continuing duties teaching philosophy, he published several articles reviewing the developments in social science in Germany and assessing their value for French social science. Although only preliminary versions of what he would write about in much more detail later, these articles gained Durkheim much attention. Some found the vision he offered of a scientific study of society attractive, while others were offended by the excessive claims made for this new field of scholarship.

Sociology Through the Back Door

The recognition Durkheim received from these articles, and his growing reputation as an innovative advocate of the emerging field of sociology, led in 1887 to a new teaching job. His appointment at the University of Bordeaux, located in southwestern France, represented a step forward in his career. Rather than teaching the French equivalent of high school students, he would now teach the equivalent of college and graduate students. Although he had not yet completed his doctoral dissertation, Durkheim's university appointment was a first step in obtaining academic acceptance for sociology.

In a sense, however, the job was not ideal. Like all other schools, the University of Bordeaux did not have a sociology department or any sociology courses. Worse, many faculty members attached to more traditional fields opposed establishing this new discipline. As a result, Durkheim was appointed primarily to teach education classes. On the side, he could teach a class on social science and introduce students to his idea about sociology, but only after he had fulfilled his duties in other areas. Acceptance of his ideas in the academic world would not come quickly or easily.

Durkheim first went to work on finishing the requirements for a doctorate—a major thesis and a minor thesis, the latter written in Latin. His major thesis would present and defend his ideas about the relationship between morality and the individual in more depth than he had been able to provide in the few articles he had published. It eventually was published as *The Division of Labor in Society*, but before that Durkheim had to defend it (as well as his Latin thesis) before an examining committee of professors in Paris. Like many at the University of Bordeaux, the more traditional members of the examining committee showed resistance to his new ideas about sociology. Still, his brilliant defense of his work at the hearing led the committee to pass him unanimously.

In the next 15 years at Bordeaux, Durkheim proved amazingly pro-ductive, both in terms of the books and papers he published and in terms of the influence his ideas began to have. Despite all his duties, he pub-lished three highly influential books and dozens of articles. He lectured on a variety of topics, supervised the research of numerous students, and created, edited, and wrote for a new journal. More than any other single person, Durkheim contributed to the establishment of sociology as a re-spected intellectual discipline at major universities in France and other countries.

5. *THE DIVISION OF LABOR IN SOCIETY*

At the University of Bordeaux, Durkheim faced numerous difficulties in gaining the acceptance of sociology as a legitimate field of study. His claims for sociology intruded on the old-fashioned ideas of the intellec-tual elite. Although all new ideas face opposition and battles about ideas in a university setting can become as heated and personal as those in pol-itics, Durkheim's aggressive views and his sharp criticism of the views of others created a special hostility toward sociology.

Opposition to Sociology

Consider some of the groups that objected to Durkheim's intrusion on established fields in his quest for the recognition of sociology. He of-fended traditional philosophers with his claim that sociology could ad-dress moral questions. He offended religious philosophers with his claim that no set of principles of right and wrong applied to all societies. He of-fended psychologists with his focus on the group rather than the indi-vidual. He offended those with more literary tastes with his insistence on scientific methods. And he offended traditional educators with his goal of making schooling more relevant to current social problems.

Perhaps many found Durkheim's style as irritating as the ideas he presented. He spoke of sociology with the moral certainty of a religious believer (Aron 1965:102). He did not treat sociology as a religion (as had Comte and some of the early sociologists), but he did present it with the fervor of a religious leader. He denounced irrationality and immorality in society like an Old Testament prophet denounced sin. Such certainty in his beliefs contrasted with the skepticism and distrust many academics had about new ideas.

Many found themselves intimidated by Durkheim's serious person-ality. He participated in social events when necessary for his career, but he remained distant and sober in conversation. He spent much more time in intellectual discussion and debate, but he remained cool and log-ical when his opponents became angry and emotional. In an especially harsh judgment, one critic claimed that Durkheim's seriousness in debate made him appear as a "death's head—thin, gaunt, severe, cold" and that his arguments "would have substantially assisted in the refrigeration of corpses" (Lukes 1985:370–371).

Although such criticisms were exaggerated, it is true that Durkheim avoided showiness in his writing and lectures. Rather, he presented his ideas plainly and with ruthless logic. He spoke not loudly and emotionally, but carefully and reasonably. He relied on the intensity of his ideas and his appeal to reason to convince his listeners and readers. Although "forbidding and serious," he had an "intense and gentle power [that] commanded respect, attention, even submission" (Lukes 1985:367). As a lecturer, his well-organized, exact, and logical arguments impressed listeners.

Given the strength of his beliefs and seriousness of purpose, Durkheim worked hard: "His work schedule was, indeed, truly amazing. ... His health undoubtedly suffered, and his letters reveal a number of mental breakdowns brought on by overwork" (Lukes 1985:100). He did have a happy marriage and two children, but even the family household helped support his academic work. His wife took care of his material needs, kept the house quiet so he could write, and on occasion helped him with his scholarly work.

Combined with his energy, ambition, and confidence, an uneventful personal life allowed Durkheim to devote himself fully to academic matters. Much as he had done during his years as a student, he could devote himself to intellectual pursuits for 11 or more hours a day, but now he could strive toward a goal in which he strongly believed. His gratification came from his enthusiasm for ideas rather than from pleasures of the senses. He had no pictures or artwork on the walls of his office, he dressed modestly and ate sparingly, and he spent his money carefully. Devoted primarily to work, duty, and discipline, he could "never experience pleasure without a sense of remorse" (Lukes 1985:40). A sense of mission in his work dominated his life.

Durkheim's nephew and most accomplished student, Marcel Mauss, told a telling story about his uncle and intellectual guide (Thompson 1982:28). Mauss once took a break from work to enjoy a cup of coffee in the café across the street. After sitting there for a few minutes, however, he saw Durkheim walking on the sidewalk near the café. Although a fully grown adult, Mauss hid under a table to avoid being seen and criticized for loafing by his hard-working and serious supervisor.

Spreading His Ideas

Despite his intimidating bearing, Durkheim attracted devoted students and colleagues. Although serious and demanding, he offered an original set of ideas for understanding and improving society that students found appealing. Moreover, he would do all he could to help those students who desired to learn about and use his ideas. Students could apply Durkheim's perspective of scientific social realism to a variety of topics that particularly suited their personal interests.

To help develop a systematic program of sociological study, Durkheim founded a journal called the *Année sociologique*. The journal provided a place for Durkheim's students to publish their work, for Durkheim himself to review other books and articles on sociology, and for those outside of Bordeaux to see the progress made in this new field. It also helped Durkheim create a cohesive group advocating sociology and defending it against its many critics. He provided a French example of the kind of cooperative social science that he had found in Germany.

Along with the journal, Durkheim used his lectures to spread his ideas. In courses on education, he emphasized the importance of logical reasoning and reliance on evidence rather than the appreciation of beauty or originality for its own sake. He convinced many students that the literary masterpieces of creative individuals were less important to progress than the effort of a scientific community to carefully observe and understand the social world. He further reinforced these views by insisting that students write precisely and directly rather than extravagantly and obscurely.

Durkheim also used his lectures on education to discuss morality, believing that educators had a duty to discuss moral topics in their teaching. Done correctly, secular and scientific moral education could replace religious education as a means of instilling modern ideas of right and wrong and improving the functioning of society. Through such ideas, Durkheim eventually came to have an immense influence on education. His students spread his ideas outside of Bordeaux in the schools and universities where they taught after graduation.

Durkheim's efforts at building a program brought success for his version of sociology. Many others offered views on the direction social science should take, but they did so more as individuals than as editors of journals or leaders of a group of intellectual followers. For example, Gabriel Tarde, a judge with wide-ranging interests and a literary bent, had written several important books on sociology that took a more psychological view than did Durkheim. Yet his work did not define a clear program of specialized study that students could follow. Durkheim's work gained more influence in France in part because of the organizational strength of his school of thought.

Types of Social Solidarity

Durkheim's first book, *The Division of Labor in Society* (a revision of his dissertation), offered original insights into the nature of social life, addressed issues of social solidarity and morality, and nicely illustrated his sociological perspective. The book began with the observation that social differentiation characterizes modern societies. In Durkheim's terms, modern societies have a more specialized division of labor. While members of smaller traditional societies share the same characteristics, members of larger modern societies differ from one another. Modern society divides tasks, roles, and duties into numerous parts that complement one another, and individuals have different positions within this complex division of labor. Durkheim asked why this change occurred and what consequences it had for morality and social order.

To answer the question about why this change occurred, he argued that social differentiation results from population growth and increases in population density. Growth and density in turn increase competition for scarce resources, and competition produces differentiation. With a growing population packed into a limited area, everyone cannot do the same thing—the environment could not support a large society in which everyone hunted or everyone farmed. Consequently, people perform more specialized tasks that complement one another.

With a specialized division of labor, members of a society come to depend on one another in a new way. The numerous, different, and narrow tasks require that persons trade for necessary goods and services created by others. This type of social dependence differs greatly from the dependence that exists in traditional societies. Whereas dependence results from similarity in traditional societies, it results from interrelated differences in modern societies (such as among students, faculty, administrators, and staff at a university). Durkheim termed the dependence in simple societies **mechanical solidarity** and the dependence in complex modern societies **organic solidarity**.

The process of specialization occurs in the realm of ideas as well as in the realm of the economy. With specialization, people have more social contact with those holding different knowledge, opinions, and values. Durkheim used the term **collective conscience** to refer to common beliefs and feelings among members of a society. As societies and social relationships become more specialized in modern societies, so does the collective conscience become more specialized.

Punishment and Crime

To illustrate the changes in the collective conscience, Durkheim compared the nature of laws and the strength of punishments across societies. In traditional societies based on similarity (except for differences of age and sex), people share and strongly adhere to their social morality. Here the collective conscience exerts a strong influence on behavior. People tend to think in concrete terms: someone either violates or does not violate moral rules, and those who violate the rules deserve a harsh penalty, such as banishment, physical punishment, or death.

In modern societies based on organic solidarity and differentiation, the collective conscience weakens as the intensity of shared beliefs declines. Laws become more flexible, and punishments consider the special circumstances and motivations that may lie behind any violation. Punishment attempts to restore individuals to their former position in society through probation, fines, or community service rather than banishing or killing them. Although the collective conscience remains influential in modern society, it takes a different form than in traditional societies.

In describing the relationship between the type of social solidarity in societies and the form of punishment, Durkheim presented a startling insight: he argued that crime is normal and valuable in a healthy society. Rather than harming society, a certain amount of crime mobilizes group members to act together to punish it. The existence of crime and punishment for committing a crime reaffirms ideas of right and wrong. It results naturally from a shared morality. Without clear instances of the violation of society's rules, the rules would lack meaning.

The function of crime appears in another way: punishment of offenders increases solidarity. Anger about crime and a desire to punish criminals create emotional bonds among members of society. This explains why persons unaffected by a particular crime nonetheless become upset by it. It explains why executions of criminals throughout history have been publicly viewed events. It explains why all groups and societies identify some form of deviance or crime, even though the types of deviance and crime can differ greatly across societies.

The comparison of societies and their moralities offered a perspective on the problems of Durkheim's time. Some thinkers viewed differentiation as part of the evolution toward a better society; that is, more advanced societies created economic wealth, increased freedom, and focused on the happiness of individuals. But Durkheim also saw the negative consequences of economic wealth and individual freedom. Individual freedom weakens the ties to social groups and shared beliefs of right and wrong that give life meaning. Rather than creating happiness, specialization results in the disintegration of social bonds and threatens the moral unity of society.

6. SUICIDE AS SOCIAL BEHAVIOR

Eventually, in 1896, the University of Bordeaux promoted Durkheim to full professor of social science. At Durkheim's urging, the faculty also voted to include social science as a required part of the curriculum. Both events represented important milestones in the acceptance of sociology. In the next year, Durkheim published another important book, this one on suicide, that bolstered his reputation.

Still, the real sign of success for Durkheim and the field of sociology would come from an appointment at the University in Paris. With the publications of his books and numerous articles, the attention his original ideas received, and the numerous students he had trained at Bordeaux, Durkheim might have expected the chance to move up to France's most prestigious university. Yet the controversial nature of his work allowed only slow progress toward that goal.

In 1902, with the determined effort of his supporters in Paris, Durkheim obtained a job at the Sorbonne (the center of arts and sciences at the University of Paris). As in Bordeaux, however, the opposition of traditionalists to sociology required his appointment as professor of education. Again, sociology had to enter through the back door. Durkheim continued to teach education in the hope that he could, like he had in Bordeaux, eventually obtain an appointment in sociology.

Intellectual Battles in Paris

After Durkheim's move to Paris, his enemies kept up the attack on his work. Criticisms came from all directions, forcing Durkheim to take time to answer the charges. Sometimes he noted that critics misinterpreted his ideas, and at other times he responded directly to the more accurate, but still critical, interpretations of his work. Although the criticism must have been frustrating, it might also have encouraged him in some ways: criticism meant recognition, and recognition was better than indifference. He felt confident that, with continued effort, his ideas would win out over those of the critics.

Consider some of the intellectual battles Durkheim had to fight to obtain acceptance for his ideas and the field of sociology. Supporters of Bergson's philosophy attacked Durkheim's reliance on science to understand human experience. Bergson's writing emphasized the importance of intuition rather than analysis. He argued, in contrast to Durkheim, that the analysis of society by carefully studying its individual parts could not capture the continuous flow of life that each person experiences. Because intuition does not divide the world into separate things, it allows people to perceive the whole of reality through their own experience. Durkheim's use of the scientific method to study humans who can freely make choices would be bound to fail.

Other critics attacked Durkheim's social realism. Gabriel Tarde, alluded to earlier, viewed society more as an aggregation of individuals imitating leaders than as something real. Psychologists and economists likewise viewed the individual as the only appropriate object of study for social scientists. To them, Durkheim's discussion of the collective conscience seemed mysterious—it referred to society as a real thing even though no one could see it. To answer these critics, Durkheim's studies provided numerous examples of how ties of the individual to the group and society reveal the existence of larger social forces.

In the political arena, religious conservatives who desired to replace democracy with a monarchy and further strengthen the military objected strongly to Durkheim's work. His opposition to Catholic education and support for secular education angered conservatives, who viewed him as a radical supporter of modernism and socialism. They worried that his new ideas about education would brainwash young students against religious values.

Ironically, radical socialists also viewed Durkheim as an opponent. His unwillingness to commit himself politically, despite an identification with some of the goals of socialism, led many leftists to view him as an enemy. He generally ignored the issues of class conflict, dialectic change, and exploitation of workers that were central to the work of Marx. Like Marx, he recognized the importance of material conditions, but unlike Marx, he also emphasized the importance of ideas as an influence on social conditions. Moreover, Durkheim considered Marx's work unscientific.

Rather than revolution, Durkheim favored reform of the current system. He saw progress in the shift from traditional society rooted in mechanical solidarity, with its repressive laws, to modern society, with its greater freedom and emerging democratic institutions. More radical critics, however, viewed the modern power of business owners and governments as more repressive than traditional societies. From their viewpoint, reform would help only those who already had power—more drastic change was needed to make workers equal to owners. Durkheim thought change could come only through steady, careful, and persistent efforts. As a result, many viewed Durkheim as a conservative defender of the status quo (and many continue to do so today).

Durkheim persevered against the opposition, however. In 1913, 11 years after he came to the University of Paris, a chair in sociology was created for him. By that time, his reputation and accomplishments had become so well known that even his opponents could not stop formal recognition. As Durkheim had hoped some 30 years earlier, sociology had obtained academic legitimacy.

Types and Causes of Suicide

Suicide, the last book Durkheim published before going to Paris, substantially contributed to the legitimacy of sociology. Suicide, he argued, represented a clear example of the weakening of the bonds between individuals and the moral order of the social community. Suicide had in fact been studied often by scholars in the nineteenth century, and a wealth of statistics and information on the topic existed. In reviewing these statistics, Durkheim had discovered that low birth rates in certain areas of Europe tended to go along with high suicide rates. Perhaps trends in both suicide and fertility resulted from the same social forces.

The trends and patterns of suicide he found could not stem from personal factors. Although rates of suicide had increased nearly everywhere, they varied across cities, counties, and nations in stable and predictable ways. Durkheim noted that those areas with relatively high suicide rates 50 years earlier still had relatively high rates. This stability in patterns of suicide suggested that social factors—which also varied in stable ways across cities, counties, and nations—strongly influenced the apparently personal decision to commit suicide.

While varied and stable patterns of suicide across social groups and geographic regions relate closely to the integration and regulation of those groups and regions, the patterns of suicide do not fit common psychological explanations. Durkheim showed in his analysis of suicide statistics that groups and areas with the highest rates of suicide were not the groups and areas with the highest rates of mental illness or alcoholism. Even such a personal behavior as suicide—a behavior that by definition involves the action of only one person—correlated more closely with social factors than psychological factors. By demonstrating the superiority of social explanations, Durkheim's study of suicide contributed to the recognition of sociology as an independent and valid field of study.

Durkheim identified two types of suicide in modern societies—egoistic and anomic. **Egoistic suicide** results from low integration of individuals into social groups. Durkheim defined *integration* as a property of groups based on the degree of social interaction and the strength of shared beliefs among group members. It is reflected, for example, in higher rates of suicide among single, divorced, and widowed persons than among married persons and in higher rates of suicide among married persons without children than among married persons with children. By giving social meaning to a person's life, the bonds between family members reduce egoistic suicide.

According to Durkheim, differences in egoistic suicide also explained rates of suicide across religious denominations. Statistics for nineteenth-century Europe showed higher rates of suicide in Protestant communities and areas than in Catholic and Jewish communities and areas. Why? Because Protestantism emphasizes the individual relationship of a believer with God and allows personal leeway in interpretation of the Bible, it loosens the social control of a congregation over its members. In contrast, Catholicism and Judaism stress the social responsibilities of adherents to the religious community. These social bonds resulted in lower suicide rates.

Anomic suicide results from the lack of external social control—again, a property of groups rather than individuals. Anomie refers to a condition of normlessness in a group or society. During periods of social and personal change, the authority of family, community, and church declines, and social norms that guide individual thoughts and actions weaken. Without such authority, moral guidance, and social control, individual desires and goals can expand without limit. Since the world seldom provides the resources to meet excessive desires, disappointment and suicide result. People do best when their goals match the means to obtain their goals. Ultimately, then, the lack of clear norms, values, and social regulation produces anomic suicide.

Social changes that produce high rates of divorce or economic boom followed by bust lead to anomie or a state of unregulated desires. One can understand that the sense of failure persons might experience after a divorce, unemployment, or loss of income would increase suicide rates. However, Durkheim identified another source of suicide resulting from these changes. The freedom given by divorce, a high-paying new job, or a huge inheritance can create desires and hopes that eventually produce disappointment. Changes in either direction reduce the group's control of the individual.

The opposite of low integration and regulation can also increase suicide rates. Too much integration can result in what Durkheim called **altruistic suicide**; that is, an individual commits suicide as part of a group action, such as has occurred in several celebrated instances of multiple suicides among cult members. Too much regulation, on the other hand, can result in **fatalistic suicide**; for example, a slave might take his own life because of the hopelessness and oppression he faces. Moderate levels of both integration and regulation, according to Durkheim, reduce the likelihood of suicide.

Increasing Social Solidarity in Modern Society

A solution to suicide and other problems of modernization would come from better integrating individuals into a complex and differentiated society. A sense of belonging and stronger ties of individuals to social groups and morality would reduce problems of isolation and unregulated desires. Social integration would cushion individuals from the frustration and tragedies of life. Rather than responding to these problems with crime, suicide, or violence, individuals could rely on the authority and support of the group to deal with their problems more constructively. Social regulation by groups would also instill the sense of duty, discipline, and sacrifice needed to hold personal desires in check.

Durkheim saw the solutions to problems in modern society as lying in belonging, duty, and character rather than in personal pleasure and happiness. He argued that happiness is an unattainable goal—regardless of their efforts, everyone will face sadness and sorrow.

Human expectations and desires rise faster than the ability to achieve them. Conforming to group authority and morality, however, gives direction and purpose to a person's life. According to Durkheim, true moral action and personal character derive from the sacrifice of selfish pleasures for the group. Conversely, society works best when it exercises control over individuals.

How, more precisely, can social integration and personal bonds be encouraged in modern societies? The means to this goal would certainly have to differ from those used in traditional societies based on mechanical solidarity. The uniformity and subordination of the individual in traditional societies would not work in societies moving toward further specialization and organic solidarity. Rather, the means would have to be consistent with the newly emerging division of labor; that is, integration would have to come from the increasing dependence of individuals on one another and from the different resources they can offer to others. It would require new social relations based on specialization.

First, solidarity in modern society could come through participation in economic groups. Where the family, church, and village once provided a sense of belonging, economic and work associations can do something similar in modern societies. For example, all groups in an industry—workers, managers, and owners—could unite as a means of advocating their common interests in society, the economy, and politics. Rather than creating conflict between workers and managers or owners, these associations would build community across these diverse groups. They would serve as a kind of minisociety in which all members share the same collective morality.

Second, society needs values that transcend membership in specialized groups. Durkheim believed that the worth and dignity of the individual provided one such value. Individualism in this sense differs from selfishness. Rather than blocking integration into social groups, shared values about the individual would contribute to social consensus. Durkheim's claim that a revised version of individualism could simultaneously reinforce both authority and the autonomy of the individual sounds like a contradiction. In Durkheim's view, however, valuing the dignity of the individual could contribute to the respect people have for society. It could create solidarity in a society characterized by differences rather than by similarity.

Although his recommendations were never implemented, Durkheim's arguments about suicide, individualism, and integration all carried forward the sociological perspective. His work identified and explained patterns of social behavior that many had viewed as being the result of individual or psychological characteristics. His arguments referred to social facts rather than individual traits and relied on observable evidence rather than philosophical debate. All this helped establish sociology as a field. With its numerous concrete examples of how one could actually use the sociological perspective, Durkheim's work began to gain recognition.

7. INDIVIDUALISM AND COMMUNITY TIES

As an advocate of the sociological perspective, Durkheim remained persistent and untiring. Despite his success as an academic leader in Paris, he worked just as hard as in earlier decades, continuing to work with students, edit his journal, and preach the virtues of sociology to believers and nonbelievers alike. As a member of numerous committees that constructed the curricula for schools throughout France, he could champion the need to teach social science. He trained France's best students, who in turn would pass on what they had learned from Durkheim about social science when they became teachers. He helped restructure the requirements at the University of Paris to emphasize modern fields of study rather than the classics. Although these changes at first created an uproar, they soon became accepted parts of French education.

To his immense satisfaction, Durkheim saw his ideas gain widespread influence over the years. By 1914, when World War I brought France and Germany into another military conflict, he had reached the top of the academic world in France. Unfortunately, however, the last few years of his life brought grief that prevented enjoyment of his status. Durkheim never recovered from the death of his son (and many of his students) in World War I. For some time after hearing the news, he would allow no one even to mention the death of his son—he found it too painful to discuss. His health began to suffer, and his work slowed. In late 1916 he suffered a stroke. He died the next year at the age of 59, an indirect victim of the war.

Elementary Forms of Religious Life

In 1912, 15 years after his last book and only 5 years before his death, Durkheim completed his most impressive work, *The Elementary Forms of Religious Life*. Some view this complex and insightful book as one of the greatest of the twentieth century (Collins and Makowsky 1989:112). It aims (among many other things) to demonstrate the essentially social nature of God and religion. In somewhat simple terms, it suggests that religion represents the worship of society by its members.

This extraordinary claim pushes Durkheim's perspective on the primacy of the social world even further beyond his previous work. He had earlier demonstrated the social nature of morality, deviance, and suicide, and he now aimed to do the same for religion, the ultimate source of morality. If the supernatural could be explained sociologically, it would extend the perspective in a novel way.

To support his arguments, Durkheim relied on new sources of data. Rather than examining statistics across communities of Europe as he did to study suicide, he relied on descriptions of the religious beliefs and activities of tribal societies in Australia. Scientists in the growing field of anthropology had begun to study the cultures of small hunting and gathering societies across the world, and the new knowledge about religion in these societies provided raw material for social theory. Durkheim would use the findings of these studies to explain the emergence of pure forms of religion in relatively simple societies, those that lacked the complexities of modern society. Religion so pervaded the social life of these societies that he could gain special insight into its true nature.

Before anything else, Durkheim began by defining religion. He argued that religion does not always involve beliefs about the supernatural or even a god (Buddhists, for example, have no conception of divine beings). Rather, what all religions have in common is a distinction between the sacred and the profane. Sacred objects have special qualities that create awe and respect and must be treated as separate and protected; profane, everyday objects have no such special qualities. In Christianity, the Bible, the communion host, and the altar are treated as sacred, while non-Christian religions and societies define other objects as sacred. Religion can be defined, then, as a unified system of beliefs and practices related to what is sacred.

In the tribal societies Durkheim studied, sacred objects took the form of totems, and religion was based on totemism. A totem is an animal, plant, or object that members of a clan come to see as sacred and having supernatural powers. Each clan within a small society is united by kinship and a common ancestor but also typically has its own totem. Members of the clan treat the totem with reverence and are forbidden to kill, eat, or mistreat the animal or plant that the totem represents. The clan follows special rules of conduct or rituals in the presence of the totem, and the totem in turn provides protection and special status to the clan. In these ways, totems (and religion more generally) come to play a crucial role in the lives of clan members.

Durkheim's definition of religion and description of totemism in primitive societies has a sociological point—to demonstrate the underlying social nature of the beliefs and rituals. In the first place, the religious beliefs and rituals help society function. The shared beliefs about the sacredness of totems help hold the group together by giving members of a clan a common identity, while the rituals and ceremonies create a sense of emotional solidarity when members act together in showing respect to the totem. Totemism further helps maintain conformity to the group's morality. Those who violate rules of the clan or society feel separated from the common beliefs and special relationship to the sacred totems.

In addition, however, Durkheim goes beyond this reasoning to suggest something more profound: he argues that totemic beliefs and rituals really involve the worship of society. As people come together through interaction, the social stimulation creates a special feeling that Durkheim called effervescence. Although not a particularly fitting term, it refers to something real, like the feeling of belonging in a crowd during a sporting event or a large family during a reunion. A similar feeling may also come from the power of the group in constraining what an individual can or cannot do. Whatever the circumstances, the feeling seems to involve a mysterious force that goes beyond or surrounds the individual.

In primitive societies, as Durkheim argued, clans come to view the force as sacred and represent it symbolically in the form of a totem. In this way, the clans give this powerful but mysterious force a concrete form and offer a supernatural explanation for its appearance. Religion involves the beliefs of clan members about the objects they treat as sacred, but it ultimately stems from social experiences. The totems that clans worship in essence symbolize forces created through social interaction.

To summarize Durkheim's theory, religious beliefs in general and totemism in particular celebrate the power and significance of society by giving it concrete form. Although people feel the influence of group membership and the constraints of social morality, they do not quite understand the nature of this force. To give meaning to these vague intuitions about social forces, they worship sacred objects that (unconsciously) represent society and its power. In this way, religious beliefs unite individuals within a moral community and form the basis for a shared morality.

Criticisms of Functionalism

Today, Durkheim still counts as one of the most influential of all sociologists. As the first scholar to give academic legitimacy to the field, his legacy endures. More than a century ago, he defined a new subject matter as well as the scientific method of study that still forms the basis of sociology. His brilliant critique of unrestrained individualism and demonstration of the nonrational foundations of social cooperation separated sociology from psychology and philosophy. His study of the causes of suicide provided a model of high-quality social research. As a result of these contributions, every student who opens a sociology textbook reads about Durkheim in the first chapters.

Sociologists have, however, rejected some parts of Durkheim's perspective on society. Of most concern to modern scholars, Durkheim overstated the analogy between society and an organism. The analogy implies that, much the way each organ in a body contributes to the survival of the organism, each part of society contributes to the successful functioning of the total society. A larger perspective based on the idea that society consists of interrelated parts that support one another in the functioning of society as a whole is called structural-functionalism or **functionalism**.

In the view of many, functionalism tends to accept or justify existing social arrangements without regard to the inequalities and unfairness that invariably arise within society. If each part of society contributes to the functioning of the whole, each part has value that justifies its continued existence. From an extreme functionalist perspective, poverty and crime appear normal and healthy. Yet this perspective ignores the fact that social arrangements may favor some groups more than others; some groups have a greater stake than others in keeping things the same. The focus on functions for the "total" society downplays these differences, even treating them as aberrations from a normally functioning society.

This criticism no doubt oversimplifies the complexity of Durkheim's work. He recognized the limitations of functional analysis and tried in his work to distinguish between causes and functions. Further, he never used his arguments to rationalize social problems; to the contrary, he hoped to use sociology to reduce social problems. While Durkheim's work showed conservative currents stemming from his concern about the harm of modernism, it also contained more liberal concerns with democracy and freedom. During his lifetime, Durkheim's reformism riled conservatives as much as radicals. His intense desire to logically understand society led him to avoid oversimplified claims in favor of either side.

Still, functional analysis played a part in his work. Durkheim tended to highlight the benefits stemming from orderly connections among individuals in society and the abnormality of social conflict. Since problems result from the incompatibility of different parts of the social system, his studies focused on social reforms designed to make the parts of a society work better together. He treated alienation, inequality, and social protest as short-term problems rather than as central components of modern society. Since most sociologists today reject functional analysis, they look critically at Durkheim's work.

Sociologists and others today also react negatively to Durkheim's traditional views about the roles of men and women in society. He thought that biological differences between men and women required different social roles in the division of labor within marriage and society. Women should remain active in the private, domestic sphere of child care and homemaking; men should remain active in the public, economic sphere of work and politics. Through a sexual division of labor, men and women would be united in a close relationship within marriage and could avoid the problems causing and stemming from divorce. Not surprisingly, many women and men today object strongly to such views.

Concern with Individualism

In contrast to his functional analysis, Durkheim's work on questions involving morality, community ties, and individualism remains important today. In some ways, a resurgence of sociological concern about individualism has occurred in the last decade in the United States. According to some, the trends identified by Durkheim in the structure of social relations have continued to promote individualism at the expense of community ties. With hindsight, the problems stemming from individualism that Durkheim studied seem worse now than in Durkheim's time.

In an influential and prize-winning book, *Habits of the Heart*, Robert Bellah and colleagues (1985) argued that the freedom of modern society has resulted in a lack of meaningful moral connections between people and a lack of public involvement in local community life. People in the nineteenth century presented their morality in a public way, by acting properly and doing good deeds that others could see. More isolated and separate from one another than in the past, people today seem intent on attaining individual success and achievement and on expressing individual talents and feelings. They like to impress others with their material belongings, lifestyles, and leisure-time activities.

Ever more income and freedom, however, have not brought happiness. In interviews with people across the country, Bellah and his collaborators found much confusion about the meaning of life today. Having reached their goals and gained the freedom to do just what they want, people still feel dissatisfied but do not understand why. Consider some examples:

✦ Brian Palmer, a successful businessman in northern California, has in recent years shifted his goals from work to family. Rather than satisfaction, his occupational success and time spent at work had brought the breakup of his first marriage and a sense of failure. Now, he devotes more time to his new marriage and children, hoping that the shift in goals from work to family will make life meaningful. Still, he tends to view the world in terms of what activities and goals will bring him the most satisfaction. Beyond that, he seems to have no larger purpose in life.

✦ Margaret Oldham, a psychologist living near Atlanta, also sets individual fulfillment as her primary goal. With no children, a job she likes, and sufficient income, she has devised a lifestyle that expresses her freedom and interests. She proudly takes responsibility for her own behavior and urges her clients to do the same. Consistent with her individualism, however, she feels uncomfortable making demands on others. Her desire for personal freedom and her unwillingness to judge others limit the attachments she has to her community. Since her personal fulfillment has little to do with others, something seems missing from her life.

✦ Wayne Bauer, once involved in protests against the Vietnam War in the 1960s, has maintained his interest in politics by becoming a community organizer. Devoted to problems of social injustice, he tries to help people improve their lives by organizing into political groups that can protest poor treatment. His work thus involves him with local groups and communities. Even so, his motives seems less concerned with others than with his own satisfaction and dissatisfaction. Rather than being guided by community morality, he uses community groups to meet his personal needs.

With each person's focus on different goals, Bellah and his colleagues saw something arbitrary about individual choices in modern society. Unless people share meaning and values with others—have a common morality—life has little meaning. Without social commitment and limitations on personal desires, individualism brings emptiness and may undermine freedom. The authors "are concerned that this individualism may have grown cancerous" (Bellah et al. 1985:vii).

People today tend to view their social problems as new and special, but the work of Bellah and others echoes many of Durkheim's concerns. Durkheim wanted to understand how persons in a modern, complex, and differentiated society could remain part of a community that could provide guidance, support, and regulation of morality.

Since these same problems face us today, sociologists continue to address the same issues Durkheim did: How can we balance the need to belong and find moral guidance from the larger community with the need to express our individuality and enjoy our personal freedom? How do we do the right thing? Durkheim not only asked these important questions but also provided a valuable perspective on them. If his solutions to the problems now look outdated, his insights into the problems themselves remain fresh.

SUMMARY

After decades of political violence, France in the late 1800s had established a democracy. Émile Durkheim hoped this democracy would survive but realized that social order in society depended on more than hope—it depended on the bonds between individuals and social groups. Durkheim devoted his career to the study of these bonds and to the sources of morality that contribute to social order. In so doing, he defined sociology as a field separate from psychology, economics, education, and philosophy.

To make the case for sociology, Durkheim needed to demonstrate that society involved something more than individuals freely choosing to cooperate with one another. He argued instead that without a set of rules of right and wrong to guide social behavior, trust would not exist and individuals would not cooperate. These shared rules must come from the larger groups and society to which individuals belong. Society rather than individual self-interest, therefore, makes social cooperation possible.

Given the importance of morality to social order, Durkheim further reasoned that scholars needed to study society in its own right rather than just the individuals that comprise it. Since the behavior of individuals results from forces outside themselves, the group rather than the individual needed to become the object of study. The study of groups and societies thus defined sociology as a new and separate field of study.

Along with an object of study for the new discipline, Durkheim offered sociology its own version of the scientific method to study the influence of the group on individuals. He wanted to replace philosophic speculation and literary description with systematic observation of social life. Sociologists could objectively study social facts (or external forces of influence over individuals) just as physicists objectively study the movement of physical matter. For example, to study the ideas of right and wrong that guide behavior, Durkheim examined the punishment, anger, and outrage exhibited by people when others violate those ideas.

Using his sociological and scientific perspective, Durkheim made important contributions to the study of social solidarity, crime, suicide, and religion. All these studies related to his central concern with social order and morality and provided unique insights into each topic that still remain fresh today.

To study social solidarity, Durkheim compared the division of labor or degree of specialization across societies. He noted that societies with simple and complex divisions of labor exhibit different types of solidarity. In simple, small societies characterized by similarities among their members, solidarity stems from common values and behaviors. In larger, more complex societies, solidarity comes from each part making a different contribution to the whole. The shift from solidarity based on similarity to solidarity based on diversity and interdependence increases the freedom of individuals but also reduces social unity and community integration.

In discussing issues of morality and solidarity, Durkheim offered a startling insight about crime, arguing that crime is a normal and valuable component of society. Rather than harming society, a certain amount of crime mobilizes group members to act together to punish it. The existence of crime and punishments for committing crimes reaffirms ideas of right and wrong. Without clear instances of violations of society's rules, the rules themselves would lack meaning. Further, anger about crime and the desire to punish offenders create emotional bonds among members of society.

Durkheim also illustrated the power of his sociological perspective in his study of suicide. He demonstrated that this behavior, which by definition involves only one person, nonetheless stems from social factors. Suicide is more common among persons lacking close ties to social groups and clear norms to follow. Persons strongly integrated into family, religious, or community groups thus have lower rates of suicide than those less strongly integrated. The relationships of individuals to groups rather than individual traits themselves best predict suicide. If something as apparently individualistic as suicide actually results from social forces, then other more social behaviors no doubt also stem from social forces.

Later in his life, Durkheim turned his intellectual powers to the study of the emergence of religion in tribal societies. With startling originality, he claimed the concept of the gods came from the organization of society. By describing how religious beliefs celebrate the power and significance of society in simple societies, his work demonstrated the social nature of both God and reality.

Durkheim's criticisms of individualistic theories and demonstration of the social foundations of morality remain central to sociology today. His study of suicide endures as a model of careful reasoning and data analysis. His definition of social facts still helps define sociology as an independent field of study. And the problems of individualism and belonging still concern sociologists and the public. Although scholars today are critical of Durkheim's use of functional reasoning, they continue to rely on his insights into a variety of topics.

DISCUSSION QUESTIONS

1. How did coming from a close-knit family in a small town affect Durkheim's reaction to the competitive Paris schools? What kind of learning and teaching did Durkheim want?

2. Describe France's political and social problems after its defeat in the war with Prussia. How did the loss of religion and the rise of modernism contribute to these problems? Did Durkheim think that a return to religion could solve the problems of nineteenth-century France?

3. What underlying assumption about self-interest and cooperation did Spencer and English philosophers make? What flaw in this assumption did Durkheim identify?

4. Give examples of how morality acts as an external constraint on the behavior of individuals. How does the focus on external restraints differentiate sociology from other social sciences?

5. If Durkheim could not study morality directly, how did he propose to study it indirectly? How did he propose to adapt the experimental method to make comparisons across societies? Give an example of how the comparative study of morality might proceed.

6. Explain how population growth and density increase the division of labor. Give examples of mechanical solidarity and organic solidarity. How does crime contribute to social solidarity?

7. What criticisms did opponents make of Durkheim's views on science, social realism, and secular education? What criticisms did radical socialists make of Durkheim's work? Do these criticisms have validity?

8. Compare egoistic and anomic suicide, and identify the groups that experience high rates of these types of suicide. How does each type of suicide reflect the influence of social rather than individual factors?

9. Describe the difference between sacred and profane objects. What form did sacred objects take in the societies Durkheim examined in *The Elementary Forms of Religious Life*? What does it mean to say that religion involves the worship of society?

10. Evaluate the strengths and weaknesses of the functionalist analogy used by Durkheim and other sociologists. How does social life today reflect the problems with individualism highlighted in Durkheim's work?

REFERENCES

PRIMARY SOURCES

Durkheim, Émile. 1933 [1893]. *The Division of Labor in Society* (translated by George Simpson). New York: Free Press.

Durkheim, Émile. 1951 [1897]. *Suicide: A Study of Sociology* (translated by John A. Spaulding and George Simpson). New York: Free Press.

Durkheim, Émile. 1982 [1895]. *The Rules of the Sociological Method* (translated by W. D. Halls). New York: Free Press.

Durkheim, Émile. 1995 [1912]. *The Elementary Forms of Religious Life* (translated by Karen E. Fields). New York: Free Press.

SECONDARY SOURCES

Aron, Raymond. 1965. *Main Currents in Sociological Thought* (Vol. II). Garden City, NY: Doubleday.

Ashley, David, & David Michael Orenstein. 1995. *Sociological Theory: Classic Statements* (3rd ed.). Boston: Allyn & Bacon.

Barzini, Luigi. 1983. *The Europeans*. New York: Penguin.

Bellah, Robert N., Richard Madsen, William M. Sullivan, Ann Swidler, & Steven M. Tipton. 1985. *Habits of the Heart: Individualism and Commitment in American Life*. New York: Harper & Row.

Bernstein, Richard. 1990. *Fragile Glory: A Portrait of France and the French*. New York: Knopf.

Braudel, Fernand. 1988. *The Identity of France* (translated by Sian Reynolds). New York: Harper & Row.

Clark, Terry. 1973. *Prophets and Patrons: The French University and the Emergence of the Social Sciences*. Cambridge, MA: Harvard University Press.

Collins, Randall. 1985. *Three Sociological Traditions*. New York: Oxford University Press.

Collins, Randall, & Michael Makowsky. 1989. *The Discovery of Society* (4th ed.). New York: Random House.

Coplestone, Frederick. 1962. *A History of Philosophy* (Vol. 9). Garden City, NY: Image Books.

Coser, Lewis A. 1977. *Masters of Sociological Thought* (2nd ed.). San Diego: Harcourt Brace Jovanovich.

Etzioni, Amitai. 1996. "The Responsive Community: A Communitarian Perspective." *American Sociological Review* 61:1–11.

Giddens, Anthony. 1971. *Capitalism and Modern Social Theory*. London: Cambridge University Press.

Gillis, A. R. 1996. "So Long as They Both Shall Live: Marital Dissolution and the Decline of Domestic Homicide in France, 1852–1909." *American Journal of Sociology* 101:1273–1305.

Jones, Robert Alun. 1994. "Ambivalent Cartesians: Durkheim, Montesquieu, and Method." *American Journal of Sociology* 100:1–39.

Jones, Robert Alun, & Douglas Kibbee. 1993. "Durkheim, Language, and History: A Pragmatic Perspective." *Sociological Theory* 11:152–170.

Knapp, Peter. 1994. *One World—Many Worlds: Contemporary Sociological Theory.* New York: HarperCollins.

Lehmann, J. M. 1995. "Durkheim's Theories of Deviance and Suicide: A Feminist Reconsideration." *American Journal of Sociology* 100:904–930.

Lepenies, Wolf. 1988. *Between Literature and Science: The Rise of Sociology* (translated by R. J. Holingdale). Cambridge, UK: Cambridge University Press.

Levine, Donald N. 1995. *Visions of the Sociological Tradition.* Chicago: University of Chicago Press.

Lukes, Steven. 1985. *Émile Durkheim: His Life and Work.* Stanford, CA: Stanford University Press.

Mestrovic, Stjepan G. 1988. *Émile Durkheim and the Reformation of Sociology.* Totowa, NJ: Rowman & Littlefield.

Nisbet, Robert A. 1966. *The Sociological Tradition.* New York: Basic Books.

Pope, Whitney. 1976. *Durkheim's "Suicide," a Classic Analyzed.* Chicago: University of Chicago Press.

Ritzer, George. 1996. *Sociological Theory* (4th ed.). New York: McGraw-Hill.

Russell, Bertrand. 1945. *A History of Western Philosophy.* New York: Simon & Schuster.

Teitelbaum, Michael, & Jay Winter. 1985. *The Fear of Population Decline.* Orlando, FL: Academic Press.

Thompson, Kenneth. 1982. *Émile Durkheim.* London: Tavistock.

Viault, Birdsall S. 1990. *Modern European History.* New York: McGraw-Hill.

REFERENCE NOTES

Citations for quotations and special points of interest are given in the text. Listed here are citations to sources for major topics covered in each section of the chapter.

1. **From Small-Town France to Paris:** Life at École Normale (Clark 1973:38–39; Lukes 1985:45–46); Durkheim's background (Lukes 1985:41–43; Coser 1977:143; Mestrovic 1988:27–33); Competition (Clark 1973:38–39); Durkheim's failure (Coser 1977:143; Lukes 1985:42–44; Thompson 1982:28); Lonely and isolated (Lukes 1985:42); Student discussion (Lukes 1985:46); Dissatisfaction with learning (Lukes 1985:53; Coser 1977:144; Clark 1973:39); Henri Bergson (Thompson 1982:29); Bergson's critics (Coplestone 1962:179; Russell 1945:803–804).

2. **Political and Social Problems in France:** 19th century France (Viault 1990:190, 312–315); Expected victory (Barzini 1983:127–132); Factions (Nisbet 1966:10–12); Lack of compromise (Coser 1977:157–159; Bernstein 1990:235); French conflicts (Bernstein 1990:237; Barzini 1983:124); Traditional authority (Nisbet 1966:107); Divorce (Gillis 1996); Fertility (Teitelbaum & Winter 1985); Suicide statistics (Durkheim 1951[1897]); Anti-Semitism (Lukes 1985:345; Thompson 1982:12); Pessimism (Nisbet 1966:268); Modern sociology in France (Thompson 1982:11); August Comte (Ritzer 1996:13); Loss of religion (Aron 1965:2; Coser 1977:137; Lukes 1985:196); Durkheim and conflict (Thompson 1982:12); Rejects

religion (Coser 1977:143; Lukes 1985:48); Problems of individualism (Coser 1977:136; Nisbet 1966:304; Lukes 1985:139).

3. The Moral Basis of Social Life: Poor performance (Thompson 1982:29); Ties to professors (Coser 1977:144); Teaching jobs (Thompson 1982:34); Ambition (Collins & Makowsky 1989:104; Ashley & Orenstein 1995:108; Thompson 1982:12); Early sociologists (Levine 1995:167); Individual and society (Lukes 1985:66; Knapp 1994:53); Critique of general principles (Jones & Kibbee 1993:163); Herbert Spencer (Collins & Makowsky 1989:88; Rizer 1996:37); English intellectual tradition (Levine 1995:129); Self-interest and social life (Collins & Makowsky 1989:104–105; Nisbet 1966:90, 270; Collins 1985:135); Social realism (Lukes 1985:79; Aron 1965:69; Coser 1977:173).

4. The Scientific Comparison of Societies: Travel grant (Lukes 1985:86); Traditional philosophical methods in France (Jones & Kibbee 1993:165; Giddens 1971:69); Experimental method and social behavior (Jones 1994:5); Literary description (Lepenies 1988:1); Auguste Comte (Lukes 1985:68–69); Durkheim's teachers (Thompson 1982:30–32); French science (Jones 1994:3; Lukes 1985:86); Advantages of scientific approach (Coser 1977:156, 173; Lukes 1985:331, 405); Compare groups (Collins & Makowsky 1989:110; Jones 1994:23); Published articles (Thompson 1982:13–15); Recognition (Coser 1977:145); Appointment (Lukes 1985:95, 108); Dissertation exam (Lukes 1985:299); Productivity (Lukes 1985:100).

5. The Division of Labor in Society: Establishing sociology (Thompson 1982:22; Coser 1977:164; Aron 1965:102; Mestrovic 1988:1–3); Personality (Coser 1977:170; Lukes 1985:40, 97–100, 367–371; Thompson 1982:28); Students (Lukes 1985:368; Thompson 1982:42); Journal (Coser 1977:146, 167); Education courses (Lukes 1985:106–110; Lepenies 1988:51–52; Aron 1965:100); Gabriel Tarde (Coser 1977:153; Lepenies 1988:55).

6. Suicide as Social Behavior: Promotion (Coser 1977:147); Social science at Bordeaux (Lukes 1985:108); Sorbonne (Lukes 1985:103; Coser 1977:147); Criticisms (Lukes 1985:363); Bergson's supporters (Lepenies 1988:71); Bergson's writings (Coplestone 1962:179; Lepenies 1988:71); Durkheim's supporters (Lukes 1985:371); Durkheim's critics (Lukes 1985:300, 302, 314; Thompson 1982:39); Opposition to Catholic education (Lukes 1985:375); Ignored class conflict (Lukes 1985:318); Durkheim on Marx (Thompson 1982:16); Radical critics (Thompson 1982:90); Sociology chair (Ashley & Orenstein 1995:104); Suicide studied often (Collins & Makowsky 1989:110; Lukes 1985:191,194); Economic integration (Ritzer 1996:96–97); Dignity of the individual (Lukes 1985:343; Thompson 1982:44).

7. Individualism and Community Ties: Continuing work (Lukes 1985:554); Trained students (Lukes 1985:379); French education (Coser 1977:148); Most impressive work (Aron 1965:45; Thompson 1982:124; Coser 1977:138); Ideas gain influence (Lukes 1985:393); Death of son (Lukes 1985:555); Health (Lukes 1985:558); Academic legitimacy (Collins 1985:123; Thompson 1982:22); Durkheim's functionalism (Lukes 1985:83; Thompson 1982:105; Coser 1977:172–173); Feminist critics (Lehmann 1995:8); Individualism (Bellah et al. 1985; Etzioni 1996).

chapter 3

A Prophet of Doom: Max Weber and the Spread of Rationality

Modern life seems more and more impersonal. We have to deal with large bureaucratic organizations that treat us as numbers rather than as individuals; waste our time with forms, long lines, and computerized phone answering; and frustrate us with half-hearted and unfriendly service. Large government agencies, universities, and corporations can make life difficult. We also have to deal with chain stores and restaurants that, although they emphasize quick and friendly service, nonetheless seem increasingly similar and predictable. McDonald's, Wendy's, Burger King, Chili's, Bennigan's, the Gap, and the Limited offer depressing sameness. At the same time that the world has become increasingly complex, in certain ways it has also become increasingly similar.

These trends reflect the spread of rationality throughout society. Rational procedures in bureaucracies make it possible to deal with large numbers of people as quickly and efficiently as possible. Rational procedures allow chain restaurants and stores to use the same efficient and successful practices in all locations. And rational procedures help make it possible to maximize profit, increase living standards, and create enormous wealth. Still, rationality and efficiency often seem so overwhelming that people continually search for less efficient and rational ways to enjoy personal intimacy, spontaneous emotion, spirituality, and faith.

How has rationality come to play such an important part in our lives? How does the reliance on rational procedures today contrast with the working of societies in the past? In the early 1900s, as he observed the emergence of bureaucracies in the government and military, the German sociologist Max Weber worried about the loss of human values in the spread of rational, efficient, and predictable behavior. During his life, he investigated the emergence of certain forms of rational behavior and organizations in modern society. The trends he described continue to affect our lives.

Along with Karl Marx and Émile Durkheim, Max Weber rounds out the dominant threesome of classic sociological theory. Unlike Marx and Durkheim, however, Weber never faced the bitter intellectual opposition, hostility, and conflict that they experienced. Because he had already gained a reputation as an economist, lawyer, and historian before moving onto sociology, his work helped give legitimacy to the new field in Germany.

Rather than battling intellectual critics, Weber had to fight his own psychological demons. In his personal life, he worked to exhaustion, never able to enjoy pleasure in general or even sexual relations with his wife—and eventually experiencing a long period of severe depression that interrupted his work and career. Eventually overcoming these problems, he wrote on an enormous range of topics with a special knowledge and sophistication that still impress readers today (and, not incidentally, make for difficult reading). Attuned to nuance and complexity, Weber rejected extreme, one-sided theories of social life, aiming instead to find a middle ground between competing ideas and political views.

Many of Weber's studies have become sociological classics. He examined the relationship between the Protestant Reformation and the emergence of capitalism in Europe. He described the components of social inequality and the different types of power and authority in society. He contrasted religious beliefs and their implications for social and economic life in Protestant and Catholic Europe with those in the Middle East, India, and China. And he described the characteristics of bureaucratic organizations. Within these varied studies, he highlighted the growing, even dominating, importance of rational thought and action.

Held in high esteem even by his critics, Weber's work is ambitious, complex, and insightful. He made so many contributions to the field of sociology that a review can cover only a small part of them. Even this small part, however, helps define modern sociology and conflict theory.

1. A TORMENTED FAMILY LIFE

In the fall of 1893, at age 29, Max Weber planned to marry and finally move out of his parents' house. Except for a few years away in college and the military, he had lived at home in a suburb of Berlin, Germany, with his father, mother, and younger siblings. Life in the Weber (pronounced VAY-ber) household had always been filled with tension, and the past seven years had intensified the strain for the young man. He had returned there from college at age 22—a tall, full-grown man with strong opinions and a fierce temper, yet unable to support himself until he finished his advanced schooling. At an age when others had become independent, Weber had to rely financially on his father.

Max Weber Sr. could easily have afforded to help his oldest, highly talented, and immensely hard-working son establish himself, but he was a domineering and manipulative person who enjoyed having even his grown children around so he could control them. For the younger Weber, however, living at home brought misery. He deeply resented his father's dictatorial rule and his own financial dependence on him. Worse, he could not bring himself to reasonably discuss his concerns with his father—or even to express them. Instead, he held his strong emotions inside during those long years while he prepared for a career as a lawyer and scholar.

In a letter to his fiancée, Weber wrote: "For years I have realized with infinite bitterness that I was unable to obtain a position that would give me independent income ... the fact that it was denied me made my family home a torment" (Weber 1975:185). To deal with his inner torment, he single-mindedly devoted himself to his work and studies, denying himself even normal pleasures and relaxation. Occupying his mind every minute of the day with work seemed a way to push aside the difficult emotions brought out by daily life with a father he loathed.

Near the end of his stay at home, Weber had begun to earn his own income by holding three jobs, any one of which would have fully occupied almost anyone else. He taught at the University of Berlin, worked for a Berlin attorney weekdays from 9:00 A.M. to 7:00 P.M., and participated in a research project on agricultural problems in eastern Germany (Mitzman 1970:85). More impressively, he succeeded in each. On top of his duties as a teacher and junior lawyer, he wrote with his collaborators a 900-page report on the research project that received much attention and praise.

Now he could look forward to complete financial and personal independence from his father: a job and marriage would set him on a course as a successful young man. After a brief period of indecision about whether to pursue a career as a lawyer or an academic, Weber decided to devote himself to a scholarly career at the University of Berlin. In 1893, he married his second cousin Marianne, the granddaughter of his father's older brother, and moved into his own home near his father's. One year later, he received and accepted an appointment at the prestigious Freiburg University. The newlyweds then moved hundreds of miles away from Berlin to establish a life of their own.

Unfortunately, but not surprisingly, the conflicts of his earlier life would stay with Weber even after his independence. The tangle of his family relationships created conflicts, tensions, and emotions that would scar the intense and quiet young man. Weber would grow into a brilliant—but deeply troubled—scholar and sociologist.

Parental Conflict

Weber was descended from prosperous Protestant families located mostly in northern and eastern Germany. His ancestors on both sides of the family had moved to these Protestant areas of Germany to escape religious persecution in the Catholic countries of Austria and France. There they established successful businesses and later made possible substantial bequests to their children and grandchildren. These family resources helped Weber's parents, Max Sr. and Helene, to live a comfortable upper-middle-class life.

Despite their similar backgrounds, Max Sr. and Helene got along poorly. Complete opposites in personality and values, they could not hide their disagreements from their children. In public, Weber's father was an outgoing and pleasure-loving man who gladly altered his beliefs and principles to avoid personal difficulties and achieve professional success. Only at home did he demand, as head of the family, that others should follow his desires and commands without question or dispute. Dealing with his powerless family members, Max Sr. was a tyrant and bully.

In the public arena, he served as a lawyer, civil servant, and member of the German parliament. He belonged to a minority political party that favored a constitutional monarchy and supported democratic rights at a time when German politics was dominated by an inflexible monarch, a wily and ruthless chancellor, and a powerful and conservative aristocracy of landowners who ruled the nation with unbending power. Rather than fighting for his democratic beliefs, however, Max Sr. accommodated himself to the ruling elite. In return, he enjoyed a successful career in the government.

In contrast to Max Sr., Helene was quiet, introspective, and disciplined, taking little pleasure in food, drink, or socializing. She reluctantly agreed to sex only for the purpose of having children—no doubt a source of conflict with her pleasure-loving husband—and worried intensely about her children's well-being. Max Jr. had faced a life-threatening bout of meningitis at age 2 and a daughter died at age 4. While these events had led Helene to long periods of sadness, Max Sr. had quickly returned to his normal life and badgered his wife to do the same. Her pessimism and seriousness contrasted with his optimism and shallowness.

Also unlike Max Sr., Helene was deeply religious. She expressed her spirituality not in emotional joy, but in daily efforts to perform acts of goodness. Although she worked to the point of exhaustion raising seven children and serving the commands of her husband, she still devoted time to helping the poor and needy. Where some responded to poverty and inequality in industrial society with calls for revolution, many others like Helene thought Christian charity could better deal with these problems. Although Max Sr. ridiculed his wife's hopes as foolish and impractical, Helene remained committed to her religious duty.

Money further worsened the problems between husband and wife. Although Helene had received an inheritance that exceeded her husband's earnings, Max Sr. felt threatened by his wife's wealth and insisted on controlling all spending. Although he spent lavishly on his own comfort, he only grudgingly gave Helene the money needed to run the household. Since he refused to give her funds for her religious charities, Helene took money meant for servants, did the servants' work herself, and then secretly gave that money to charity (Mitzman 1970:45).

Weber's Early Years

An intelligent and observant child, Weber felt the strain of parental conflict; bitter and heated arguments must have occurred often as his parents became increasingly estranged. Weber felt caught between both sides. On one hand, an emerging sense of honor and sympathy for his mother's devotion to duty made him resent his father's treatment of her; on the other hand, he identified with the authority and power of his father, his famous political and intellectual friends, and the respect he received in German society. This sort of ambivalence would mark Weber's thoughts and actions throughout his life.

As a young man, Weber initially seemed most attached to his father. Whatever sense of duty his mother might have instilled in him, it did not yet show up in dealing with others. In school, he consistently underperformed, but because he read widely on his own, he received good grades and other students admired his knowledge. Even so, he impressed teachers as lacking industry, maturity, and respect for tradition.

Like his father, he later attended the University of Heidelberg to study law. In some ways, he even imitated his father's behavior in college. Although never one to enjoy sports, he took part in the fencing activities common in German universities at the time (he even had his face scarred in one duel); although never one to mingle easily, he joined fraternity drinking parties and put on weight that bloated his body and face. On returning home after the first semester, Weber presented a shocking appearance to his mother—he now looked so much like his father that she slapped his face. He had changed from a thin and sickly young man to a heavy-set drinker (Coser 1977:236).

In the remaining years of college, several events conspired to shift Weber's allegiance to his mother. Like all young men, Weber had to serve in the military, where he found the physical demands, tedious drills, and verbal abuse of basic training hard to endure (observing Weber perform a gymnastic drill, a sarcastic drill-sergeant told him he looked "like a barrel of beer swinging on a trapeze" (Gerth & Mills 1946:8)). Not until promoted to an officer did he come to tolerate military life. The army made him realize how much he enjoyed intellectual pursuits and how much he would dislike a life like his father's that did not require full use of his brain.

In addition, he spent time during his military service with an uncle and aunt who lived near the training base in Strasbourg, relatives who presented a refreshing contrast to his own parents. The uncle, a professor and historian, held political views similar to those of Weber's father, but had the courage to express them. He also valued his nephew's opinions—another contrast with Weber's domineering father. The aunt, although deeply religious like his mother, expressed her beliefs with a more appealing sense of confidence and forcefulness. Both relatives provided attractive role models, his intellectual uncle highlighting the shallowness of his father and his religious aunt displaying the values of his mother in an admirable light. As a result, Weber gained more respect for his mother and less for his father.

A Frantic Work Pace

His experiences in the military and with his relatives encouraged a new maturity that led Weber to reject the selfish pleasures of his early years in college. His new discipline showed during the last semester of his undergraduate studies, spent at the University of Göttingen in central Germany. His routine there revealed the trait of self-denial that would come to rule his life: "He continued his strict work routine, regulated his life by the clock, divided his day into exact segments for the various types of instruction" (Weber 1975:105). At the end of the day, he would prepare a meal consisting of "a pound of chopped raw beef and four fried eggs" (Weber 1975:105). Other than a short card game after the evening meal, Weber rarely joined the activities of other students. He never exercised and spent little time outdoors.

Worried that her son had become a recluse, Weber's mother encouraged him to socialize with other students. After attending a dance at his mother's urging, Weber teasingly complained in a letter to her of the time he had wasted there. The people he met at the dance discussed boring topics like skating, singing, recent engagements, the room heat, and the weather; he said he could instead have worked "through all of the general part of the German Criminal Code, and the specific part up to the 'criminals dangerous to public welfare'" (Weber 1975:108). Weber much preferred intellectual conversation.

After completing his military service and undergraduate studies, he returned to Berlin to begin postgraduate work. His experiences with his relatives and years of independence made returning home difficult. He could no longer accept the bossy and pleasure-loving behavior of his father, but he felt unable to confront him; instead, "a frantic work pace helped divert him from the tension at home" (Coser 1977:238). He would submit himself to a rigid schedule of work that he would follow with monkish discipline.

This strategy of hiding from family problems through work would have tragic consequences in years to come, but for now it brought some benefits. It not only prevented open conflict between father and son while they lived together but also offered a prod for the enormous hard work needed to master his chosen fields of study—law, economics, and history. And within these already demanding fields, he concentrated on such difficult and technical topics as medieval trading law, Roman land tenure, and agricultural workers in eastern Germany.

Others recognized Weber's wide-ranging knowledge and remarkable productivity. After finishing his doctorate and performing well at both the University of Berlin and Freiburg University, he received a prestigious appointment at the University of Heidelberg. Thus, at the age of 32, he returned as a professor to the same place he had come as an immature student many years earlier, quickly reaching a goal it took others decades to attain. His hard work had given him the independence from his father he had always wanted. Yet even rapid academic success could not protect him from the disastrous personal problems that would eventually result from the tensions and contradictions in his life.

2. GERMANY: A NATION OF EXTREMES

Weber's changing attitude toward his father as a young adult reflected the uncertainty he felt toward his family life. More generally, he felt the same sort of uncertainty toward life in Germany under the authority of an increasingly powerful government. The fact that the German government in some ways represented a symbol of his father's authority (Coser 1977:234) helped shape Weber's political and scholarly views. Much as he at first had identified with his father's success, he at first admired his nation's government and leadership. Later, as he had come to dislike his father, he would also become hostile to Germany's leaders.

The years between Weber's birth in 1864 and his leaving home in 1893 were a period of drastic change in Germany. During the first half of the nineteenth century, Germany lagged behind England and France in modernizing its economy and politics. While England and France had united into powerful, centralized nations during wars of the late Middle Ages, Germany had remained a loosely organized confederation of small states, making it difficult to extend trade and commerce across German state boundaries and build markets for the sale of factory products.

Germany's largest state, Prussia, which extended eastward from the area around Berlin in central Germany toward the Polish and Russian borders, was ruled by a hereditary monarch and conservative landowners who opposed democracy and personal freedoms. Similar conservatism in the nearby and more powerful Austro-Hungarian Empire also obstructed German movement toward political rights and industrial development. As a result, many perceived Germans as backward peasants and feudal masters unable to compete in the modern world.

The military weakness of Germany generally and Prussia specifically seemed to confirm this contemptuous view. In the early 1800s, German and Prussian fighters typically performed poorly; after all, Napoleon had easily defeated them. Only the efforts of England and Russia had freed Germany from the control of the French. Yet, by the mid-twentieth century, Germany had become an aggressive military power that nearly conquered all of Europe in World War II under its power-hungry leader, Adolf Hitler.

German Unification

Germany's change from backwardness to militarism occurred in the second half of the nineteenth century, during the formative years of Weber's life. Under the leadership of its monarch, William (or Wilhelm) I, and, more importantly, its chancellor (or prime minister), Otto von Bismarck, Prussia united the German states into one nation. After launching policies of industrial development and military modernization, Prussia stunned all of Europe with successive victories in wars with Denmark, Austria, and France (recall that this latter victory in the Franco-Prussian War profoundly shaped Durkheim's view of France's future).

These victories allowed Prussia to create a new German empire in 1871, ruled by the former Prussian monarch, now called Kaiser William I (*kaiser* being a German derivative of *Caesar,* and thus meaning "emperor"). The new nation contained some 40 million people—making it larger than France or England (Mitchell 1978). Germany then continued its policies of industrial growth, became the Continent's economic leader, and nearly matched England in its financial and military power.

The military and economic power of the new nation came in part from an important social innovation: the use of bureaucratic procedures in the army and civil service. Throughout history, single military leaders like Napoleon had directly commanded the forces they led. Standing on a hill from which he could view the battle, a general would send commands to his officers and soldiers by courier. As the nineteenth century progressed, however, armies had become so large that no one person could follow all the action and efficiently send orders to the masses of soldiers, causing breakdowns in coordination and "chaos, as different units marched off in different directions and to defeat" (Stark 1996:616).

To deal with this problem, Prussia became the first nation to organize its armed forces into a kind of bureaucracy. Prussian generals devised a system of identically trained and equipped divisions led by a well-trained staff of officers, the most talented of whom received training in the principles of battle and experience with mock maneuvers. As leaders of the divisions, these officers could make decisions on their own but still follow the principles used by their commanders. Since these procedures proved enormously effective, Prussia defeated its enemies with surprising ease.

A bureaucratic organization also emerged to run the state in Germany. Rather than relying on relatives, friends, and supporters of the emperor to administer the nation, Germany employed professional civil servants. They efficiently collected taxes, enforced laws, set policies, distributed government benefits, and regulated the large number of citizens contained in the new empire. Not surprisingly, public bureaucratic organizations gained an increasingly large degree of power.

Political Backwardness

Despite the modernization of the economy, military, and government, the politics of Germany remained backward. The German state gave power to the military and to a bureaucratic civil service, but not to an elected parliament. The kaiser appointed the chancellor, who in turn set policies that the civil service administered and enforced. A legislature elected by all adult male voters existed and included representatives of workers and the growing middle class of small business owners, but the new German constitution gave little real power to the legislature. As a result, Germany combined modern industrial power with an outdated, undemocratic political system.

Most political power resided with the large landowners in central and eastern Germany, called Junkers (meaning "young noblemen" and pronounced YOON-kurs). A Junker himself, Bismarck made sure that they controlled the legislature, made up the core of the military officers, and supported his nation-building policies. The Junkers strongly favored the goal of increasing the international power of the German nation; in return, Bismarck helped them keep agriculture profitable by taxing cheaper food products from abroad.

Once, addressing the parliament, Bismarck declared that the great issues of the day would be settled by "blood and iron" rather than by democratic debate and majority rule (Viault 1990:300). Another time when the parliament refused to approve new taxes to pay for a military buildup, Bismarck collected and spent the taxes anyway. Despite the growing political rights in England and France, Bismarck and the kaiser refused to allow any steps toward real democracy.

This authoritarian political system proved helpful in speeding industrial growth and military expansion. Because Germany had industrialized relatively late, it could change much more quickly than England could. Having an industrial model to copy, and no political opposition to block industrial policies, Germany could quickly adopt the latest technology and equipment. Companies laid vast new railways, built gigantic steel mills, manufactured consumer goods, and created central banks with huge financial resources. Similarly, a generous military budget, a national draft, innovative methods of officer training, and the efficient production of military weapons further strengthened the army.

With the growth of industry, the urban working class grew as well, but it did not share equally in the higher income enjoyed by others. In these years, discontented workers united behind the Social Democratic party, which, following radical calls for collective ownership of property, threatened Bismarck's policies of industrialization and militarization. In 1878, Bismarck tried to outlaw meetings of Social Democrats and restrict their fund-raising. Later, he attempted to buy the loyalty of workers with highly popular social insurance policies that provided benefits to disabled and retired workers.

Along with efforts to isolate the growing working class, Bismarck maneuvered to limit the power of the growing class of capitalists. He could succeed because the new business class tried to imitate rather than battle the old aristocracy. Although richer, they wanted the same honors, titles, and lifestyles as the hereditary Junker landowners. Partly as a result of this attitude, big business became subservient to the conservative power of Bismarck's state rather than an independent force for political change.

The lack of conflict between landowners and capitalists gave Bismarck and Germany advantages in foreign affairs: with order at home, Bismarck could focus on expanding Germany's international power. Again proving his talents, he created alliances with Russia and Austria that isolated the angry and still potentially powerful nation of France. With foreign enemies held in check and domestic opposition isolated, Bismarck could devote Germany to further developing its economic and military power.

Given its sudden economic changes and political inflexibility, Germany became a nation of extremes. On one hand, many took pride in Bismarck's accomplishments of unifying the German nation and making it an international power. They adopted a nationalism that sought even wider German borders, new foreign territories, and greater economic and military power. Weber's father, although part of the democratic political center, celebrated Germany's newfound power and respect. On the other hand, German workers found themselves isolated from political decisions and deprived of their share of the growing wealth, making them increasingly radical and powerful opponents of the government.

Approaches to Scholarship

The scholarly and intellectual world displayed much the same conflict as existed in the world of politics. At one extreme, some scholars glorified the growing power of the German state (Weber's father praised these scholars, while his uncle denounced them). They discarded any attempt at objectivity in their support for the government and selectively interpreted historical facts to advance their own values and obtain favorable treatment from the monarchy.

At the other extreme, Marxist socialism offered an intellectual and political alternative to conservative scholars and philosophers. Given the power of the state to control the appointment of professors at German universities, socialists could not advocate their views from the privileged position of the academy. Yet intelligent and well-educated leaders of the Social Democratic party championed socialist thought. Even those who rejected Marx's theories and political views had to become familiar with them.

A third group, those who fell between the extremes and wanted to maintain objectivity amidst the pressures of both conservatives and socialists, adopted still another style of scholarship: they avoided drawing political implications from their studies and dedicated themselves instead to carefully compiling detailed descriptions of historical periods and places. Avoiding the search for general laws, they emphasized the slow accumulation of reliable facts.

Some historians went further to argue that, in addition to accumulating facts, they needed to discover the subjective experiences behind human action in different times and places. Unlike animals, people act according to the interpretations they give to the world; without understanding these interpretations, the study of history would be incomplete. Although no one could ever know exactly how people had experienced the world in the past, historians should do more than describe human behavior in the same way that physical scientists describe the motion of planets or the law of gravity.

This descriptive approach provided new historical understandings and a wealth of new sources for scholars to learn about the past while also avoiding political controversy. Still, it had a drawback: it could easily bog down in a mass of historical trivia. The more facts that accumulated, the more difficulty one would have grasping the essential themes behind them. History would become an unending sequence of separate and increasingly detailed descriptions that would provide little understanding of the larger forces that guided social behavior and organized societies.

Thus, the descriptive approach did not provide the basis for an effective social science. As in France, where Durkheim had to struggle to establish the field during the 1880s and 1890s, sociology courses, professors, students, associations, or journals did not exist in Germany. Indeed, most historians opposed the generalizations a science of society might try to provide. They likewise avoided the emerging methods of sociology—observation of primitive societies, use of simple samples and surveys, and direct comparisons across nations. Students could receive training in law, economics, and history, but not sociology.

In response to these intellectual currents, Weber would carve out his own perspective. He would harshly criticize both the conservative national leadership of the Junkers and the naive idealism of the radical socialists. He would favor a strong German nation and seek to preserve the accomplishments of Bismarck but reject the authoritarian methods used to reach these goals. He would recognize the need for worker representatives to participate in the government but reject their socialist goals.

Concerning the role of values in scholarship, Weber realized that all scholars have values that influence their choice of topics and political opinions, yet he also thought they could put those values aside in their research. He would call for objective methods in social scientific studies but apply those methods to understanding subjective human experience and meaning. And he would rely on the wealth of information accumulated by German historians but use it to make scientific generalizations and address political controversies. He wanted to use the historical detail he had mastered in his studies as a way to make general comparisons across societies and historical epochs. Although not perfect solutions to the intellectual problems of the times, Weber's ideas would help define and shape the emerging field of sociology.

3. PROTESTANTISM AND THE EMERGENCE OF CAPITALISM

As a professor, Weber's powerful mind, encyclopedic knowledge of history, and hard work impressed his academic colleagues. His formidable and severe appearance—"tall, stout, black-bearded, and moody"—likewise must have impressed others (Collins & Makowsky 1989:119). He seemed destined to become one of Germany's top scholars.

Success did not, however, slow Weber's work pace. When his wife Marianne urged him to rest, he illogically said, "If I don't work until one o'clock, I can't be a professor" (Weber 1975:202). Given his already quick rise in academia, that statement reveals the neurotic anxieties underlying his compulsive activity. Driving himself mercilessly, he denied himself nearly all worldly enjoyment. The problems that underlay his work habits manifested themselves in another way: Weber had not yet had, and indeed would never have, sex with his wife. Nonetheless, the couple had a close—if highly intellectual—relationship. Only in an affair some 20 years later would he find sexual release (Mitzman 1970:277).

A Severe Psychological Depression

It was only a matter of time before Weber's crushing workload, inner torment, and unhealthy family relationships led to a collapse. An incident with his father and mother triggered this collapse in 1897, soon after he began his job at the University of Heidelberg. When Weber and

Marianne moved to Heidelberg, his mother, Helene, wanted to visit them by herself. She wanted time to enjoy her oldest son and daughter-in-law peacefully, free of the commands of her husband. As controlling as always, however, Max Sr. insisted on coming anyway.

When both showed up in Heidelberg, and his father continued to treat his mother poorly, Weber finally exploded. Now independent and more sure of himself, he let out the anger he had previously withheld, banning his father from his home until he stopped treating his mother as a servant. While his mother stayed, his father left and, in anger at both his wife and son, began to travel on his own. Weber would never again see his father: seven weeks after the incident, Max Sr. died unexpectedly during his travels.

Soon after his father's death, Weber began to exhibit symptoms of remorse, exhaustion, sleeplessness, and anxiety. When these symptoms worsened into a severe depression, he had to take a leave of absence and eventually resign from his job. In the words of his wife, "Everything was too much for him; he could not read, write, talk, walk, or sleep without torment" (Weber 1975:242). When he tried to teach, "his arms and back became temporarily paralyzed. He found it difficult to speak; serious thinking was impossible" (Collins & Makowsky 1989:120).

Weber found travel helpful, and he spent much of his time during the next few years in Italy, in Switzerland, and on the shores of the Mediterranean Sea. Unable to involve himself in even the simplest activity during his travels, he often spent his time staring out of his hotel window. Although some viewed the illness skeptically, as something that willpower could overcome, Weber felt physically unable to perform his duties. Every time he tried to resume his writing or teaching, he found the tasks torturous. Every time he thought he was improving, he would suffer another relapse. During the worst periods, he even entered a sanitarium.

His mental problems came from many sources. Tension over conflict between his mother and father and guilt over the death of his father appear to be the most obvious causes. In addition, however, the malady ran in the family: several of Weber's close relatives experienced similar symptoms—one cousin and one sister even committed suicide. Overwork, sexual repression, childhood sicknesses, and physical weakness may also have played roles. Whatever the cause of the breakdown, Weber's extremely stern conscience and rigid standards made it difficult for him to forgive himself for this weakness. This of course made recovery agonizingly slow and difficult.

By 1902, Weber had begun to show more permanent improvement and to renew his academic interests. In 1904, he accepted an invitation to visit the United States, where he gave a lecture in St. Louis—the first since leaving his teaching position at the University of Heidelberg. The positive reception to the talk and the stimulating observations he made of life in the United States encouraged him to return fully to his writing. Although he would suffer relapses throughout his life, the worst of the depression seemed past.

As he began to improve, Weber's personal problems led to a new topic of study: the values and beliefs of Protestantism. Although not himself religious, his own compulsive work habits and inability to enjoy simple pleasures reflected and exaggerated the traits of his family's Protestantism. If he could understand these traits and the Protestant beliefs that led to them, he might better understand the sources of his own behavior and problems. The study of the Protestant ethic could offer a way to self-liberation.

Religion and Success

The study of Protestantism conveniently related to his longer-term interests in the emergence of capitalism. Trained as an economist and historian, Weber had studied how economic motivations under modern capitalism differed from those in ancient civilizations and the Middle Ages. Beyond his concern with the sources of his own problems, he realized that Protestantism might relate to his larger intellectual concerns with economics and history: the study of Protestantism and capitalism would direct his previous technical and narrow research to larger intellectual questions about the nature of modern society.

Two facts suggested a relationship between Protestantism and the emergence of capitalism. First, in nations, areas, and cities of Europe whose populations included both Protestants and Catholics, Protestants had become more successful. In Weber's (1958:35) words, "business leaders and owners of capital, as well as the higher grades of skilled labor, and even more the higher technically and commercially trained personnel of modern enterprises, are overwhelmingly Protestant." Weber had also observed firsthand the tremendous economic energy in the United States, then a predominantly Protestant nation. The gigantic skyscrapers, numerous businesses, and bustle on the streets there symbolized the capitalist spirit he wanted to study.

Second, worldwide comparisons demonstrated that modern capitalism had emerged only in a small part of Western Europe. It had not emerged in any of the great civilizations of China, India, or the Middle East, nor in the Eastern or Southern European nations of Russia, Greece, Italy, or Spain. It had emerged in parts of England, the Netherlands, Germany, and Switzerland that were also centers of the Protestant Reformation. In fact, Weber's own Protestant relatives exemplified the kind of Protestant capitalism that appeared only rarely across the world's civilizations.

Weber hoped to use this association between Protestantism and capitalism to address a larger issue: Could ideas cause economic behavior in the same way that economic behavior causes ideas? Marx's claim that ideas stemmed from the material or economic interests within a society had intrigued Weber since his graduate studies. He thought the claim useful—economic position certainly influenced people's thoughts, values, and beliefs—yet overly simple. A more complete understanding of social life would also have to consider the potential for ideas to shape economic success.

To examine the causal relationship between Protestantism and capitalism, Weber first tried to isolate the essential characteristics of the kind of capitalism that had emerged in Europe and North America over the previous centuries. One characteristic, which he termed the **spirit of capitalism**, involves the rational and calculating pursuit of maximum profit. Only in modern capitalism does the desire for unlimited profit combine with the efficient use of reason.

The writings of Benjamin Franklin, whose autobiography and popular writings gave practical advice to his American readers, illustrated the spirit of capitalism. Franklin hated wasted time and wasted money. He believed that, since time is money, those who spend their hours in relaxation or idleness rather than working for pay are throwing away money. Similarly, since invested money generates more money, spending one's earnings also wastes money. Franklin noted how "wonderfully small trifling expenses mount up to large sums [that] may for the future be saved" (Weber 1958:50). This spirit—the desire to earn more and more money without spending it—characterized capitalism in the northeastern United States and parts of Europe.

A New Form of Economic Behavior

The capitalist spirit represents a major break with the past. Rather than a way to meet daily needs and pleasures, the pursuit of profit becomes an end in itself. Historically, persons making a profit or earning a wage would stop work to enjoy their good fortune with food, drink, and leisure. Spending their gain as soon as they received it, workers in the past would do just enough to meet daily needs. Greed existed in the past, as it exists under capitalism, but it took a different form in premodern societies. It resulted in efforts to make a huge gain quickly through adventure, piracy, military conquest, or risky schemes. The most effective way to wealth—inheriting land—also involved little individual effort.

Catholicism in the Middle Ages did not encourage the steady and unceasing effort needed to produce more and more wealth. Rejecting the pursuit of worldly gain, Catholics admired the behavior of priests, monks, and even beggars who isolated themselves from the temptations of the material world. By devoting themselves to prayer, poverty, and humility, many believed they became closer to God and salvation in the afterlife. Even if the peasants or craftsmen in the Middle Ages could not imitate the extremes of the religious orders, they could limit their pursuit of profit.

Modern capitalism therefore involved a completely new and, in some ways, unusual behavior. It seemed foolish to aim for maximum wealth but then save and invest that wealth rather than spend it for pleasure or distribute it to charity. Yet such strange behavior was necessary for the development of capitalism. How could one account for its emergence?

The Marxist claim that Protestant religious ideas emerged to bolster the growing strength of capitalism failed to answer this question. It could not explain how capitalism could emerge in such an unsuitable context in the first place. It seemed to Weber that a solution to the question required another approach. Although the behavior of early capitalists appeared strange from the perspective of the dominant Catholic worldview of the Middle Ages, it might make more sense if scholars could understand the larger worldview of the capitalists. He wanted to understand the meaning early capitalists gave to their behavior and how religious values contributed to that meaning.

The Protestant Ethic

A study of Protestant theology did indeed suggest to Weber some religious motives for capitalist behavior. In *The Protestant Ethic and the Spirit of Capitalism,* first published in 1904–1905, Weber identified how Protestant beliefs encouraged the use of rational decision-making in pursuit of unlimited profit. In general terms, he focused on **ascetic** Protestantism, a theology based on self-denial of spontaneous enjoyment and worldly pleasure. More particularly, he focused on an ethic of Protestantism exemplified by Calvinists, at first in Geneva, Switzerland, during the 1500s and then as the ethic spread among Puritans, Presbyterians, and Methodists to various parts of Europe.

The Protestant ethic, original and unique in the history of the world's religions, accepted the rule of the world by an absolute, infinite God. Yet, for reasons humans could not understand, this all-powerful and mysterious God predestined some to salvation and some to damnation. Regardless of how they acted on earth, some would join God in heaven while others would suffer in hell. The mysterious rituals, sacraments, and prayers of Catholicism could do nothing to gain salvation from God. Believers must instead submit themselves to God's will.

But if people could do nothing to influence their ultimate end, why not have fun in the meantime? After all, if good behavior did not guarantee salvation and bad behavior did not guarantee eternal punishment, Calvinists might reasonably enjoy the delights of food, drink, and sex. However, Calvinism contained another central tenet besides predestination. Whether saved or damned, people should act in this world so as to give glory to God. God wants His people to build a kingdom on earth in His image. Although Calvinism did not precisely explain how ordinary affairs of everyday life could glorify God, moral conduct would certainly include active involvement in the world's affairs rather than the isolation of Catholic monks.

To deal with the psychological anxiety caused by an uncertain and unchangeable destiny, believers might look for signs that God had chosen them as one of the select few predestined for heaven. Consistent with God's plan for humans on earth, the sign would likely relate to both daily work and freedom from sinful pleasures. In crude terms, the sign would involve worldly success in terms of pursuit of profit, use of that profit for saving and investment, and the creation of even more profit and wealth. Being poor came to be seen as an offense to God.

John Wesley, the English founder of Methodism in the mid-1700s—the same time that industrial capitalism began to emerge in that country—urged his followers to adopt an ethic similar to that of Calvinism: "We must exhort all Christians to gain all they can, and to save all they can; that is, in effect, to grow rich" (Weber 1958:175). Why? Hard work and frugality will bring riches, but "as riches increase, so will pride, anger, and love of the world" (Weber 1958:175). Therefore, believers must remain industrious and thrifty, avoid desires of the flesh, and save rather than spend their earnings.

Protestant believers wanting to accumulate wealth would rely on rational decisions, careful calculation, efficient action, and limited spending. This was the calling of Protestant businessmen: their daily activities fulfilled their religious duty, signaled their good standing in God's grace, and helped eliminate any doubt over their ultimate destiny. Traditional businessmen acting only to satisfy their physical needs were quickly driven out of business—their more rational, disciplined, and efficient competitors had a moral and religious purpose behind their business activities.

Strange as it may seem on the surface, then, accumulation of wealth proved consistent with denial of the benefits of that wealth. Thus, Weber had identified a link between ascetic Protestantism and capitalist success: the desire of some Protestants to act for the glory of God and receive an indication of their predestined salvation encouraged a new form of economic behavior. Weber had demonstrated that social and religious ideas can define interests and shape material conditions of society.

Critics often misunderstood Weber's arguments, faulting him for ignoring other factors that contributed to the growth of capitalism. In fact, Weber claimed not that ideas *always* or ordinarily cause economic behavior but that they *sometimes* do. He did not posit the Protestant ethic as the only cause of the emergence of capitalism, but as an important contributing factor. Overall, he offered new insights into the complex historical processes that led to capitalism in the West (and influenced his own life and personality).

4. SOURCES OF SOCIAL INEQUALITY

With the publication of *The Protestant Ethic and the Spirit of Capitalism,* Weber began a period of staggering output. He had lost nearly seven years of his career to depression, and in the years to come he would continue to experience shorter episodes of inability to work. Still, he had "manic spurts of extraordinary intense intellectual work" (Gerth & Mills 1946:11) and produced "work in the next sixteen [years that] has never been surpassed" (Collins & Makowsky 1989:120). Although now 40 years old, and just beginning his career as a sociologist, he would make up for the late start with sheer effort and brilliance.

Stability in his personal and family life helped make for a calm environment that aided his productivity. He received a substantial inheritance from his grandfather in 1907 that gave him the funds to continue his scholarship without a university job. He remained close to his mother until her death and to his brothers and sisters for the rest of his life. He could also rely on the loving acceptance of his wife and the intellectual support of a set of scholars and friends who often visited his home to discuss current issues.

Resigning from his university job both eased Weber's guilt over failing to perform his duties and aided his scholarship. He could avoid teaching, a time-consuming activity that he viewed with dread, and be free of faculty meetings, university committees, and long discussions about school policies. The life of an independent scholar even allowed him to avoid rushing his work to publication. Although a prolific writer, he could take advantage of his freedom to develop the complexity of his arguments and employ his vast store of historical knowledge.

For example, revolutionary activity in Russia in 1905 sparked Weber's interest. In order to read about the events in the daily Russian newspapers, he spent time in bed each morning studying Russian, soon mastering the language and writing several insightful articles on these events—something a busier (and less intelligent) scholar could not have accomplished. In years to come, he would devote enormous time and effort to understanding the civilizations and religions of ancient India, China, and Israel. His study of these topics helped him explain why rational capitalism had failed to emerge there as it had under Protestantism in Europe.

Despite this calming stability, Weber remained a difficult person in some ways. To those he dealt with, "his demanding conscience and rigidity of honor was highly inconvenient and somewhat troublesome"

(Gerth & Mills 1946:26). The volcanic temper and general moodiness that lay below his scholarly writing often appeared in public. He harshly criticized his former university colleagues who showed anti-Semitism and political bias in their decisions. He protested vigorously when a promising scholar was denied a position as a professor because he belonged to the Social Democratic party. He even sued those who questioned his honor.

Weber and Sociology

Weber's intellectual freedom to pursue whatever interested him contributed to the emergence of the field of sociology in Germany. His interest in the religious sources of capitalism moved him from the fields of economics and law toward social behavior. He also began to propose methods for the new social science that would combine his desires to interpret social behavior and to employ objective scientific research. In 1904 he joined with others to edit a new and influential journal for sociological articles, and in 1910 he helped found the German Sociological Society.

Because he had already established an imposing reputation, he could advance the field of sociology without the opposition Durkheim faced in France. Resistance to the new field existed in German universities, as it existed in other nations, but Weber did not need the imprint of respectability that a formal professorship of sociology would give—he already had intellectual respectability. If he acknowledged sociology as a valuable field of study, others felt they should do the same. Despite the debates his ideas sometimes sparked, he never experienced the widespread intellectual hostility that Durkheim faced in France.

Weber differed from other sociologists in another way that helped smooth the acceptance of his work in Germany. Both Marx and Durkheim sometimes expressed their views in blunt and undiplomatic terms; their writings magnified rather than moderated their differences with the jealously guarded doctrines of their opponents. In contrast, Weber presented his claims more carefully, with his immense knowledge of the complexity of world history leading him to qualify, restrict, and complicate his claims. This makes it difficult to read Weber's work: anyone looking for a clear and brief statement of his thesis or a convenient summary becomes quickly frustrated by the seemingly endless definitions, careful distinctions, and intricate reasoning. Yet it was Weber's recognition of the complexity of the social world and his carefully qualified claims that restrained potential opposition to his original ideas and sociological views.

Weber's complex insights into the nature of the social world appeared in his work on the topic of social inequality. He thought that Marx, who stressed the centrality of class and the conflict between business owners and workers, provided valuable insights into the sources of social inequality in capitalist economies. Ownership of factories, banks, and corporations concentrated wealth, social respect, and power in the hands of a small elite, while denying others a fair share of these social rewards. However, he also thought that positing class as the single or dominant source of social inequality oversimplified the complexity of society.

According to Weber, three potentially independent sources of inequality existed. Corresponding to the economic, cultural, and political components of societies, Weber distinguished among class, status, and party groups. Class groups struggle over resources of income and wealth, status groups struggle over resources of prestige and esteem, and party groups struggle over political power. Consistent with Marx's claim, the three dimensions often overlap, with the advantages gained from one reinforcing the advantages gained from the others. The dimensions could also, however, vary independently.

Class

First, Weber defined **classes** as groups that share similar life chances. Life chances stem from favorable positions in economic markets and are visible in the possession of goods and opportunities for income. This definition overlaps with Marx's in its focus on the objective positions of workers in relation to market employment. Owners of property have greater income and wealth, and more opportunities to invest that income and wealth, than those who do not own property. Weber could see, for example, that class groups in a small mining town might consist of only two distinct groups: mine owners and miners.

In most situations, however, differences also exist within groups of owners and groups of nonowners. Because some owners have more valuable property than others, they earn more income, contribute more to savings, and can afford a better lifestyle. For example, Bill Gates, the founder and primary owner of Microsoft who is worth billions of dollars, has economic resources that the owner of a local computer store does not. Similarly, some workers have more skills and education than others, and thus they earn more in the labor market. Although neither a bank manager nor a taxi driver relies on ownership of property for income, the banker will enjoy advantages that the cabby does not.

Status

Second, Weber defined **status** in terms of social evaluation or prestige rather than objective economic position. Members of high-status groups separate themselves from others by a distinctive and highly respected lifestyle, acknowledging their similarities with one another and striving to distance themselves from outsiders. They travel widely, speak distinctively, purchase fashionable products, attend cultural events, and involve themselves in charities—all activities that separate them from the majority of a society.

High-status groups can also maintain their prestigious positions through family and legal barriers. In terms of family barriers, membership in a high-status group might require descent from an aristocratic family. Although outsiders might hope to join the group through marriage, parents typically try to restrict the marriage partners of their children to fellow group members. In terms of legal barriers, status-group membership often involves easily recognizable racial differences. Until the 1950s and 1960s, for example, the former slave states in the southern United States outlawed interracial marriage and required racial segregation in schools, hotels, and restaurants. Today less formal, but still effective, barriers to racial integration exist throughout the world.

In capitalist societies, class and status groups overlap. Those with better life chances and more wealth can afford a distinctive lifestyle that others cannot afford to imitate. However, money itself means less to high status than does the kind of lifestyle the money is used to support. For example, members of traditional European aristocracies slowly began to lose their wealth with the replacement of agriculture by industrial capitalism, but they could maintain their status through their designations as noble princes, lords, barons, and dukes, as well as their fashionable ways of living.

Weber did not have to look far to find an example of how status could differ from class. The landowning Junkers of Germany maintained their social prestige despite declining economic dominance. Newly rich capitalists tried to imitate their lifestyle by buying estates with farmland, mansions, and hunting lodges in eastern Germany and often tried to marry their children into the aristocracy. The Junkers, and more generally the traditional aristocracy throughout Europe, in turn labeled the newly rich as unsophisticated pretenders who lacked the breeding, honor, and dignity of those descended from many generations of nobility.

Even today, status-based honors gain much attention. The royal family of England acquires its celebrity in part from its status and selectivity (as well as its substantial wealth). Although they bring no income, lordship and knighthood remain highly sought honors—Paul McCartney of the Beatles and Elton John, two of the world's richest and most famous celebrities, have been knighted by Queen Elizabeth. In the United States, members of the Kennedy and Rockefeller families seem to have become part of a modern American royalty based as much on prestige and celebrity as on income.

Party

Third, Weber defined **parties** as groups organized to obtain power. To help realize the goals of their members, parties participate in the struggle over social power and control. In the United States, they include the Democratic and Republican parties and factions within those parties that aim to shape public policies and legislation. Parties also include special-interest groups—such as trade unions (the AFL-CIO, the Teamsters), professional organizations (the American Medical Association, the American Bar Association), religious groups (the Moral Majority, the Christian Coalition), and pressure groups (the American Association of Retired Persons, the Welfare Rights League, the National Organization of Women)—as well as government bureaucracies that seek more power to fulfill and expand their duties.

Because parties often use power to gain economic advantages or higher status, this third dimension of inequality overlaps with class or status. Yet powerful trade unions may consist of members with relatively low income and status. In Weber's time, the Social Democratic party gained considerable influence through political channels even though it consisted of low-status workers with low income. Without this third dimension, Weber could not make sense of modern patterns of inequality.

Together these three dimensions represent the potential for a different type of stratification system than that envisioned by Marx. Both Marx and Weber treated conflict as central to inequality: those with economic, status, and political advantages struggle to maintain them, and those without these advantages struggle to gain more. However, unlike Marx, Weber viewed differences more in terms of small increments that overlap across the three dimensions. He depicted the stratification system in terms of a ladder with numerous and closely spaced positions rather than in terms of two separate and distinct classes.

5. RATIONALITY AND BUREAUCRACIES

Over the years, Weber's view of the world became increasingly pessimistic. Depression can result in excessively negative perceptions, and Weber's difficult personal experiences could easily have been generalized to the larger world. He became a twentieth-century prophet of doom: "Max Weber saw himself in a role similar to that of Old Testament prophets, those harbingers of disaster and doom who castigated their contemporaries for the errors of their ways" (Coser 1970:vii).

Political Disillusion

The political situation in Germany added to his growing disillusion about the future. Having grown up during the military and diplomatic successes of Bismarck, Weber entered adulthood devoted to a strong German nation. As an older adult, however, he saw Bismarck's successors blunder in the country's foreign and domestic policy. The kaiser, government bureaucracy, and military staff became increasingly arrogant in their national pride, ultimately hurting rather than serving German interests.

A new leader, Kaiser William II, dismissed Bismarck as chancellor in 1890 and assumed many leadership duties himself. Conceited and undiplomatic, he lacked Bismarck's slyness and vision in protecting Germany from the threats of nearby nations. In a speech stating that "no one can dispute with us the place in the sun that is our due," William II bluntly called for expansion of German territory (Viault 1990:326). Combined with continued growth of the German army and navy, the call for expansion rightly worried other nations.

Allowing the alliance with Russia that protected Germany's eastern border to lapse, William II then tried to negotiate a treaty with Britain. British leaders, however, refused to enter an alliance with an undemocratic and increasingly belligerent military state. Since France had remained a bitter enemy since the Franco-Prussian War, Germany found itself nearly surrounded by enemies. As these other nations armed themselves in response to Germany's militarization, an arms race pushed them all toward war.

Weber thought these trends threatened to destroy the gains the country had made under Bismarck. He blamed a foolish emperor, an undemocratic government, and a rule-obsessed and unimaginative bureaucracy for leading Germany astray. Never one to shy away from battles, he made his views public. At the same time, he defended advocates of unpopular causes, such as pacifism, opposition to anti-Semitism, and feminism (his wife was one of the leaders in the feminist and suffrage movement in Germany). All this made for considerable controversy.

Despite his dislike of the current government, Weber had mixed feelings about a more democratic alternative. On one hand, he thought democracy would provide better leaders for the country. Relying on Junkers to staff the bureaucracy and military, Germany lacked fresh ideas, independent thinkers, and powerful personalities. Those who had the potential to become leaders in the mold of Bismarck found the restraints of a powerful bureaucracy difficult to overcome. A democratic government (including a parliament with real power), however, would allow talented leaders with courage, toughness, and the ability to inspire others to rise to the top of the power structure. Such leaders would balance the rigidity of the current government.

On the other hand, he looked at the petty squabbles among democratic political parties with disdain. Weber would later say, "In a democracy the people choose a leader in whom they trust. Then the chosen leader says, 'Now shut up and obey me.' People and party are then no longer free to interfere in his business" (Gerth & Mills 1946:42). However much he favored democracy as a way to replace rigid bureaucrats and military officers with talented leaders from less powerful parts of society, he still had doubts about the ability of a democratic leader to act for the long-term good of the country.

The Growth of Rationality

The last few pages of *The Protestant Ethic and the Spirit of Capitalism,* which he finished shortly after his breakdown, expressed concern about the future. Where the Protestants of centuries past, like Ben Franklin, had a sense of religious duty that gave meaning to their pursuit of profit, modern capitalism by Weber's time had destroyed the ideals and spirit that had once motivated business leaders. Now, the sheer size and organization of capitalism controlled the lives of individuals, and the pursuit of wealth destroyed their spiritual values. Weber worried that modern capitalism had become an "iron cage."

Modern capitalism differs from both precapitalist economies and the emerging capitalist economies of earlier centuries in the importance of a certain type of rationality. Weber defined **formal rationality** as the use of calculation to weigh costs and benefits and the search for maximum efficiency to guide conduct (subject to existing laws, rules, and regulations). With modern capitalism, formal rationality in pursuit of profit had become an end in itself rather than a means to salvation.

Weber knew that formal rationality brought enormous benefits in dealing with problems of size. Business organizations have to use rational principles to deal efficiently with large numbers of people, sales, products, and payments, and in the last century, industrial capitalism had led to gigantic markets, huge organizations, and an expanding population. Without formal rationality, organizing the large-scale activities of modern economies would be impossible.

Weber saw that governments had to deal with the same problem of size and develop similar solutions. With unification, a population of 40 million, and demands from citizens to participate in public affairs, the German government needed to deal precisely and quickly with millions of people, forms, and pieces of information. Only formally rational rules that regulated conduct could deal with the massive size of the modern nation-state. The civil service and military in Germany had, accordingly, become increasingly professional over the last century.

Rationality in Bureaucracies

Formal rationality had reached its highest expression in the bureaucracies that had come to dominate both business and government. Many people in the early twentieth century took bureaucracy for granted, assuming that rational procedures for governing and doing business had always been the norm. Yet Weber's thorough knowledge of history revealed how rationality had revolutionized modern life. Although officials once administered the historic empires of Egypt, China, and Rome, their actions had been guided more by tradition and values than by formal rationality. In contrast, **bureaucracies** in modern societies had, according to Weber, the following characteristics:

1. Bureaucracies assign fixed duties to officials. In the past, officials did whatever their rulers told them to do, and duties could change depending on the circumstances, the people involved, and the personal desires of the rulers and officials. Modern bureaucracies divide duties into clearly defined and specialized tasks.

2. Bureaucracies consist of a hierarchy or pyramid of precisely defined authority. In the past, persons held power and could use it as they saw fit. In modern bureaucracies, power resides in a position in the hierarchy, and the position defines how the officeholder can use the power.

3. Bureaucracies operate with written rules and documents. In the past, officials and subjects had to rely on informal discussions, crude notes, and individual memories in their work. Modern bureaucracies turn to detailed records to clarify duties, policies, and authority.

4. Bureaucracies rely on the expert training of officials. In the past, rulers selected relatives and friends as officials or required applicants to perform favors or pay for their position. Modern bureaucracies appoint officials based on their merit or ability to perform the position's tasks.

5. Bureaucracies require separation of the public and private lives of their salaried employees. In the past, official business overlapped with the personal lives of officials, who used their position for personal profit. Modern bureaucracies detach the position from the person, thereby making life outside the organization separate from job duties.

6. Bureaucracies manage by applying standard rules to a variety of circumstances. In the past, decisions were based on personal feelings, selfish needs, and even the momentary whims of the rulers or officials. Modern bureaucracies require officials to follow organizational rules and remain within their specified authority.

In practice, these characteristics do not appear exactly as Weber described them, but they still illustrate the underlying principles behind rational organizations. Even if real bureaucracies deviate from the ideal, Weber's description reveals the special nature of modern organizations.

Consequences of Rationality

Since the efficiency of formal bureaucracies had never been approached previously in human history, Weber might have viewed their development with optimism. After all, modern societies could not have emerged without them. Nonetheless, Weber found himself concerned, like other sociologists before him, with the harm modern societies do to individuals. The oppressive and mechanical efficiency of bureaucracies deadened individual creativity, independence, and initiative, while the specialized tasks, detailed rules, and impersonal authority allowed little room to satisfy the human needs for personal bonds, emotional expression, and release from routine.

Take, for example, the problem of organizational "red tape." Bureaucratic officials deal poorly with individuals as special cases. They force everyone to fill out forms that have little relevance to their particular concern; they often refuse to make decisions or give information, sending clients to other departments or other officials. And they become so oriented toward following rules that they lose sight of the goals of the organization and the need for innovation. Nearly everyone in modern societies has had to deal with these problems.

However, Weber saw these problems as the inevitable result of the search for efficiency. Rather than stemming from unqualified workers or poor leaders, the problems of bureaucracies follow directly from the efficient methods of dealing with large numbers of people and information. Bureaucratic procedures often do not fit individual cases precisely because they are designed to efficiently deal with the masses. Given problems caused by size, modern societies are destined to confront both the benefits and problems of bureaucratization.

Weber sadly realized that formal rationality and bureaucratization would steadily spread to all parts of social life, that individuals would be unable to escape the specialization and impersonality of formal rationality in any part of their lives. Religion, music, art, war, law, education, and family life had already entered the cage of rationality. Rationality would further result in a "disenchantment of the world" as it continued to replace the meaning people once received from their religious, irrational, and emotional visions of life.

Disputing the hope for freedom and equality under socialism, Weber argued that rationality and bureaucracies would grow even stronger under such a system. By giving the state the additional tasks of coordinating a large-scale economy, socialism would increase the power of the public bureaucracy and speed the trends toward bureaucratic control. Rather than replacing the rationality of capitalism, the merger of the state and the economy under socialism would worsen the dehumanizing consequences of bureaucracy.

If socialism could not counter Weber's pessimism about the spread of rationality, neither could democracy. Although he recognized the need to allow the masses of citizens to participate more fully in the leadership of the country, he also worried about the limitations of democracy. The mass participation of citizens would require the bureaucratization of political parties under the control of party officials and professionals, and even the simple reliance on counting votes for electoral victories would require the discipline of calculation and increase the role of party bureaucracies.

Thus, few aspects of life can escape from the mindless bureaucratic machine. Weber summarized his concerns not long after his breakdown: "So much the more terrible is the idea that the world should be filled with nothing but those cogs who cling to a little post and strive for a somewhat greater one...[It's] as though we knowingly and willingly were supposed to become men who need 'order' and nothing but order, who become nervous and cowardly if this order shakes for a moment...the central question is not how we further and accelerate it but what we have to set against this machinery, in order to preserve a remnant of humanity from this parceling-out of the soul, and from this exclusive rule of bureaucratic life ideals" (Mitzman 1970:177–178).

6. POWER AND AUTHORITY

In 1914, World War I began, with Germany and Austria-Hungary allied against France, Great Britain, and Russia. In one sense, Weber found the declaration of war a relief from his constant anxiety about the future of Germany. Although he suspected that Germany could not withstand the might of the nations allied against it, war would at least substitute action for worry. In this sober view, he differed from the loud boosters of German power who wanted to use the war for the nation's political and economic gain. Rather than as a romantic adventure, he viewed the war as necessary to protect Germany from its enemies.

Always the pessimist, Weber viewed war as part of the normal course of history, resulting from the ever-present differences across nations in cultures, values, and resources rather than from issues of right and wrong. Like class, status, or political groups within a society, nations contend for power, territory, and prestige. To guarantee its security and maintain its way of life, Weber thought Germany would have to participate in the war.

A Critic of the Government

Given the necessity of the war, Weber naturally hoped to limit the military risks to Germany. Given the presence of enemies to the east (Russia), southwest (France), and nearby seas (Britain), Germany needed a quick victory because a long war would stretch the resources it would need to defend itself on two fronts. Weber worried that the boastful and overconfident leaders failed to recognize the seriousness of Germany's position, and he would become increasingly critical of the leadership of the kaiser and the generals as the war progressed.

Now 50 years old, Weber could not serve as a soldier. Instead, he was commissioned a captain and put in charge of running nine hospitals in the Heidelberg area. Although he performed his duties with distinction, his growing disgust with the operation of the war made it difficult to continue with them. As hopes for a quick victory ended with a military stalemate in France, his worries intensified. He resigned his commission to become "a self-appointed prophet of doom" (Gerth & Mills 1946:22), publicly criticizing the military for its continued quest for a total victory, the kaiser for his blindness to the serious threat to Germany, and the munitions makers and landowners for supporting the war for their own selfish interests.

Weber predicted, for example, that Germany's use of its submarine power to sink British ships would draw the United States, still officially neutral, into the war on the side of Britain. In fact, the sinking of a British passenger liner, the *Lusitania,* killed 139 Americans and contributed to the eventual entrance of the United States into the war against Germany and its undemocratic government. Germany would consequently lose the war once the fresh troops from the United States helped Britain and France on the western front.

Calling for peace and frustrated by the government's lack of responsiveness, Weber became increasingly harsh in his criticisms of the kaiser and other leaders of imperial Germany. At a conference in 1917, he challenged the authorities to indict him for treason so he could invite civilian and military leaders to testify as witnesses under oath, an outburst that genuinely frightened some of the audience. Worried that the police might arrest some delegates because of these remarks, someone asked to have Weber calmed down. An acquaintance and admirer of Weber answered, "Can you put out a volcano with a glass of water?" (Mitzman 1970:293).

His extreme criticism of the war effort moved Weber from the political center toward the social democracy of the workers and further away from conservative nationalists. He continued to advocate democracy and a new constitution as a means to provide new leaders. Still, he remained too much of an individualist, too dependent on investments from his inheritance, and too critical of Marxism in intellectual terms to join a worker's party advocating socialism.

During the war years, Weber juggled his political activities with his scholarly writing. Although he avoided the compulsive activity that had contributed to his breakdown years earlier, he still worked hard by ordinary standards. He concentrated in particular on his masterpiece, *Economy and Society,* a multivolume effort that would connect his wide-ranging interests in capitalism, religion, rationality, organizations, and stratification. The work also addressed another topic central to sociology—the use of power. Such concerns no doubt occupied Weber's mind during his political battles with Germany's rulers before and during World War I.

Sources of Legitimate Power

Exhibiting his usual effort to describe carefully the phenomena he wanted to study, Weber began by defining **power** as the "chance of a man or of a number of men to realize their own will in a communal action even against the resistance of others who are participating in the action" (Weber 1946:180). In simple terms, power involves a social relationship between at least two people in which one person gets his or her way over another. Rather than a personal trait, power is a social phenomenon because it exists as a part of relationships.

Obeying the commands of someone with power can derive from self-interest; for example, physical force or economic threats can lead someone to follow commands. A more stable form of power relationships, however, involves established **authority**, which Weber defined as the legitimate or accepted use of power to give commands. Societies work more smoothly when the use of power has legitimacy in the eyes of both the rulers and the ruled.

The legitimacy of authority comes from three broad sources. First, traditional authority comes from a belief in the sacred quality of traditions or long-standing ways of acting. By tradition, for example, the oldest son of the current ruler gains authority on the death of his father, or the oldest family members make decisions that younger members follow. Once assigned, traditional authority resides in particular persons who have considerable freedom in the actions they take.

Second, legal authority comes from laws, regulations, and rules that specify the appropriate actions of those holding particular positions in organizations. This is the type of authority that guides bureaucracies in modern societies. Officials must follow written guidelines in their use of power, and those subordinates accept the use of that power because they accept the laws, regulations, and rules as legitimate. Legal authority thus resides in the office or position rather than directly in a person. Consistent with the spread of bureaucracies and rationality, history exhibits an increasing shift from traditional authority to legal authority.

Third, charismatic authority differs importantly from both traditional and legal authority, coming from the devotion of followers to leaders with extraordinary qualities. Weber used "charisma" in its narrow sense to refer to a state of divine blessing or a special power endowed by God. More broadly, it refers to a variety of physical, personal, or social qualities that others find rare and special. Based on social relationships, charismatic authority involves both leaders and followers. The followers accept the use of charismatic power because of their devotion to the extraordinary qualities and mission of the leader.

Weber used "charisma" to mean more than having an attractive and energetic personality. Many people are enthusiastic, good looking, and able to inspire loyalty, but they do not generate the awe-inspired worship among followers that charismatic leaders do. The holiness of Jesus, the selfless leadership of George Washington, and the tough persistence of Winston Churchill exemplify charismatic authority. Less positively, the military heroics of Napoleon, the nationalist and racist appeals of Hitler, and the call for a worker's state of Lenin also fit the definition of charismatic authority. The special, sometimes even supernatural, gifts of charismatic leaders make this type of authority rare in history.

Charismatic Authority and Change

In its reliance on the innovative qualities of a single person, charismatic authority disrupts the accepted social order and challenges traditional and legal authority. As such, perhaps it could offer an alternative to the dominance of rationality and legal authority. Weber had once asked, "What have we to set against this machinery of mindless bureaucracy?" (Mitzman 1970:232). Here was one answer and one source of hope. A gifted and creative leader could bring the spontaneity, freedom, and emotion lacking in modern society; the flexibility and informality of charismatic authority could counter the fixed and impersonal routines of bureaucratic organizations.

Charisma might even provide a solution to the problems of leadership in Germany. Far from charismatic, William II appeared clumsy, nervous, and overexcited, lacking the self-conscious assurance of a heroic leader. Germany needed a leader with the strength to overcome the power of the traditional monarchy and inflexible civil service and to act for the good of the nation. Such a leader could, even in the face of opposition from current leaders, inspire the masses to support his vision. Unfortunately, the lack of democracy in Germany made the emergence of such a leader unlikely.

In the larger scheme of history, Weber could not avoid drawing pessimistic conclusions about charismatic authority. By its very nature, it lasts only as long as the charismatic leader lives, and the extraordinary nature of charisma makes it rare and difficult to replace. To become permanent, charismatic authority must change in the direction of traditional or legal authority. The leader may choose a successor, who can then choose another successor, and so on, or the leader can specify a rule of hereditary leadership. These procedures, however, eventually result in a form of traditional authority. Alternatively, the ruler can appoint disciples, officials, and staff to carry on his mission, but this eventually transforms charismatic authority into legal authority. Either way, what was once special becomes routine.

7. RATIONALITY IN CONTEMPORARY SOCIETY

Recognizing certain defeat in 1918, the kaiser abdicated and Germany surrendered. Leaders of the Social Democratic party declared Germany a republic, and an assembly was elected in 1919 to design a new constitution. Meanwhile, in the Versailles palace outside of Paris, leaders of the victorious nations set severe terms for a peace settlement that German leaders had no choice but to accept. Since newspaper censors had blocked reports of military setbacks, many Germans refused to recognize defeat, instead blaming the democratic leaders for submitting to Germany's enemies.

Weber's wartime writings had brought him to national prominence, and his opposition to the failed leadership of the kaiser even raised the possibility of elective office. Indeed, he helped found a new German Democratic party and ran as a candidate in the elections of the new democracy. However, given his hostility to political organizations, Weber refused to campaign on his own behalf, work with party officials, or flatter other politicians. Not surprisingly, he gained few votes.

He also served in the German delegation to the Versailles peace conference, another experience that led to disappointment. The efforts of Germany's former enemies to destroy the honor of a great nation with their terms for peace outraged Weber. He opposed the treaty, preferring instead the invasion and rule by the enemies. Once the treaty was signed, he pessimistically wrote, "I fear this peace means only the beginning of our misery. ... I fear there will be a 'terror without end'" (Weber 1975:657). That the demanding conditions of peace contributed to the rise of Adolf Hitler and the coming of World War II some 20 years later confirmed Weber's pessimism.

The end of the war seemed to renew his energy and desire for an academic career. During a visiting professorship at the University of Vienna in 1918, Weber found the room where he lectured filled to capacity with students, professors, state officials, and politicians—such was his reputation that he required the largest hall available. Although stressful, these lectures gave Weber the confidence to consider accepting a permanent position. Universities throughout the country sought to hire the famous scholar, but the University of Munich won his services with a promise to let him lecture primarily on sociology.

At the University of Munich, Weber's teaching and scholarly discussions gave him a great deal of pleasure—to his surprise, he was able to participate fully in his duties, even supervising his first dissertation. He also continued to work on *Economy and Society*. His wife wrote that "Weber regarded his renewed strength as miraculous, but he wondered if it would last" (Weber 1975:672).

In fact, it would not. The death of his mother in October 1919 was followed by the suicide of a younger sister in April 1920. These events filled his thoughts with death. Soon after, he succumbed to chills and fever, experienced periods of delirium, and was diagnosed with pneumonia. On June 14, 1920, soon after beginning his new job in Munich, he died.

During his 56 years, Weber began as a lawyer, economist, and expert on agricultural workers. He then shifted his interests to the sociological study of religion, culture, and capitalism, and still later to subjects of inequality, power, and politics. This diversity of topics makes continuity in his writings hard to discern. Had he lived longer, Weber might have provided a framework to integrate this diversity; more likely, however, he would have continued to avoid any effort to develop a grand system of sociological theory.

Weber's Methods

Rejecting the overstated claims of truth made by others, Weber realized that he could gain only a partial understanding of the complexity of reality because the infinite diversity of the world requires social scientists to investigate only selected slices. No single perspective or theory could incorporate all that we know about social life. More than constructing a wholly original system of thought, then, Weber added his own interpretations to existing theories or perspectives, trying to reconcile competing ideas rather than dismiss one as wrong and accept another as right. Consider a few examples.

His work on the Protestant ethic demonstrated the effect of ideas on economic behavior as a way to revise Marxist claims of the dominance of economic factors. Still, Weber did not attempt to replace materialism with an alternative theory positing the general dominance of ideas. More generally, his work connected religion and economics in a way that improved on the work of both Marxists and non-Marxists.

His work on rationality and bureaucracy identified general trends that seemed to affect a wide variety of institutions in Western societies. However, he balanced the attention to rationalization with his studies of charismatic leaders who disrupted the existing legal–rational order, believing, as did other German scholars, that unforeseen events, great leaders, and social passions can influence the course of human history. Thus, rather than being a mechanical law that proceeds without interruption, the trend toward rationalization allows for the unexpected.

His use of historical evidence and illustrations relied on the careful description of societies and people in past times and different places.

Based on the tradition of German historical scholarship, Weber's "knowledge of world history probably exceeded that of any other person who had ever lived" (Collins & Makowsky 1989:119). At the same time, however, his use of that detailed knowledge to draw conclusions became an essential part of his sociological studies.

His methodology made the case that values should influence the choice of topics to study but should not distort the findings of scientific analysis. Science cannot evaluate values, tell people how to live, or answer moral questions; it can, however, rely on objective methods in answering questions about social life. Balancing political values with objective observation would not be easy, but it would be necessary.

His view of science also incorporated the need both to understand subjective human experiences and to employ objective methods. Indeed, Weber defined sociology as the scientific study of what he called **social action:** human conduct oriented toward others and based on the social meaning given to that conduct. This perspective focuses on the personal intentions of individuals who participate in groups rather than on the characteristics of groups alone. He used the German word *verstehen* to refer to the understanding of the meanings individuals give to their actions. Yet he believed that scientists can and should interpret the social meanings of actions in a way that is logical and able to be replicated by others.

Overall, Weber's effort to find a middle ground between competing ideologies and methodologies has greatly influenced the field of sociology. His work on class, status, and party contributes importantly to a conflict perspective that guides much sociological theory and research today. Additionally, his studies of competition among class, status, and party groups, as well as his recognition of the constant struggles among nations, support the conclusion that "Weber deserves to be named as the individual who set off modern conflict sociology" (Collins 1985:92).

Extreme Rationality

Consider one example of how Weber's concepts continue to prove useful to sociologists. In an intriguingly titled book, *The McDonaldization of Society,* George Ritzer argues that the principles of formal rationality identified by Weber have continued to transform the world. These principles have reached an extreme form in fast-food restaurants, but now they also dominate education, work, health care, travel, leisure, politics, and the family. In Ritzer's (1996:1) words, "McDonaldization is the process by which the principles of fast-food restaurants are coming to dominate more and more sectors of American society as well as the rest of the world."

The four principles of fast-food restaurants identified by Ritzer build on Weber's description of bureaucracies but now extend outside their normal location in large organizations. Consider some examples.

1. The principle of *efficiency.* The desire of customers for quickly served and inexpensive meals in fast-food restaurants requires a rationally designed system for cooking food, taking orders, serving customers, and providing seats and tables. The popularity of fast-food restaurants reflects the efficient way in which they meet these needs. However, the aim for efficiency in, say, educational institutions may make less sense. Large classes and multiple-choice exams allow universities to educate large numbers of students efficiently; students, in turn, can save time by relying on textbook summaries and purchased lecture notes rather than attending classes and completing the readings. Although efficient, such methods lose sight of the ultimate goal of learning.

2. The principle of *calculability.* Fast-food restaurants emphasize quantity over quality in calculating the number of customers served; the time needed to cook and serve the food; the size of burgers, fries, and drinks; and the minute-to-minute sales or profits. Dealing in numbers makes it possible to identify precise goals and ways of acting to reach those goals. However, applying the principle of calculability to areas such as medical care makes many uneasy. Medical practices often calculate the number of patients served per hour, the time spent in hospital beds after surgery, the cost of special procedures, and the payments available from the government. As spurs for higher productivity, greater profits, or lower costs, these numbers may worsen the quality of health care.

3. The principle of *predictability.* Fast-food restaurants use the same recipes, greetings, decors, and menus in their franchises. As a result, no matter where they travel, people know they can expect the same kind of food and service in McDonald's or other chain restaurants that they receive in their hometown. Perhaps more surprisingly, the principle of predictability also shows up in entertainment today. Successful movies spawn sequels with the same actors and similar plots. Packaged tours to foreign countries carefully plan sightseeing to avoid any surprises. Disney World and other resorts make possible vacations without the risk of disorder, messiness, or the unexpected (one can even cruise the jungle without mosquitoes, dangerous animals, or discomfort). These types of entertainment lack the crucial ingredient of excitement and the newness of the unexpected.

4. The principle of *control.* Being inefficient, imprecise, and unpredictable, humans as either employees or customers threaten the rational design of fast-food restaurants. To the extent possible, businesses increase their control by substituting computer-controlled machines for people, since machines can reduce human error and cut wage costs. In fast-food restaurants, they slice, grind, and package food; control the temperature and cooking time; dispense drinks and ice cream in set amounts; and list and sum the cost of a customer's order. In other businesses, too, the principle of control requires that customers increasingly deal with inflexible machines. Obtaining cash from ATM machines, selecting a course schedule on the computer, and facing a menu of options when calling a business all represent the sometimes maddening consequences of the rational principle of control.

Like Weber, Ritzer worries about the iron cage of rationality. "As McDonaldization comes to dominate ever more sectors of society, it will become even less possible to 'escape' from it." Today rationality even more seriously frustrates human needs for creativity, freedom, and emotional expression than it did in Weber's time. Of course, rationality brings advantages, too: if people did not benefit from McDonaldization in some ways, the trend would not continue. In ways demonstrated in Ritzer's book, however, rationality creates its own irrationalities.

One could easily continue citing examples of the recent application of Weber's concepts to modern society, for many of his ideas and insights seem as fresh today as they did 80 years ago. Although Weber was influential in his own time, his status has risen over the decades as sociologists continue to find his work essential to the field.

SUMMARY

Although trained in law, history, and economics, Weber moved toward the study of more sociological topics after a long period of depression. In one of his most important studies, *The Protestant Ethic and the Spirit of Capitalism,* he examined the influence of Protestant beliefs on the emergence of capitalism, defining and describing two characteristics of modern life that emerged in a select few Western European nations. The first characteristic, the Protestant ethic, involved a special belief common among several Protestant denominations: namely, that material success in life reflected God's grace and predestination for eternal salvation, but that enjoying the pleasures of success was sinful. Although Protestants often worked hard to earn money, they saved rather than spent their money.

The other characteristic, the spirit of capitalism, represented a major break with the past and overlapped with the Protestant ethic. Historically, persons making a profit or earning a wage would stop work to enjoy their good fortune with food, drink, and rest. In contrast, the capitalist spirit involved the desire to accumulate and invest wealth as well as the use of rational and efficient practices to achieve those goals. Protestant businessmen, who fulfilled their religious duties by accumulating wealth but not spending it, thereby contributed to the emergence of capitalism.

To support his view, Weber noted that modern capitalism emerged in Europe rather than in other civilizations throughout the world and in Protestant rather than Catholic parts of Europe. The evidence thus demonstrated how social and religious ideas common in only certain parts of the world can produce differences across groups and societies in material success. Weber's claim that ideas affect economic behavior contrasts with Marxist arguments about the dominating importance of material production. Weber did not deny the importance of economic forces in shaping ideas, but he also recognized that ideas can affect economic arrangements.

Further exploring the themes he presented in his study of capitalism, Weber considered more generally the role of rational behavior in modern capitalism. What he saw did not reassure him. Unlike early capitalism, modern capitalism relied on rationality without underlying religious values, thereby treating efficiency and calculation as ends in themselves rather than as means to larger goals. In its ideal form, rationality in modern society appeared in bureaucracies. And better than anyone else, Weber described the essential characteristics of these bureaucracies and large organizations. However, he worried that the specialized tasks, impersonal relationships, and absence of emotion brought about by bureaucracy and rationality make modern life meaningless and inhuman.

Weber also demonstrated the growing importance of rationality in power and authority. He defined *power* as the ability to realize one's will against the resistance of others and *authority* as the legitimate or socially accepted use of power. In the past, authority came from long-standing traditions that gave certain families and persons the right to lead, or sometimes from charismatic leaders whose extraordinary qualities inspired devotion among their followers. In modern societies, however, legal–rational authority dominates. Such authority, which comes from laws, regulations, and rules tied to positions and offices rather than people, dominates bureaucratic organizations.

In his work, Weber developed a broad-based conflict perspective on social life. Although recognizing the central place of conflict in social life, he also recognized that conflict involves more than groups defined by their economic position. He considered how multiple dimensions of social inequality—such as class, status, and power—contribute to conflict between social groups in modern societies. The complexity of his thinking on inequality, and the helpful illustrations he provided for his arguments, make his work especially valuable to scholars today.

In studying religious ideas, rationality, and the emergence of capitalism, Weber demonstrated remarkable knowledge of other historical periods, nations, and societies, writing insightfully about the civilizations of China, India, and the Middle East. Along with presenting an astounding amount of detail about these civilizations, he was able to isolate characteristics that distinguished Europe from the rest of the world. In his large-scale studies of civilizations, however, Weber did not ignore the people who inhabited them, for his view of science included the goal of understanding the social meaning people give to their conduct. As in his study of the early Protestants who fostered modern capitalism, he focused on the goals, beliefs, and values of individuals as well as on their behavior. To avoid political bias in social theory, however, Weber's method requires scholars to put aside their own values and try to understand the values of others.

In his attention to ideas and economics, the complexity of social life, and the importance of intentions and behaviors, Weber's work has provided a model for sociological theory. In his use of historical data, study of diverse societies and civilizations, and efforts to minimize the influence of political values on research results, his work has also provided a model for sociological research.

DISCUSSION QUESTIONS

1. How did Weber's tormented family life affect his personality and ambition? In what fields of study did Weber specialize?

2. What innovation contributed to the growing military and political power of the new German nation? In what ways did Germany remain backward?

3. Compare the competing views of scholarship that existed in Germany in the late 1800s. How did Weber's view of scholarship differ from these views?

4. What evidence demonstrated the economic success of Protestants? If religious beliefs led to economic success, what would it say about claims that economic position determines ideas?

5. What is the spirit of capitalism and how does it relate to ascetic Protestantism? Explain how a doctrine about predestination and God's kingdom on earth could lead to the desire to accumulate wealth. Does the relationship exist today?

6. Compare class, status, and party. Give examples of how these components of inequality can differ from one another.

7. Compare the benefits and problems of formal rationality and bureaucracies as presented by Weber. Have the problems identified by Weber worsened since he wrote of them?

8. Define power and authority, and then compare traditional, legal, and charismatic authority. Give examples of each type of authority.

9. What did Weber mean by social action? How do his views about the scientific study of human behavior differ from those of Marx and Durkheim?

10. How, according to Ritzer, do McDonald's and other fast-food restaurants represent an extreme example of the dominance of rationality in modern society? Give examples of this dominance in other parts of modern society.

REFERENCES

PRIMARY SOURCES

Weber, Max. 1946. *From Max Weber: Essays in Sociology* (translated by H. H. Gerth & C. Wright Mills). New York: Oxford University Press.

Weber, Max. 1947 [1920]. *Max Weber: The Theory of Social and Economic Organization* (translated by A. M. Henderson & Talcott Parsons). New York: Free Press.

Weber, Max. 1958 [1904–05]. *The Protestant Ethic and the Spirit of Capitalism* (translated by Talcott Parsons). New York: Charles Scribner's Sons.

Weber, Max. 1968 [1921]. *Economy and Society* (three volumes). Totowa, NJ: Bedminster Press.

SECONDARY SOURCES

Aron, Raymond. 1965. *Main Currents in Sociological Thought* (Vol. II). Garden City, NY: Doubleday.

Ashley, David, & David Michael Orenstein. 1995. *Sociological Theory: Classic Statements* (3rd ed.). Boston: Allyn & Bacon.

Barzini, Luigi. 1983. *The Europeans.* New York: Penguin.

Bendix, Reinhard. 1962. *Max Weber: An Intellectual Portrait.* Garden City, NY: Doubleday.

Collins, Randall. 1985. *Three Sociological Traditions.* New York: Oxford University Press.

Collins, Randall. 1986. *Weberian Sociological Theory.* Cambridge, UK: Cambridge University Press.

Collins, Randall, & Michael Makowsky. 1989. *The Discovery of Society* (4th ed.). New York: Random House.

Coser, Lewis A. 1970. "Preface." Arthur Mitzman, *The Iron Cage: An Historical Interpretation of Max Weber* (pp. v–viii). New York: Knopf.

Coser, Lewis A. 1977. *Masters of Sociological Thought* (2nd ed.). San Diego: Harcourt Brace Jovanovich.

Gerth, H. H., & C. Wright Mills. 1946. "Introduction: The Man and His Work." In H. H. Gerth & C. Wright Mills (trans.), *From Max Weber: Essays in Sociology* (pp. 3–74). New York: Oxford University Press.

Giddens, Anthony. 1971. *Capitalism and Modern Social Theory.* London: Cambridge University Press.

Kasler, Dirk. 1988. *Max Weber: An Introduction to His Life and Work* (translated by Phillippa Hurd). Chicago: University of Chicago.

Knapp, Peter. 1994. *One World—Many Worlds: Contemporary Sociological Theory.* New York: HarperCollins.

Miller, S. M. 1963. *Max Weber.* New York: Crowell.

Mitchell, R. B. 1978. *European Historical Statistics: 1750–1970.* New York: Columbia University Press.

Mitzman, Arthur. 1970. *The Iron Cage: An Historical Interpretation of Max Weber.* New York: Knopf.

Morrison, Ken. 1995. *Marx, Durkheim, Weber: The Formation of Modern Social Thought.* Thousand Oaks, CA: Sage.

Nisbet, Robert A. 1966. *The Sociological Tradition.* New York: Basic Books.

Ritzer, George. 1996. *The McDonaldization of Society* (rev. ed.). Thousand Oaks, CA: Pine Forge Press.

Schroeder, Ralph. 1992. *Max Weber and the Sociology of Culture.* London: Sage.

Stark, Rodney. 1996. Sociology (6th ed.). Belmont, CA: Wadsworth.

Viault, Birdsall S. 1990. *Modern European History.* New York: McGraw-Hill.

Weber, Marianne. 1975 [1926]. *Max Weber: A Biography* (translated by H. Zohn). New York: Wiley.

REFERENCE NOTES

Citations for quotations and special points of interest are given in the text. Listed here are citations to source for major topics covered in each section of the chapter.

1. **A Tormented Family Life:** Family strain (Mitzman 1970:47–48; Weber 1975:185); Work habits (Kasler 1988:11; Mitzman 1970:42, 85); Career choice (Mitzman 1970:41); Marriage (Gerth & Mills 1946:10); Job (Gerth & Mills 1946:11); Family background (Weber 1975:7, 24); Father (Kasler 1988:2–3; Coser 1977:236; Mitzman 1970:17); Mother (Kasler 1988:2–3; Mitzman 1970:19–21, 44–45; Weber 1975:29); Weber's youth (Mitzman 1970:22; Gerth & Mills 1946:4–6); College (Gerth & Mills 1946:6–8; Coser 1977:236); Uncle (Kasler 1988:4); Aunt (Coser 1977:236); Work pace (Weber 1975:105–108; Coser 1977:238); Technical topics (Giddens 1971:120–124); Prestigious appointment (Coser 1977:238).

2. **Germany: A Nation of Extremes:** Prussia (Viault 1990:299); Military weakness (Barzini 1983:72); War victories (Viault 1990:301–304); Population

(Mitchell 1978; Ashley & Orenstein 1995:269); Military bureaucracy (Stark 1996:616); Professional civil servants (Coser 1977:254); German politics (Coser 1977:254; Viault 1990:300, 323–324; Mitzman 1970:78–79); German capitalists (Miller 1963:4; Coser 1977:254; Viault 1990:376; Mitzman 1970:35); Scholarship (Coser 1977:245–248; Gerth & Mills 1946:45; Aron 1965:255); Weber's approach (Aron 1965:242).

3. Protestantism and the Emergence of Capitalism: Appearance (Collins & Makowsky 1989:119); Work pace (Weber 1975:202); Sex (Coser 1977:238; Mitzman 1970:277); Parent's visit (Weber 1975:230; Mitzman 1970:149; Gerth & Mills 1946:29); Symptoms (Gerth & Mills 1946:11; Weber 1975:242; Collins & Makowsky 1989:120); Travel (Coser 1977:239; Gerth & Mills 1946:12); Unable to perform (Weber 1975:239–240; Coser 1977:239; Mitzman 1970:157); Sources of problems (Gerth & Mills 1946:28; Kasler 1988:11; Bendix 1962:8–9); Improvement (Gerth & Mills 1946:14); Visit to U.S. (Gerth & Mills 1946:16); Study of Protestantism (Collins & Makowsky 1989:120; Mitzman 1970:172–175); Weber's Protestant relatives (Coser 1977:235); Work in past (Giddens 1971:125–126); Early capitalists (Aron 1965:215–218; Giddens 1971:130); Critics misunderstood (Aron 1965:218).

4. Sources of Social Inequality: Work productivity (Gerth & Mills 1946: 11; Collins & Makowsky 1989:120); Inheritance (Kasler 1988:14); Close to mother (Coser 1977:253); Freedom to work (Gerth & Mills 1946:19, 24); Difficult person (Gerth & Mills 1946:19, 26); Weber sued (Kasler 1988:17); Sociology (Kasler 1988:13; Coser 1977:240); Style (Gerth & Mills 1946:26; Giddens 1971:133); On classes (Weber 1946:180–185); On status (Weber 1946:186–194); On party (Weber 1946:194–195).

5. Rationality and Bureaucracies: Weber's view of the world (Mitzman 1970:167); Political disillusion (Aron 1965:242; Collins & Makowsky 1989:139; Viault 1990:326, 377; Coser 1977:254); Defends unpopular causes (Coser 1977:242–243); Weber as a statesman (Aron 1965:234, 243, 249; Gerth & Mills 1946:42); Formal rationality (Weber 1946:298–299; Giddens 1971:183; Morrison 1995:341, 346; Coser 1977:231); On bureaucracy (Weber 1946:196–203); Problems of bureaucracies (Coser 1977:255; Giddens 1971:159, 183); Disenchantment (Aron 1965:214); Socialism (Aron 1965:250; Giddens 1971:179; Weber 1946:225).

6. Power and Authority: World War I (Collins & Makowsky 1989:139; Ashley & Orenstein 1995:266; Aron 1965:248, 258; Collins 1986:12; Viault 1990:393–394); War involvement (Gerth & Mills 1946:22, 40; Collins & Makowsky 1989:139); War critic (Mitzman 1970:293; Coser 1977:256; Gerth & Mills 1946:41); On power (Weber 1946:180; Giddens 1971:154–155); On authority (Weber 1947:324–406; Mitzman 1970:244; Aron 1965:236; Gerth & Mills 1946:52–55); Pessimism about charismatic authority (Mitzman 1970:250; Giddens 1971:162; Gerth & Mills 1946:54).

7. Rationality in Contemporary Society: Surrender (Viault 1990:435); Weber's national prominence (Mitzman 1970:300; Coser 1977:241); Opposed treaty (Weber 1975:651–657); Lectures (Weber 1975:604, 671); Death (Weber 1975:689, 698); Diverse topics (Kasler 1988:212; Schroeder 1992; Knapp 1994; Aron 1965:201; Collins & Makowsky 1989:119); Values (Coser 1977:258–259; Aron 1965:191); Social action (Giddens 1971:146; Aron 1965:245); McDonaldization (Ritzer 1996).

chapter 4

Impressions of Everyday Life: Georg Simmel and Forms of Social Interaction

Many of our experiences with the social world involve daily interactions with small numbers of people we know well—our family, intimate partners, friends, roommates, and co-workers. At the same time, however, we experience the social world with others we know less well—teachers, students, administrators, store clerks, bus drivers, waiters and waitresses, secretaries, and strangers that pass us on the street, view movies with us in a theater, and eat with us in a restaurant.

The growth of cities in modern societies has contributed to the importance of impersonal and fleeting ties relative to personal and longlasting ties, a fact that has brought both negative and positive consequences. On the negative side, people in large cities often seem unwilling to help strangers in need, lack the close neighborhood ties of small-town residents, and treat people according to their looks, jobs, and money rather than their inner value as persons. On the positive side, modern city life brings excitement, stimulation, and innovation and enhances opportunities for economic success.

Georg Simmel, a German sociologist during the late 1800s and early 1900s, grew up in Berlin at a time of drastic population growth and cultural change. Born and raised in the very center of a noisy, active, and growing city, he experienced the changes brought about by modern urban life more intensely than others. He could not help but notice the special traits of city residents—indeed, he had many of these traits himself. In his work, Simmel attempted to understand and compare the interaction he saw in large groups and cities with the more personal and intimate social interactions that occur in small groups.

Unlike many early sociologists, Simmel studied the social interaction of individuals in everyday life, writing about the relationships between people in families, at parties, and on city streets and focusing on the basic elements of social life—how people become angry, jealous, or bitter, fall in and out of love, find and enjoy friendships, help or fail to help strangers, or try to impress others. The essence of social life, according to Simmel, appears in these commonplace and familiar dealings with other people.

In his studies of everyday life, Simmel highlighted the social nature of human behavior. The forms that social behaviors take—whether they involve small or large groups, conflict or cooperation, or intimates or strangers—affect how individuals act, and his goal for sociology was to describe and explain these forms of behavior. By identifying the underlying patterns of interactions across diverse situations, he hoped that sociology could make sense of the complexities of social life.

As the first German academic to use the word *sociology* in a book title, Simmel made contributions to a variety of topics. He described forms of social interaction involving conflict that apply as much to understanding the actions of leaders of nations at war as to couples getting divorced. He described forms of social interaction involving domination that apply as much to government authorities and citizens as to lynch mobs and their victims. He described the changes in social interaction that result from the use of money for economic exchange in modern society. And he discussed how city residents respond to the daily overflow of people, ideas, and events they face.

Despite publishing dozens of books and hundreds of articles, however, Simmel failed to gain respectability among German academics. His writings were too clever, too original, and too popular to suit his critics, who found his work stimulating and insightful but did not think it added up to a unified perspective on the social world. Indeed, the uniqueness of Simmel's work has made it difficult for others to emulate, and he did not attract close followers during his life.

American sociologists, however, have found Simmel's work more intriguing. Early in the century, several of the nation's first sociologists adopted Simmel's approach, and in the last two decades, his work has enjoyed renewed interest. His work on city life, culture, and modernity has influenced those still concerned about the direction of change in today's society. And his attention to social interaction has attracted much interest among those concerned with behavior in everyday life.

1. THE ATTRACTIONS OF CITY LIFE

When he finished his doctoral studies at the University of Berlin in 1885, Georg Simmel (pronounced GAY-org ZIM-mel) knew what he wanted to do: he wanted to stay in Berlin, where he had been born and raised, and establish a successful career as a professor at the prestigious University of Berlin, where he had gone to school as both an undergraduate and graduate student. Although most scholars with a new Ph.D. looked for jobs at other universities, where they could start fresh in a new environment with new colleagues, Simmel loved Berlin too much to leave. Rather than work in one of the many smaller university towns throughout Germany, he wanted the exciting intellectual and social life of a large city.

Having lived all his life in Berlin, he had become thoroughly accustomed to life in a modern city. He was born in 1858 in the very center of the growing metropolis; rather than residing in a homey neighborhood on the outskirts of town or in a nearby suburb, he grew up near the intersection of Berlin's two busiest and most important streets. In comparable terms, Simmel might have grown up near Times Square in New York City or Piccadilly Circus in London (Coser 1965a:1). With a high volume of business dealings, traffic, visitors, and shoppers, such a location might seem poorly suited to a family and children. But Simmel had always enjoyed the noise, activity, and excitement of the city center. Where others found such an environment overstimulating, he had adjusted to it early in his life and, indeed, seemed more attached to the city of Berlin than to his family or relatives. He once said that none of his family members had influenced his intellectual goals in an important way, yet life in a large city had clearly shaped his personality and social development.

As Simmel would later argue in his writings, city living tends to make people detached and distant from others: one can observe the variety of activity and the diversity of people in a city without becoming personally involved with them. In much the same way, Simmel grew up somewhat aloof from and unconcerned with those around him. His father, who died when Simmel was 16, did not have much influence on him, nor did a family friend who became his guardian after the death of his father. He disliked his mother, whom he found domineering and suffocating, and he seems to have wanted little contact with any of his six older brothers and sisters.

Instead of having close ties with his family, Simmel devoted himself to the world of art and ideas. As a young man, he became close to a painter named Gustav Graef, whose family provided a substitute for Simmel's own, and later involved himself as much with painters and poets in Berlin as with scholars and scientists. He eventually married a young and well-educated painter, Gertrude Kinel, in 1890.

Given his broad interests, Simmel attempted to explore topics of art and music while a student of philosophy. He wanted to study and write about ideas he found stimulating rather than limiting himself to what his philosophy professors studied. The modern urban culture of Berlin—where he enjoyed artistic innovation, personal freedom, and stimulating activity—provided the ideal environment to explore his wide-ranging concerns. Why should he leave all this for a job at another university?

An Academic Nonconformist

Unfortunately, Simmel's goals for an academic career in Berlin did not match the views of the professors and educational bureaucrats who controlled his job opportunities. The professors of philosophy at the University of Berlin and the government officials in the department of education in charge of hiring had some doubts about his suitability for a job there. They knew the young man well, since many had taught him in their classes, supervised his dissertation work, and interacted with him in department seminars. Based on their experiences with him, they wondered if he would pursue the kind of career they expected of new professors.

Simmel certainly showed exceptional talent, but many thought he misdirected that talent by trying to apply his ideas to a wide variety of topics and problems rather than concentrating on the narrow confines of the field of philosophy. In late nineteenth-century Germany, scholars pursued their studies with extraordinary rigor, detail, and thoroughness, and professors were expected to study topics in depth and read all the relevant literature. These high standards of scholarship made German universities the world's best.

Simmel, however, never fully accepted these standards and traditions. As demanded by his teachers, he mastered the works of the great German philosophers and could present their perspectives on questions about the nature of reality and knowledge. Yet he tended to stray from the dominant topics of study to those with less prestige and respectability, venturing into the study of psychology, sociology, art history, medieval Italian, and music. This tendency left some professors wondering about his goals: Would he bring himself to specialize in a narrow philosophical topic, as success in the academy would require? Would he devote himself to the in-depth study of one topic?

Simmel gave his doubters good reasons to think that he would not. His intelligence made it clear that he had the ability to move smoothly and quickly across diverse topics, and his independent nature made it clear that he lacked the desire for sustained concentration on one topic. Not surprisingly, his supervising committee rejected his first dissertation on psychological studies of music because it deviated so far from the normal topics of philosophical study. He then quickly submitted some of his more conventional work so as to finish his doctorate with due speed. But later, when giving a presentation of his work, Simmel bluntly criticized and offended a high-ranking member of the faculty.

Academic Anti-Semitism

Another concern of Simmel's opponents involved his religious background—he came from a Jewish family. His paternal grandfather, born Isaac Israel, had changed his last name to Simmel in 1812 in order to become a German citizen. Isaac's son, Simmel's father, later converted to Catholicism and married a young woman from his hometown who had converted to Lutheranism. Simmel himself was baptized as a Protestant. With a family background of Catholics, Lutherans, and Jews, he never identified with any of the religions and never attended church or synagogue. Just as he lacked close ties to his family, he never developed close ties to a religious community. Even so, his Jewish background affected how others evaluated his work.

As in other countries, Jews suffered from prejudice and discrimination in German society. For those hoping to avoid religious bigotry, it took several generations of intermarriage, a change in name, and a new residence to erase a Jewish background. In the meantime, most converts faced suspicion from both Christians and Jews. Christians viewed them as opportunists who had changed religion to gain economic success and social acceptance and Jews viewed them as renegades who had denied their background and religious beliefs.

Treatment of Jews in the academic world likewise reflected prejudice and discrimination. No formal laws existed to prevent Jews from university employment, and German Jews entered the academic world in large numbers. Even so, they found advancement difficult because universities placed limits on the number of Jewish professors they would promote: although about 12 percent of lecturers came from Jewish backgrounds, only about 3 percent reached the position of tenured professor (Gay 1978:114). Although possible, success for Simmel, as for other Jews, would come with more difficulty than for Christians.

Given Simmel's intellectual nonconformity and this academic anti-Semitism, it is not surprising that a decision on his initial application to join the University of Berlin was delayed. In 1885, he received the appointment as a lecturer that he wanted, but the position came without a regular salary—university lecturers at that time in Germany depended on irregular fees paid by students who attended the lectures. Unfortunately, these fees barely provided enough to live on. Only a promotion to a professorship would provide a decent and regular salary, the chance to participate in departmental governance, and the qualification to supervise students.

Fortunately, Simmel did not have to worry about his finances. His father owned part of a successful chocolate factory that still manufactures candy bars in Germany today, and his guardian, the founder of a well-known international musical publishing house, left a considerable fortune to each of his adopted children when he died. This inheritance would support Simmel for most of his life. Although he could accept a poorly paid job without financial deprivation, he still hoped his position as a lecturer would not last long—he wanted the prestige and esteem that would come from recognition of his work and promotion to a professorship.

Perhaps Simmel should have taken the skeptical attitudes of his superiors more seriously. At the University of Berlin, he would never gain the respect he felt he deserved or obtain the promotions he sought, nor would recognition come from other major universities in Germany. His decision to stay at the University of Berlin, and follow wherever his intellectual interests led him, would take him far afield from the philosophical traditions of the last decades of the nineteenth century. It would ultimately harm rather than help his career.

2. JEWISH LIFE IN GERMANY

Simmel emerged from the same national and political environment as Max Weber, experiencing the unification of Germany under Bismarck and the growing military and economic power of the new nation. Unlike Weber, however, Simmel showed little interest in politics. He did little to protest the lack of democracy, the excessive power of the Junkers, and the authoritarian rule of Bismarck and Kaiser William I. The growth of Berlin as a city and the artistic changes in Europe concerned Simmel more than politics.

Growth of a Modern City

As the German nation grew during Simmel's early life, Berlin became one of Europe's largest and most important cities. Although the capital of the German state of Prussia during previous centuries, Berlin had remained relatively unimportant and backward compared to London, Paris, Rome, or Vienna. With its establishment as the capital of the new German nation, however, Berlin grew quickly; it had a population of nearly 1 million people by 1874 and 1.7 million by 1894 (Poggi 1993:35). The 74-percent growth rate during those 20 years gave Berlin an energy and sense of confidence equal to or greater than that in other major European cities.

The changes brought about by a growing population and new residents made life in Berlin exciting, restless, and stimulating. New ideas flowed into the city along with migrants from all over Europe, and the city's large size also contributed to the kind of diversity that produces artistic and literary innovation. Less positively, the emerging greatness of Berlin made its residents boastful and arrogant, and the city's enormous influence on the rest of the nation gave them a sense of superiority over those located in rural areas and smaller cities. Berliners took excessive pride in living in Germany's largest and most important urban center.

Along with its population growth, Berlin experienced dizzying economic growth. Germany's military victories under Bismarck brought riches from the defeated nations into the capital of the victorious nation. Stock market and real estate prices rose, new factories and businesses hired more workers, and employees received better pay. Rampant speculation on stocks and real estate brought financial ruin to some and great wealth to others. To service the new wealth, large stores replaced homes on the fashionable streets of Berlin.

Berlin also contained many cultural and intellectual attractions. It boasted good museums, art galleries, theaters, orchestras, and opera companies. The University of Berlin, although relatively new compared to some of the German universities founded in the Middle Ages, had emerged as the scholarly equal to others in Germany, France, and England. And a variety of books, newspapers, and respected journals were published there. Despite lacking a strong artistic and literary tradition, Berlin became a cultural center that contributed to Germany's greatness.

Jewish Migration to Cities

Migration from Germany's rural areas to Berlin during this period of growth brought another important change to the capital: it became the center of Jewish life in Germany. For centuries, Jews had lived in small communities in Eastern Europe, where they suffered daily from discrimination in their contacts with the surrounding Christian community and on occasion from violence at the hands of resentful governments and other citizens.

Partly because of discrimination, they resided in segregated areas, maintained a distinct style of life, and kept close ties to their religious community. They spoke Yiddish, sent their children to Jewish schools, and observed special religious traditions such as worshiping on the Sabbath (Saturday) and eating kosher food; Jewish men wore distinctive long felt coats, wide-brimmed hats, and long beards. Since they were not permitted to own land, they supported themselves in small businesses and by money lending; this involvement in commerce further contrasted with the farming activities of the majority of the Christian population.

During the period from 1780 to 1910, however, the European Jewish community gained the opportunity to break free from their traditional ways of life (Cantor 1994:232). In the 1800s, they received the full rights of citizenship, which allowed them to migrate from small communities, enter previously restricted occupations, attend public schools, vote, and own property. German leaders gave Jews this new freedom less from a sense of religious tolerance than from national self-interest—to industrialize and grow, Prussia and then Germany needed to utilize fully the skills of all its population. Their background in commerce and traditional emphasis on education and learning made Jews valuable to the nation-building goals of German leaders.

Once freed from legal constraints and extreme forms of anti-Semitism, Jews in Germany experienced rapid social mobility. Having had weak ties to agriculture, they adapted well to market capitalism, founding and running successful banks, factories, stores, newspapers, and shipping businesses. Having a strong tradition of education, they also entered the professions of law, medicine, journalism, and teaching in large numbers. Many other Jews who worked as laborers in the growing number of factories became heavily involved in labor union movements in Germany. Jewish contributions thus proved important to the economic growth of Germany during the nineteenth century.

Many socially mobile Jewish migrants in Berlin attempted to integrate themselves into German social life, becoming loyal to the German state, attending public schools, and adopting German culture and learning. Although many Jews remained Orthodox followers of their religion or affiliated with the new Reform movement, others converted to Christianity, intermarried with Christians, or lost interest in Jewish traditions. Economic success and participation in the modern industrial economy gave many Jews confidence that they could become fully accepted members of German society.

Emerging Resentment

By the 1880s, however, religious tensions and resentment against Jewish success had begun to emerge. A slowdown in economic growth made Jews less valuable to the state and made less successful groups resentful of Jewish prosperity. According to one historian, "The social mobility [of the Jews] occurred so rapidly and visibly as to instill fear and hatred among the Christian petty bourgeoisie and working class" (Cantor 1994:232). Many Christian civil servants, small tradesmen, schoolteachers, and skilled workers resented the concentration of Jews in higher-status professions.

Hostile images stereotyped successful Jews as devious, greedy, selfish, and corrupt; the stereotypes depicted Jews as intelligent, but lacking character and too ambitious. Some people blamed Jews for economic speculations that resulted in sudden declines in stock and real estate prices and fluctuations in interest rates. One anti-Semite wrote, "For the sewer of speculations and the influence of the stock exchange, the world has to thank the Jews" (in Masur 1970:75). Others blamed Jews for social problems such as labor unrest, crime, and the conflict that came with modernization. Extremists blamed Jewish owners of newspapers for conspiring to spread anti-German propaganda.

Many successful Christians and Jews felt particularly hostile toward the newer and less successful Jewish migrants who continued to flow into Berlin from eastern Germany and Poland. These migrants still exhibited the traditional rural Jewish ways of life and thus became an easy target for prejudice. If some Jews appeared too successful and too German, others appeared too different, too unsophisticated, and too poor; if some tried to hide their Jewish background, others exhibited it all too clearly.

A special form of anti-Semitism existed in the academic world. Believing they were the defenders of traditional culture, German academics reacted negatively to many of the changes brought about by modernization. They considered themselves an educational elite, comparable to the aristocratic elite, charged with protecting the nation from the modern threat to traditional values and culture. They rejected merely practical and technical knowledge as unworthy of the spirituality and beauty of their own ideas. The entrance into the academy of Jewish scholars, who had few ties to the traditional culture and often represented the modernism that traditional academics disliked, led to suspiciousness and discrimination.

Despite its unfairness, anti-Semitism in Berlin did not take the open form it had in rural areas many decades earlier. No laws prevented Jewish equality, and no organized riots against Jews occurred in Berlin or other large cities during Simmel's time; in fact, most citizens rejected these extreme forms of anti-Semitism. As a result, Jews in Berlin did not view the anti-Semitism as a return to the hatred and violence of the past. Having moved toward the mainstream in Berlin, Jews rightly believed they differed little from other Germans in their language, culture, and patriotism. Most felt no inconsistency between their Jewish background and German citizenship.

However inaccurate and misguided, the general stereotypes and underlying resentment of Jews still had consequences. They resulted in the imposition of informal quotas for Jews in many professions, such as college professors, as well as in daily slights, rude jokes, and a sense of social distance that kept Jews from full participation in German society. Despite economic and occupational success, Jews remained distrusted by the dominant culture and social community.

In hindsight, we can see how the early emergence of a mild form of anti-Semitism contributed to more serious discrimination and genocide decades later. A young Adolf Hitler growing up in Vienna during the late 1800s and early 1900s adopted the worst forms of anti-Semitism, and in the 1920s and 1930s, many Germans joined his movement and accepted his goal of annihilating the Jewish population. From 1939 to 1945, during the years of World War II, the anti-Semitism of the Nazis resulted in the death of 6 million Jews. In Simmel's day, however, few recognized the potential for extreme violence that lay dormant in this form of religious hatred.

3. SOCIOLOGY AND SOCIAL FORMS

Despite the difficulties he might face as a Jew, Simmel began his career as a young lecturer in philosophy at the University of Berlin with enthusiasm and curiosity. Just as some of his professors had expected, his pressing desire to explore new ideas prevented him from concentrating on a single and narrowly defined topic, propelling him instead to study the new field of sociology. Rather than deserting philosophy, however, he incorporated sociology into his wide-ranging interests, teaching courses on logic, metaphysics, the history of philosophy, the philosophy of art, religion, and sociology. Throughout his life, he would work as both a sociologist and a philosopher.

Too Original, Too Popular

Reflecting his diverse intellectual concerns, Simmel avoided systematic theory and argument in favor of an unconventional style. His growing list of publications took the form of separate essays rather than a set of carefully organized and tightly connected volumes. Each essay impressed readers with its original and imaginative insights about social life and philosophical thought but failed to explain its connections to his other essays. Colleagues compared Simmel to a philosophical squirrel: he would jump from one topic to another like a squirrel jumps from one branch to another, each time rejoicing in the sheer beauty of the acrobatic leaps (Coser 1965a:3).

Critics attributed Simmel's scattered style to a lack of persistence and to shallowness in his personality and interests, whereas supporters viewed the same characteristics of his work as displaying the courage and confidence to follow his own vision. Either way, the costs to his academic career would prove great.

As Simmel's writing style evoked contradictory reactions, so did his teaching and lectures. He became one of Berlin's most popular teachers and well-known lecturers; in fact, his lectures became public events that attracted "anyone who was anybody" (Laurence 1975:34). Intellectuals, politicians, and artists looking for a way to spend a stimulating hour attended the lectures—and Simmel always provided them with a superb performance. Using abrupt gestures, dramatic pauses, and an intense delivery, he enlivened his ideas and enthralled his audience. Although he prepared his lectures with care, he delivered them as if he were, at that very moment, struggling to create and express exciting new ideas.

Some of his superiors, however, viewed his popular lectures with no more approval than they did his wide-ranging writings. In their minds, his popularity meant that he catered to his less sophisticated lecture audiences by ignoring careful, but dull, scholarship. The students and non-academics who most appreciated the lectures could not adequately judge the merit of Simmel's work—they were swayed by his superficial cleverness. Established scholars, who believed that only they could judge the contribution of Simmel's lectures to their field, did not give him the acclaim he received from others.

As with his writing and lecturing style, the content of Simmel's work excited many but repulsed others, in part because of his advocacy of the new field of sociology. In an 1894 essay, "The Problem of Sociology," he claimed he had successfully identified an approach to the new field of study that avoided the problems of previous approaches. Lacking any false modesty, he told others of the important contribution to the scholarly world he had made with this paper. He felt so confident that he sent a copy of it to a powerful Berlin civil servant in charge of university affairs, asserting in an attached note that, in part because of his efforts, sociology would grow quickly and soon obtain official recognition everywhere. In Simmel's words, "I have contrived to substitute a new and sharply demarcated complex of specific tasks for the hitherto lack of clarity and confusion surrounding the concept of sociology" (Frisby 1981:33). With assurance and perhaps naiveté, he believed his solution would overcome opposition to the field.

The Importance of Social Interaction

According to Simmel, a basic problem in the work of his sociological predecessors came from a major mistake: they tended to treat groups and societies as things separate from people, even developing general laws of societal change that made little reference to real individuals. The historical materialism of Marx and Engels treated the mode of production as the dominant cause of social relationships and social change; the French sociologist Auguste Comte wanted to identify laws of social life similar to the laws of physics or chemistry; the English sociologist Herbert Spencer wanted to apply laws of evolution to human societies and social behavior.

In contrast to these grand schemes, Simmel claimed that groups or societies do not exist as objects separate from individuals. We cannot see a society or a social group—we can only see individual people who act certain ways toward others and infer that those behaviors reflect common membership in a society or group. Thus, society exists only in the minds of individuals who participate in relationships with others. In Simmel's view, the efforts of Marx, Comte, and Spencer to develop broad and sweeping laws about something as intangible and elusive as "society" must fail.

Of course, even if invisible, society has importance in the way it ties people together in social relationships. Simmel did not want to return to the isolated study of individual psychology, but he did want sociologists to understand more precisely the object of their study. Rather than treating society as an external object, he wanted to study the people that created society in the first place.

With this goal in mind, Simmel developed an approach that focused on **social interaction**. Individuals form groups when, as a way to satisfy their needs and desires, they interact or associate with and influence one another. By creating bonds among otherwise separate individuals, social interaction unifies people into larger groups and societies. From this point of view, the term *society* represents a convenient way to describe stable forms of association. Rather than speak of groups or societies, then, Simmel more precisely spoke of the social interactions that make up groups or societies. In fact, he defined *society* simply as the sum of interactions among its members.

The Importance of Everyday Life

If, as Simmel argued, society represents less a set of forces operating *over* individuals than a set of forces operating *between* individuals, sociologists needed a new approach to the study of social life, one that focused on the small and intimate patterns of relationships that underlie groups and create society. Rather than investigating the large institutions of society, such as the state or capitalism, he advocated the study of the basic elements of social life—individuals interacting with one another. He wanted to study the hidden networks of human relationships that make up society.

In Simmel's (1959:327–328) own words:

> That people look at one another and are jealous of one another; that they exchange letters or have dinner together; that … they strike one another as pleasant and unpleasant; that gratitude for altruistic acts makes for inseparable union; that one asks another to point out a certain street; that people dress and adorn themselves for each other—these are a few casually chosen illustrations from the whole range of relations that play between one person and the other. They may be momentary or permanent, conscious or unconscious, ephemeral or of grave consequences, but they incessantly tie men together. At each moment such threads are spun, dropped, taken up again, displaced by others, interwoven with others. These interactions among the atoms of society are accessible only to psychological microscopy.

One can see how the study of total societies would neglect the variety of social interactions that Simmel mentions in this quote. Further, the study of a total society implies a stability not present in the highly creative interactions that make up any society. Social relationships change quickly and often; the social ties between people increase, decrease, cease, and begin again. Even the more stable social relationships that make up the institutions of the state, the family, and the economy change more than it might at first appear. Rigid laws concerning the development of societies and institutions could never capture the complexity of social interaction that takes place every day.

In studying everyday life, Simmel avoided any effort to construct a sociological system with assumptions, definitions, and deductions, believing such a system would be possible only in the distant future. In the meantime, he much preferred fluid and creative thinking to the use of rigid systems, offering isolated contributions to the study of social forms in a series of separate essays that would illustrate the application of his approach to different topics.

To those who responded that the study of apparently trivial and minute aspects of social life would tell us little about the totality of society, Simmel had an answer. He noted that, because all parts of a society fit together, one cannot understand one element of society as separate from the others. Therefore, the study of one part—no matter how minor it may seem on the surface—helps us understand the unity and totality of society. He backed up this claim by using the study of aspects of everyday life—such as fashion, rules of chess, the use of knives at the table, and flirting—to shed light on the nature of the larger society. For Simmel, study of the parts provided the means to understand the whole.

He realized, however, that his proposed object of study raised a new problem for sociology. The micro-level social world of interaction consists of infinite complexity—but how could any field of study comprehend this complexity? Here again he presented an original and valuable answer, one that derived from his background in philosophy.

The Form and Content of Behavior

Simmel had written his dissertation on the work of Germany's greatest philosopher, Immanuel Kant, who noted that people cannot directly know the outside world; they can only know it through their own sight, hearing, and other senses. Yet humans do not passively observe the complex external world—they actively interpret reality to make sense of it. They might, to take a simple example, notice a variety of round objects of different sizes, colors, weights, and materials and classify them as balls used in sports and games. Basketballs, soccer balls, baseballs, tennis balls, and golf balls differ from each other, but the human mind can interpret them as part of a larger category.

Simmel realized that the same sort of interpretation is needed to organize, simplify, and make sense of social life. After all, millions of people associate with one another in daily life. Each person has different needs, desires, traits, and goals, and each interaction involves different people, places, and times. Scholars could never understand the complexity of what takes place in social life without some way to interpret, classify, and organize the details.

Indeed, in daily life people constantly identify patterns in the way people act toward one another. We might notice that when two people approach each other, they sometimes smile, nod, wave, hug, shake hands, bow, kiss, or say "hello." These behaviors all represent a more general form of greeting. Further, the greeting might lead people to talk about any of a wide variety of topics, such as the weather, family, friends, work, a party, sports, shopping, health, or current events. Despite the dissimilar behaviors and conversations that take place, the underlying similarities lead us to identify all these interactions as a form of greeting.

Simmel suggested that the social understandings used by people in daily life provide a simple model for sociological understanding. People actively interpret and impose order on the innumerable contents of their lives and experiences. **Contents** consist of everything present in individuals that brings them together in social interaction (e.g., the different ways that individuals act and converse upon meeting). **Social forms** reflect common patterns and routines of behavior that select from and organize the diversity of social contents (e.g., the category of greeting that organizes individual ways of acting and conversing). In Simmel's view, sociology should identify and classify different forms of social interaction.

Consider another example. Huge differences exist among nations at war, married couples going through a divorce, businesses competing for the same customers, attorneys involved in an expensive lawsuit, street-gang members fighting over turf, religious groups denouncing others as unbelievers, and protesters demonstrating against the police. However, these diverse social interactions have something in common: they all involve conflict. Further, all interactions involving conflict, despite obvious differences, have certain similarities or common properties. Sociology should aim to identify the social forms of interaction, such as conflict, that underlie the outward diversity.

If people organize and interpret social forms in everyday life, do we need sociologists to do the same thing? Simmel would say that, although people organize and interpret the social world, they typically do not try to understand how they do it. An analogy exists between social forms and grammar. Although people use rules of sentence syntax and structure in speaking and writing, they typically cannot explain the rules they use. We know rules of grammar exist and study them in school, but few of us fully understand them. Sociologists should work like grammarians—they should identify the underlying forms of social interaction that people use unconsciously and routinely.

The goal of studying social forms greatly simplifies the task of sociology. Similar forms of interaction occur with dissimilar content and across diverse situations. Sociology can thus focus on the routine patterns of social life rather than on the specific individuals that participate in them. Simmel's definition of the field avoids the problem of trying to study all aspects of society. Sociology can never understand everything that occurs in society, but it does not need to if it focuses on forms rather than content.

4. FORMS OF DOMINATION AND CONFLICT

By 1901, Simmel's 16 years at the University of Berlin had resulted in notable accomplishments. Besides his popularity as a lecturer, he had gained worldwide fame as the author of 6 books and 70 articles, with translations into English, French, Italian, and Polish (Coser 1977a:195). His work in sociology in particular attracted many new scholars to the field; in the United States, for example, the editor of the country's first sociology journal, a professor at the University of Chicago, translated and published several of Simmel's essays. Max Weber wrote that Simmel "deserves his reputation as one of the foremost thinkers, a first-rate stimulator of academic youth and academic colleagues" (Turner 1992:164).

Continued Professional Rejection

Despite his fame and international publications, his accomplishments were slighted by leaders at the University of Berlin and the German ministry of education. Because they had so far refused to give him a promotion, he remained a lecturer who did not receive a regular salary and did not fully belong to the academic community. He finally received a promotion in 1901, but it was honorary and thus did not bring with it the salary, status, and power of a real professor. Lacking the respect of many of his academic colleagues, Simmel seemed destined to remain in the position of an apprentice at the university.

Although he loved Berlin, he reacted to the rebuff by seeking a job as a professor at the University of Heidelberg. Although located in a small, less sophisticated town, the University of Heidelberg had great prestige and an opening for the professorship Simmel thought he deserved. Strong recommendations for the job from Max Weber and other famous scholars gave him hope that his career would finally advance. Unfortunately, the same objections to his work that existed in Berlin kept officials in Heidelberg from making the offer.

Why had Simmel failed to gain formal academic recognition? Although anti-Semitism certainly played a role, as discussed earlier, those prejudiced against Jews found other reasons to justify their bias. For the job at Heidelberg, the regional minister of culture requested Dietrich Schaefer, a scholar specializing in medieval history at the University of Berlin, to evaluate Simmel's work (quoted from Coser's (1965b:37–38) translation of the letter). Schaefer began by noting Simmel's Jewish background: "I do not know whether or not he has been baptized, nor did I want to inquire about it. He is, at any rate, a dyed-in-the-wool Israelite in his outward appearance, in his bearing, and in his manner of thinking." The letter then claimed that Simmel's "academic and literary merits and successes are very narrow and limited" and that one does not come away "with too much of positive value."

Schaefer denigrated Simmel's popularity as a lecturer by noting the Jewish composition of his audience. "A Semitic lecturer ... will find fertile soil, no matter what the circumstances, at a university where the corresponding part of the student body numbers several thousand, given the cohesion that prevails in these circles." In contrast to Christian and German male students, Jewish students are swayed, according to Schaefer, by shallow cleverness. Showing his prejudice, Schaefer wrote, "I do not imagine that the University of Heidelberg would be especially advanced by attracting that kind to its lecture halls."

The letter also made condescending references to the women and foreign students attracted to Simmel's lectures. Schaefer continued, "He spices his words with clever sayings. And the audience he recruits is composed accordingly. The ladies constitute a very large portion—even for Berlin. For the rest, there [appears at his lectures] an extraordinarily numerous contingent of the oriental world, drawing on those who have already settled here as well as on those who are still flooding in semester after semester from the countries of the East. His whole manner is in tune with their orientation and taste."

In point of fact, Simmel's work followed closely from the insights of previous German philosophers rather than from Jewish or foreign scholarship. In the words of a respected historian, "Georg Simmel's sociology was no more Jewish, no less German, than Max Weber's" (Gay 1978:125). Even so, that seemed to make little difference to those intending to discover so-called Jewish characteristics in his work.

An Impressionistic Style

Other reasons might have contributed to Simmel's lack of acceptance. For one thing, he may have threatened other scholars. Too much success can create jealously, and, in Simmel's case, his popular lectures took students away from those given by senior professors. His publications likewise received popular attention—something that few of his colleagues could claim—and sometimes offended scholars with criticisms of commonly held ideas. Perhaps Simmel could have smoothed things over, but he did not involve himself in the kind of academic politics that requires young professors to flatter or show deference to senior professors.

In addition, his work was simply too unconventional to obtain widespread recognition as serious scholarship. He wrote on too many subjects, made little effort to integrate his insights, and risked "the danger of ending in scattered fragments" (Ashley & Orenstein 1995:306). He wrote for too many nonacademic publications and also neglected to use footnotes and references to other sources. Even if his essays, like the paintings of the French Impressionists, illuminated the details of life, they did not contribute to a cumulative science based on tests of hypotheses, the search for causes, and the development of theories. Scholars who respected intellectual disciplines and traditional boundaries between fields of study found Simmel's work shallow.

Reflecting his impressionistic approach, Simmel wrote dozens of separate essays on a variety of aspects of social life. In 1908, he published a compilation of these essays in a book entitled *Sociology*. Any summary cannot do justice to the diversity of topics he studied, but a few examples can give the flavor of his work. Consider domination and conflict, two common forms of interaction that Simmel described in his sociological writings.

Domination

Many interactions in social life involve a relationship between a leader and a follower or a superior and a subordinate; this form of interaction exists between parent and child, teacher and student, boss and employee, police officer and citizen, bureaucrat and client, and any number of other pairs of persons with unequal power, authority, or prestige. We might view this relationship as one-sided: one person actively gives orders and the other follows them, or one person exerts influence and the other passively accepts it. Simmel argued, however, that these relationships involve a considerable degree of personal freedom for both participants to influence each other.

In response to the commands of a leader, for example, followers have choices in how they act. They can respond to the domination with enthusiasm or apathy, can resist or submit fully to the leader, and can oppose or accept the power over them. Although some followers respond with passive or active opposition, most accept the authority of the leader, many of them perhaps actually relying on the leader's assumption of responsibility. In any case, the response of the follower to commands will in turn influence or change the behavior of the leader. The participants in the interaction thus mutually influence one another.

Although all forms of domination involve mutual influence, the type of mutual influence differs depending on the circumstances. Simmel divided domination into that exerted by an individual, a group, and a principle. First, a group can be under the power of an individual, such as subjects to a monarch, a congregation to a minister, or a class to a teacher. Relationships between a single leader and a group have something in common: they tend to foster unity among the subordinate group as strong bonds among group members emerge in reaction to their common position relative to the leader. Army groups, for example, foster unity among new recruits by instilling dislike and fear of the drill sergeant. In societies and religious communities, belief in a single, all-powerful God connects members in their submission to God.

Second, individuals can be subordinated to a group. For example, a government, a church, or corporation leaders set policies that others must follow. Compared to domination by an individual leader, domination by a faceless committee seems impersonal, unemotional, and distant. Sometimes the group takes the form of a crowd, such as in a lynch mob. In this case, the treatment of the victim depends on the emotional swings and moods that flow through the crowd. Since no single leader has responsibility for the actions of the group, crowds can act with vicious cruelty toward enemies.

Third, individuals and groups can be subordinated to an impersonal principle. In the past, this rarely occurred. Subjects preferred domination by a personal ruler rather than by a rigid and impersonal principle. Medieval servants or traditional English butlers, for example, took pride in catering to the wishes of their masters. In modern society, however, workers often resent being subject to the demands and whims of a single person, who might ask them to run personal errands or treat them unfairly. Domination by objective rules, norms, and principles rather than by single persons often guides our lives in modern society.

Conflict

Along with domination and submission, conflict characterizes many social relationships. Although people tend to view conflict as a negative form of interaction, Simmel identified its positive components. In a negative sense, conflict can sometimes end a relationship, but in a positive sense, it can also help integrate members of a group. Consider a few characteristics of interaction involving conflict.

1. *Conflict has positive consequences.* Conflict can correct the harmful behavior of group leaders or members, link group members together in opposition to another group, give group members a sense of energy and purpose in their actions, resolve tensions between different group interests and factions, and encourage group effort and achievement. Given these benefits, it would be foolish to eliminate all conflict from social relationships and social interaction. A completely harmonious group would have trouble improving, adapting, or identifying leaders.

Although the degree of conflict between groups may vary from less intense to highly intense, conflict still presents these benefits. At one extreme, conflict in contests and competitive games takes a mild form. It exists more for the enjoyment of the effort to achieve victory than for the gains in income and power that might come from victory. Softball teammates prefer victory but obtain satisfaction from competition for its own sake even if they lose. Regardless of the outcomes of the varied types of contests, competition unites participants. By accepting the rules of the game, enjoying the hard-fought contest, and sharing the camaraderie of the experience, competitors become close to their teammates and gain respect for the opposition.

2. *Conflict over impersonal interests involves greater intensity and seriousness.* When people struggle on behalf of a larger principle rather than directly against others, a dispute takes on special importance. Because the principle seems more important than the personal feelings of individuals, those who submit themselves to a cause can be merciless in attempting to make others submit to it as well. They feel motivated by a sense of purpose that views compromise—no matter how much easier it would make life—as treason to the cause. Wars, revolutions, and genocide, the worst forms of conflict in history, commonly involve leaders and their followers acting on the basis of some principle, such as nationalism, communism, or fascism. Even religious denominations that advocate peace and forgiveness have used their principles to justify armed conflict, such as in the Christian–Muslim wars during the Crusades or the Catholic–Protestant wars during the Protestant Reformation.

3. *Conflict between groups can generate extreme solidarity within groups.* As the conflict between groups escalates, members of each side unite to eliminate differences within their group and heighten the differences between their group and the opponent. While peace allows for individuality and freedom of the group members, conflict creates a strong need for unity against the enemy. Groups treat dissenters much more harshly during conflict than during peace; for example, unions on strike respond especially negatively to strike-breakers and nations at war respond especially negatively to antiwar protesters.

Leaders can take advantage of the consequences of intense group conflict. By identifying a serious threat posed to a community or nation by a foreign power, they can enhance solidarity, quiet their opponents, and gain popular support. In World War II, citizens in the United States and Great Britain supported the strong leadership of President Franklin Roosevelt and Prime Minister Winston Churchill. The famous search for communist spies during the 1950s in the United States may have helped mobilize the nation against the Soviet Union during the Cold War. In both cases, conflict enhanced internal national solidarity.

4. *Conflict between those who share common qualities and a strong sense of solidarity can result in bitterness and hostility.* Although we might expect the greatest conflict to exist between individuals and groups with the greatest differences, Simmel described how similarities increase conflict. In homogeneous groups, members become sensitive to minor differences and thus make greater efforts to maintain harmony. When harmony does break down, the resulting conflict becomes heated because the previous closeness makes the rift all the more hurtful. Hatred of traitors, those who once shared closely in the life of the group, often reaches special extremes.

Intense conflict between those who share common qualities is particularly evident in intimate relationships. Here, hate and love often seem to exist together. Simmel noted that "sometimes between men and women, a fundamental aversion, even a feeling of hatred ... is the first stage of a relation where a second phase is passionate love" (Simmel 1955:45). The intense passion of hate is more easily transformed into love than indifference. Conversely, an especially deep hatred can grow out of broken love. Although divorced couples typically blame their bitterness on the flaws of their former partner, Simmel noted that emotional hostility may follow from the previous emotional intimacy of the couple.

5. THE CONSEQUENCES OF GROUP SIZE

Over the years, Simmel slowly distanced himself from the moral failings and prejudices of the academic system. He did not actively fight anti-Semitism, although he protested in letters to his friends over his unfair treatment. He wrote after one rejection, "I have given up protesting against this nonsense ... but I cannot and will not deceive you that the decision is painful" (Frisby 1981:30). Rather than go on the attack, he focused his energies on the activities that he found most rewarding.

For example, he began to publish more of his work in popular magazines and newspapers rather than in scholarly journals. He had seen the positive responses to his lectures from students and from Berlin society. Why not target more of his work to popular audiences that nearly always gave him support and encouragement rather than to scholarly audiences that often did not? As a way to ensure the popularity of his publications, he often wrote articles directly from the notes of his already-successful lectures. Of course, the popular articles gave his more scholarly critics further justification to withhold their approval.

Similarly, he began to associate more with members of the Berlin counterculture of artists, poets, and writers who rejected the goals and materialism of the middle class. The most innovative poets and artists also rejected the rationalism of science and traditional philosophy. Simmel's involvement in these groups pushed him further away from the more narrow world of academic scholarship.

Association with these groups may also have contributed to another radical strand in Simmel's thought. Compared to the sexism of many men at that time, he developed more progressive views about women's roles in society, supporting the entrance of women into the University of Berlin and writing with insight into the problems of women. He argued that men have an advantage over women because the norms and values used to judge both men and women are created and maintained by men. Given their position of power, men set standards that assure their dominant position. Women are expected to act according to a female role, and then are judged inferior by male-created standards.

All these changes had a negative influence on Simmel's interest in sociology. From 1909 to 1914, the years after his failure to obtain the professorship in Heidelberg, he wrote little on sociology, concentrating instead on art and culture. After having helped found the field of sociology, he refused the presidency of the German Sociological Association in 1909 and, after 1910, stopped attending its meetings. He even reduced the number of sociology courses he taught during these years.

Small-Group Interaction

Despite the increase in his nonscholarly publications and eventual movement away from sociology after 1909, Simmel had already done much to demonstrate how the study of social forms should proceed. He perhaps best illustrated his formal sociology with an analysis of the influence of numbers on social interaction. Many sociologists recognized that the size of a social group shapes the kind of association that takes place within it. However, Simmel went beyond broad generalizations to identify in surprising detail how the number of other persons in a group could affect the behavior of each member.

The simplest form of a group consists of a **dyad**, or two persons. Because a dyad would by definition no longer exist if one person leaves, it lacks a structure independent of the two members. Each member must commit fully to the group for it to survive. The dependence of the group on each of the members requires a sense of trust and closeness between them. Compared to members of larger groups, members of a dyad are more likely to share their personal thoughts, feelings, and goals with the other.

Sometimes formal rights and rules exist for two-person groups that give them more stability and durability. Marriage and business partnerships, for example, are recognized by the government, courts, and other people and therefore are bound by certain rights, duties, and permanence. These dyads exist in a formal sense even when the partners informally separate. More generally, however, two-person groups exist for the satisfaction each member gets from interaction with the other. Without close interaction, the group disappears.

A **triad**, or three-person group, differs from a dyad: if one person leaves, the group will survive in the form of a dyad or can recruit a replacement member to re-form the triad. Since one person cannot destroy the group, the group can achieve domination over the individual; each member must submit to the rules and goals of the group and the other members. In practice, efforts to make members submit to the group often involve the formation of coalitions, with two weaker members possibly uniting against a stronger third member or one member trying to manipulate each of the others to gain special power.

Because these sorts of coalitions could not occur in a two-person group, the entrance of a third person into a two-person group changes the nature of the relationship. Two best friends who become close to a third person experience a change in their relationship. Similarly, a husband and wife who have a child change the nature of their relationship. The new size of the group affects the kind of interaction that occurs among the members.

The power of Simmel's arguments about dyads and triads comes from the generality of the principles he identifies. The consequences of group size for social interaction emerge regardless of the individuals that compose the groups. The principles apply to family members sharing intimacy, friends deciding how to have fun, business partners aiming for economic success, co-workers completing a job, religious believers trying to agree on scripture, students studying for an exam, roommates trying to share their space, government officials setting regulations, astronauts circling the earth, or lawyers trying a case.

The logic of dyads and triads also applies to groups that consist of specific subgroups. Alliances between nations, political factions, business organizations, families, sororities, clubs, or Mafia families may differ depending on the number of groups in the alliance. The focus on general forms simplifies the maze of social reality.

Interaction in Larger Groups

For groups of four or more, the size of the group continues to exert influence on the interaction among the members. Among small groups, unity still comes from face-to-face interaction and intimacy, and informal rules develop to control the behavior of members. Given the frequency of interaction and the intense social ties among members, arguments, disagreements, and dislike often appear. Each of the members must help enforce the informal rules through the direct criticism of deviant members. Street gangs, for example, must remain small to maintain close ties and group loyalty, but they consequently experience much conflict within the group over leadership, group rules, and unacceptable behavior.

By virtue of the number of members, larger groups produce different types of interaction. Ties become less intimate and more superficial, behavior becomes more standardized and impersonal, and members involve themselves less completely in group activities. Members often have little contact with one another, and most of the contact they do have involves routine and formal interactions. As in a bureaucratic organization, unity comes less from face-to-face interaction and discussion of personal feelings than from sets of formal rules and specialized duties.

Large groups create a greater sense of freedom among members than do small groups, but this freedom can result in a sense of isolation and lack of meaning. The larger the group, the less control the group has over each of its members. Ironically, as large groups themselves become more similar in their formal organization and rules, individuals within the groups have greater opportunity to be different. Workers in a large company must follow certain rules, but otherwise they have more freedom and autonomy inside and outside the organization than, say, members of a small religious cult. At the same time, however, members of large organizations become more distant from others and lose a sense of common belonging.

City Life and Interaction

If large group size increases the differences and individuality of the members, we might expect this process to reach its peak in cities. In a well-known article, "The Metropolis and Mental Life," Simmel explored the consequences of city life for interaction much the way he explored the consequences of group size for social interaction.

Simmel first considered the physical and economic characteristics of large cities. In physical terms, cities concentrate huge numbers of persons in a small area. This population density creates overwhelming stimuli that bombard the senses of city residents. Compared to the slower routine of rural areas, city life intensifies "emotional life due to the swift and continuous shift of external and internal stimuli" (Simmel 1971:325). In economic terms, large cities contain specialized and diverse interactions. Every day people make numerous exchanges, deal with a variety of people from different backgrounds, and choose among a vast array of products and services. The number and variety of economic contacts thus contribute further to the intensity of city life.

To avoid mental exhaustion in dealing with the overwhelming commotion of city life, people must screen out or distance themselves from their own sensory experiences. One method of screening simply involves ignoring surrounding activity. Accordingly, city residents seem indifferent to much of what goes on about them. They often do not know the names or faces of those who live nearby or who work in the same building. In crowded spaces such as trains or elevators, they act as if other passengers do not exist or do not matter. They commonly do not involve themselves in the problems of others, sometimes walking by someone who is hurt or in trouble without offering help; they often seem to care only about things that affect them directly.

Another method of screening involves devoting only partial attention to others in social interaction. This method shows in the impersonal way city residents deal with others. In buying something or asking a question, city residents care mostly about how the other person can fulfill their need for service or information. People's thinking compartmentalizes other people's actions into those that further their own interests and those that do not. To minimize sensory overload, city residents focus mostly on the actions related to their self-interest. By necessity, they commonly use people for what they can get from them.

This method of screening also shows itself in another way: city residents often seem unconcerned or unsurprised when confronted by something new or unexpected. They remain calm and continue their activity as an ambulance races to an injury, a police officer chases a criminal, or someone begins yelling about the coming end of the world. Thus, people protect themselves from the disruption of city life and conserve their mental energy by responding coolly and impersonally rather than emotionally and intensely to the unexpected. If they cannot ignore something, they distance themselves from it.

This environment of indifference and reserve in cities tends to highlight the superficial. Since encounters are often fleeting and seldom occupy the total attention of the participants, people need to make a quick first impression with how they look or how they act. No one has the time or energy to understand the deeply held personal values and moral strengths of everyone they meet. Yet they might notice someone who acts eccentrically, displays the latest fashion or unusual attire, or drives an expensive car. People become known for their outward appearance more than for their inner selves.

Benefits of City Life

If this discussion sounds negative, note that Simmel did not judge city people as morally inferior to those in rural areas. Their characteristics stem from the nature of their interactions in areas with concentrated populations rather than from ethical weakness. If people in cities appear showy or seem always to strive to impress others, these actions stem from efforts to counteract urban anonymity. If people in cities exhibit a certain hardness and lack of sympathy, their attitudes stem from their inability to respond emotionally to the innumerable problems they can observe every day. If city people seem devoted to their own interests, their selfishness stems from the need to conserve mental energy in dealing with all the stimuli they face.

To balance this negative picture, Simmel also described the many benefits and positive consequences of city life. Remember that Simmel, having spent nearly all his life in Berlin, loved living in a large city. Many of the traits of city residents—detachment, isolation, distance—also characterized Simmel. Whatever their drawbacks, cities offer excitement and a fast pace of change that for centuries have attracted migrants from rural areas. Similarly, the impersonality and anonymity of cities give individuals personal freedom that they would never have in smaller, and sometimes suffocatingly intimate, villages. This freedom releases creativity and makes cities the center of art, intellectual pursuits, and politics. Further, the fascinating intersection of diverse people, occupations, classes, and groups contributes to the flourishing creativity and vast economic opportunities that cities offer.

6. MONEY IN MODERN SOCIAL LIFE

Outside of his scholarly pursuits, Simmel devoted himself to his artistic interests. Keeping current with the latest trends, experiments, and innovations of the artistic world in Berlin, he socialized with the cultural elite—Germany's most famous poets, artists, and writers. Unlike the conservative university scholars who wanted to preserve the accomplishments of the past, Simmel and other members of this group welcomed modern innovations in the world of art that challenged the traditions most respected by conventional society.

Life Among the Cultural Elite

Simmel and the cultural elite also distanced themselves from the world of economics and politics. In regard to economics, their dedication to a cultivated life of beauty and art led them to reject the pursuit of money and economic advancement, along with the unrefined and common materialism of Berlin's middle classes. Their disdain for purely commercial activity meant that they had to find other means of support, such as teaching, writing, artwork, or inheritances. In Simmel's case, his inheritance eliminated any worry about finances.

In regard to politics, the cultural elite paid little attention to problems of government, including the lack of democracy and the authoritarian power of the kaiser. One writer described the attitude of intellectuals like Simmel as follows: "To serve the true and the beautiful, to delve into the beginnings of man's history or into the secret recesses of the human soul—these matters appeared immensely more important than the political crisis over Morocco or the elections of the Reichstag" (Coser 1977a:206).

Simmel's home—notable for its large windows overlooking a beautiful garden, paintings of the great masters, valuable Persian carpets, an impressive grand piano, and exquisite antique vases, bowls, and Buddha figures—demonstrated his refined and cultured devotion to intellect, art, and beauty. There he and his wife, Gertrude, entertained favored students and honored guests with stimulating discussion. Simmel proudly described his art treasures to visitors, played piano duets with professional musicians, and discussed art with poets, painters, and writers.

Much harder to obtain than a seat at his lectures, invitations to his home became highly desired.

Simmel's elitist and artistic style of life had similarities with his scholarly work. The discussion groups at his home or the homes of others contained free-wheeling and witty conversation but lacked systematic exploration of ideas. Much as in Simmel's essays and writings, the conversation meandered from one interesting topic to another. Any insights that came from these meetings did not accumulate into an ordered and unified whole.

In addition, the detachment of the artistic world from the outside world of economics and politics matched Simmel's style of observation in his writings. His scholarly studies reveal a distance or lack of involvement with the world; he preferred to observe and analyze social life from the outside rather than involve himself closely in the activities he studied. In this regard, he differed from Marx, Durkheim, and Weber, all of whom involved themselves closely in the social and political problems of their day.

The Philosophy of Money

Simmel's interest in modern art and culture related to a more general issue that linked many of his studies—the nature and consequences of modernity. Simmel devoted much effort to describing how social forms of interaction change with modernization. His most focused and carefully organized study, *The Philosophy of Money*, examines the consequences of the reliance on a money economy for modern social life.

Although a study of money, the book has little to do with the economics of supply and demand. On the surface, money appears simply to be a means of economic exchange, providing a standard of value that makes it possible to compare different products and services for the purpose of exchanging them. Below the surface of economic exchange, however, money has a social meaning that influences the nature of interpersonal interaction. Although people seldom realize it, modern social life takes on a form consistent with the nature of money.

Consider first the properties of money set forth by Simmel. Money has no meaning on its own—it simply stands for other things that people want to exchange. Rather than trading actual products or services, people exchange a product or service for money and then spend that money for other products or services. As a tool for exchange, money has clear advantages: it is easy to transport, divide into exact amounts, and use to buy any variety of objects or services.

The alternative—trading real objects or services—causes all sorts of difficulties. Objects and services are hard to transport (e.g., bringing a bag of corn into a store to trade for clothes). Objects and services are sometimes not divisible (e.g., trying to trade half a horse or half a doctor's diagnosis). Objects and services may not match seller and buyer (e.g., a carpenter wants clothes from a store owner, but the store owner wants food from the farmer). Money solves these problems, allowing people to obtain what they need.

Consider next the consequences of monetary exchange. Because it eases economic exchange, money contributes to the dominance of certain types of relationships in modern society. Note the overlap here with Simmel's arguments about cities: since large cities are the center of money economies, many of the same aspects of social interaction that occur in large cities occur in economies dominated by monetary exchange.

1. *Money increases individual freedom.* Because it represents a general medium of exchange, money allows individuals to use it for whatever they want. They don't have to take whatever their neighbors might have to trade; instead they can sell their products or services for money and use that money to purchase something from someone else. Similarly, other people can freely choose how to spend the money they get in an exchange. In this sense, community members are less closely tied to other people when making money exchanges.

In another sense, people become free from the objects they produce in a money economy. In the past, the objects people produced limited what they could do with them. Inheriting the tools of a carpenter or blacksmith defined the occupation of a child because trading these tools would be difficult. Similarly, peasants had to pay for their land with crops, which tied them to the land and the landlord. With money, however, no such limits exist. People are less closely tied to the objects they own or produce because they can sell them for money.

2. *Money makes interaction more impersonal.* In a money economy, people often interact with others only for the purpose of exchanging products and services for money. The reliance on money eliminates personal aspects of exchange. If someone has money for an exchange, we do not need to know much about that person's feelings and qualities. In dealing only with the parts of a person relevant to the narrow exchange of money for a product or service, the remaining parts outside the impersonal interaction remain hidden. We usually do not want to know about the personal life of a clerk when we buy a product or a waiter when we order a meal.

Given the huge number of contacts with others in a specialized and modern economy, interaction must remain impersonal. Money ties us to many more people than in the past, but these ties are a means to an end rather than ends in themselves. At the extreme, prostitution symbolizes the impersonal nature of economic exchange in modern society: even sex, something that potentially involves closeness, emotion, and personal sharing, becomes merely an impersonal economic exchange in prostitution. The exchange of gifts by sex partners involves commitment and caring, but the exchange of money for sex remains impersonal.

3. *Money emphasizes intellect rather than emotion and feeling.* Use of money requires an objective calculation of value that excludes personal feelings and distances people from their emotions. Exchange transforms qualities into quantities, and people come to think in terms of "how much." Even the most personal qualities become quantities—courts designate how much money someone should get for pain and suffering caused by someone else, and insurance companies designate how much policyholders should get for the loss of their eyesight, legs, or ability to work.

Even in daily life, people continually make calculations. People ask themselves questions such as "Will I get enough pleasure from traveling to Europe to justify spending $1,500?" or "Should I give up the fun of going to a party to make an extra $25 working overtime tonight?" These kinds of calculations dominate modern life.

The emphasis on calculation and intellect can lead people to lose sight of the nonmonetary value of things—to paraphrase a famous quote, the modern person "knows the price of everything but the value of nothing." Beyond the economic value objects give, people often take little joy in what they own. The price of a work of art seems more important than the enjoyment the owner gets from looking at it. Thus, people become more focused on selling rather than owning and on prices rather than subjective satisfaction.

4. *Money speeds the tempo of life.* By allowing for quick exchange of a variety of products and services, the symbolic nature of money allows for more interactions within a given time and thus quickens the pace of social life. People walk, talk, and act faster than in rural, premodern societies. Modern life requires punctuality in order for a variety of people to meet for the purpose of efficiently exchanging money.

Even relationships between employees and employers change quickly. Where in the past apprentices had to commit themselves to work for their more skilled employers for long periods in exchange for their training, money makes it possible to change jobs for higher pay. Likewise, modern employers do not have to agree to employ workers for many years; they can fire them with a few weeks' notice. Their major obligation is to pay workers for the time they work rather than to promise a lifetime job.

5. *Money allows specialization and personal development.* Because money represents a common currency that applies to all types of products and services, it helps create unity from diversity. In a money economy, people can specialize in their work, knowing that the money economy will allow them to exchange their relatively rare product or service. With money, people can trade with those who are quite different from them, live in another city or country, and have their own specialized tasks. Money reveals the interrelationships among all parts of society.

In summary, Simmel's study of the consequences of monetary exchange provided a unique perspective on modern social life. Where Marx highlighted economic production, Simmel claimed that the value of products comes from the money other people are willing to exchange for them rather than from the labor used to produce them. This shift in emphasis from capitalist production to modern forms of money exchange extends historical materialism. Simmel stated, "I complement the position of historical materialism, which derives all forms and contexts of culture from the economic relationships obtaining at a given time" (Poggi 1993:62).

7. SIMMEL'S LEGACY

After his failure to obtain a full professorship at either Berlin or Heidelberg, Simmel reluctantly accepted one at the University of Strasbourg in 1914. Here he would finally obtain a regular salary and the respect due to a full professor. Unfortunately, the years in Strasbourg brought sadness.

Final Years

He desperately missed Berlin. Strasbourg, formerly part of France, was far enough in distance and ideas from Berlin that Simmel felt exiled. After his last lecture in Berlin, his devoted students and listeners decorated his desk with rose petals to show their appreciation. In contrast, he found small and unenthusiastic audiences when he began teaching in Strasbourg. Worse, the outbreak of World War I shortly after his arrival required the university to turn the lecture halls into military hospitals and the dormitories into barracks. His audiences shrank further, and he had little to do as a professor.

He admitted in a letter the sadness and exhaustion he felt in Strasbourg: "How hard these years were and still are cannot be expressed; they have had the effect of aging me twice or three times what is normal (I was 60 years old some weeks ago). The whole external life is very quiet and runs almost monotonously. ... [My] academic activity equals zero, and [I find] the people alien and inwardly distant" (Frisby 1981:31).

His personal life brought some difficulty as well. Some years into his marriage, Simmel had developed an intimate relationship with a poet, art critic, and writer named Gertrude Kantorowicz. She bore a daughter named Angela, but Simmel decided never to see his child, and the mother kept her secret from her own relatives. During this time, Simmel's wife "remained at his side after agreeing to 'give him his freedom'" (Laurence 1975:40).

The start of World War I evoked an initial wave of patriotic enthusiasm in Simmel, much as it had in Weber. He thought victory in the war would uphold what he viewed as the civilized and enlightened ideals of Germany against its more materialistic and less cultured European neighbors. However, the war's unexpected destructiveness and casualties dampened his enthusiasm considerably, and he soon became disillusioned (again, much like Weber). As the war neared its end and Germany faced likely defeat, Simmel cared so little for political events that he did not even want to read the newspaper.

In 1918, the last year of the war, Simmel was stricken with cancer. Continuing to write as best he could during the remaining months, he managed to finish his last book—ironically, a study of the philosophy of life. Because he died two months before the surrender of Germany in November 1918, he avoided the humiliation German residents of Strasbourg experienced. Because Strasbourg reverted to France after Germany's defeat, Simmel's widow and son were forced to leave without their belongings. Tragedy continued when, many years later, Simmel's son, Hans, was imprisoned with other Jews in the Dachau concentration camp during World War II; he died after his release from the consequences of imprisonment.

Over his career, Simmel published 31 books and 256 articles (Ashley & Orenstein 1995:307). He was the first German academic to use the term *sociology* in a book title, and he even preceded Weber in his interest in the new field. However, because the individualistic nature of Simmel's work made it difficult for others to emulate, he did not attract close followers. Before his death, he wrote in his diary, "I know that I shall die without intellectual heirs—and this is as it should be" (Ashley & Orenstein 1995:329). Although one of the most original of the founders of sociology, he was also one of the loneliest (Levine 1971:x).

Culture and Modernity

By the time of his death, Simmel had influenced American sociology more than Marx, Durkheim, or Weber. Several important American sociologists in the early twentieth century adopted Simmel's perspective on social forms, numbers, and city life in their own work. Since the 1930s, however, Marx, Durkheim, and Weber have become more important than Simmel. Critics found the distinction between social forms and content difficult to use. Further, the field of sociology has increasingly emphasized systematic theory, specific hypotheses, and precise measurement of facts, making Simmel's insightful, but unscientific, style unpopular.

In the last two decades, however, Simmel's work has enjoyed renewed interest, in large part because of his work on the consequences of modernity. His thinking on this topic reflects a pessimism about the direction of change in modern culture that resonates with scholars today.

According to Simmel, despite enjoying wealth and freedom unmatched in human history, people in modern society feel threatened and alienated by the forces of cultural change. Ideally, culture should absorb, challenge, and enrich a person's mind. Yet modern society accumulates too much knowledge and too many products for persons to assimilate, and modern culture encourages superficial acquaintance with many artistic styles and objects rather than an in-depth understanding of a few. Consequently, the modern world becomes impersonal, distant, and routine and fails to satisfy the personal and intimate needs of its inhabitants.

To develop this thesis, Simmel distinguished between objective culture and subjective culture. **Objective culture** refers to the external forms of life, such as tools, products, technology, art, language, laws, norms, beliefs, knowledge, values, ideals, and philosophies. The objective culture expands with the increasing freedom, knowledge, and specialization brought about by modernization. **Subjective culture** refers to how individuals absorb, understand, and make use of objective products for personal growth. It comes from the interaction with objective culture, such as in reading a book, writing a paper, or collecting art.

The tragedy of modern culture comes from a contradiction between the objective and subjective. Modernity brings more freedom and innovation to the objective sphere but less ability to appreciate the products of that freedom in the subjective sphere. As is true for the city, modern culture brings so many accomplishments that they overwhelm people. Perhaps a small elite could take advantage of the new opportunities for cultural development, but most members of modern society do not. Instead of learning to truly appreciate art and culture, people focus on spending money and acquiring objects. This insight applies as much to our times as to Simmel's—perhaps more.

The Importance of Numbers: Willingness to Help

Another strand of Simmel's work has had an equally or even more important influence on recent theory and research. Following Simmel's arguments about the importance of numbers, many studies of small groups and organizations have demonstrated how group size shapes social interaction. To illustrate the continuing importance of Simmel's insights, it might be helpful to review one set of studies on group size, helping behavior, and individual effort.

During the 1960s, two social psychologists, Bibb Latané and John Darley, noted how people in cities often ignored serious crimes that occurred around them. In one famous and terrifying example that occurred in 1964, 38 residents of an apartment complex in New York City did nothing in response to the screams of a young women being repeatedly stabbed in an attack by a stranger. In response to this horrible tragedy, many quickly condemned the moral selfishness of modern city residents.

Latané and Darley considered other possibilities. Perhaps the apartment residents assumed that someone else would call the police for help. Or perhaps the residents did not know for certain exactly what the situation involved—it might be a private argument between a couple rather than an attack by a stranger. Latané and Darley reasoned that the large number of people present in the apartment building during an ambiguous and unexpected event allowed each person to place the responsibility for action on someone else.

To Latané and Darley, this reasoning suggested a hypothesis: the larger the size of a group that someone belongs to, the less responsibility a person will feel for what goes on in the immediate surroundings. In large groups—including large cities, where dozens or even hundreds of others may be present—individuals feel little personal responsibility for what occurs around them and will do little to help people in trouble. In smaller groups, people will take more responsibility for their surroundings.

This reasoning very much follows the insights of Simmel, but Latané and Darley also devised an original set of experiments to test this proposition. In one, students agreeing to participate in a study entered an office, where an assistant asked them to wait. The assistant then left to go to the room next door, then turned on a tape recording that sounded like someone falling with a loud crash and a yell. Would the naive subject come to help the apparently injured assistant? When alone, nearly all subjects immediately rushed to help.

In a variation on the experiment, subjects were left in the waiting room with another subject. In the presence of others, fewer subjects provided aid; if one subject did not leave to provide help, the other typically would not. In still other experiments, Latané and Darley found that the more subjects who participated, the less likely it was that any single one would help. The experimental results thus illustrate the diffusion of responsibility to others in ambiguous situations. Group size rather than individual morals affected the action of individuals.

The Importance of Numbers: Social Loafing

Latané extended his experiments on helping behavior to study the effect of group size on human performance. We might expect that, compared to acting alone, persons could increase their efficiency by cooperating with others. Like tiny threads combined into a strong rope, weak individuals could gain strength as members of teams, committees, armies, and other groups. Based on his previous studies of helping behavior, however, Latané suspected that groups might weaken each member's sense of personal responsibility. Individuals might unconsciously reduce the effort they put forth when part of a group. Terms such as *shirking* and *not pulling one's weight* reflect this tendency. Latané expected that group size would increase what he called "social loafing."

In another clever experiment, he asked a group of subjects to scream or clap as loud as they could, and he measured the loudness with a sound meter. Telling subjects that they wanted to know how much noise people make in social settings and how loud they seem to those who hear them, the experimenters encouraged the subjects to be as noisy as possible in their cheering and clapping. Each subject shouted and clapped in the following situations: alone, in a pair, in a foursome, and in a group of six. In each situation, the experimenters kept track of the sound.

The results demonstrated that the sound made by two persons together was less than the sum of the separate sounds of each of those two persons. Similarly, the sound made by four persons was less than the separate sounds of each of those four persons added together, and the sound made by six persons was less than the separate sounds of each of those six persons added together. Simply put, the sound emitted per person declined with the size of the group. These same results emerged when each subject wore headphones to hear the sound of others and when experimenters used machines to record the sound of each subject individual separately. Even when the subjects were offered money for cooperating, the experiments demonstrated lower group effort than the sum of the individual efforts.

Simmel himself would have had little attraction to these types of experimental studies—he preferred to rely on his less scientific and more artistic observations of social life. Still, his sociological impressions have over the years received scientific support in studies like the ones described here. More generally, Simmel's attention to micro-aspects of social life has attracted much sociological interest since the early 1900s, and his insights continue to prove helpful to those pursuing the study of the social forms of everyday life (Scaff 1988:2).

SUMMARY

Simmel's approach contrasted with that of many other early sociologists, who treated groups and societies as things separate from individuals. He wanted to study the social interaction that takes place among individuals within groups and societies, as well as the mutual influence individuals have on one another in daily life. He noted that we cannot see a society or social group but can only see individual people who associate with others in certain ways. We can study society by studying how people interact with one another.

Simmel's reasoning about the importance of social interaction led him to focus on the basic elements of social life—friendship, love, conflict, domination, exchange, art, and city life. He studied aspects of everyday life such as fashion, rules of chess, use of knives at the table, and flirting to shed light on the nature of the larger society. In Simmel's view, study of the small parts provided the means to understand the whole of society.

However, when Simmel looked at the busy, chaotic world around him, he wondered how he could make sense of the infinite complexity it included. His answer noted that, behind the complexity of individual behavior, common patterns and routines exist. Understanding these underlying patterns could organize the tremendous diversity of social life. For example, the interactions between parent and child, teacher and student, boss and employee, police officer and citizen, bureaucrat and client no doubt differ. Yet because the interactions involve persons with unequal power, they contain common characteristics. The same thesis about similarities behind apparent diversity would apply to other social interactions. For example, he described forms of interaction such as conflict and competition.

In aiming to identify the common forms of interaction, Simmel offered an innovative approach to the field of sociology: rather than focusing on a general topic, such as society or social life, sociology should involve more of a special perspective on the topic. In this way, Simmel helped define sociology as a field with its own goals. He also simplified the task of sociology by limiting it to the study of general forms of social interaction rather than to the specific and infinite details of social life.

To illustrate the importance of social forms, Simmel described with insightful detail how social interaction differs across groups of varying size. Regardless of the unique personalities of group members, the sheer number of persons in a group produces similarities in behavior among them. Two-person groups require closeness and trust, since the withdrawal of one member destroys the group. Three-person groups can survive the exit of one member, and therefore they encourage alliances of two members against another. Larger groups, in contrast, involve more formal and less intimate interaction.

Life in cities also reflects the influence of numbers. Large cities throughout the world differ in their location, culture, residents, and history, but according to Simmel all reflect certain tendencies in social interaction. The high population density bombards the senses of city residents. To avoid the mental exhaustion of dealing with the overwhelming commotion of city life, people must screen out or distance themselves from what goes on around them. They therefore tend to ignore much of the surrounding activity and to seem calm and unconcerned when something new or unexpected happens. Further, they tend to deal with others in an impersonal, often unfriendly, manner in order to minimize sensory overload.

Modern life—especially in cities, which are centers of economic activity—is affected by another element: the emergence of money as a means of exchange. Money makes for the efficient exchange of goods and services in society and for growth of income. However, the use of money has implications for social interaction. Money makes interaction more impersonal, as people deal with one another mostly for the purpose of exchanging money for goods and services. Since money also emphasizes intellect and calculation rather than emotion and feeling, people come to think in terms of price rather than in terms of real value.

Simmel described other consequences of modernity. The wealth and diversity of modern society create opportunity for cultural innovation—new ideas, theories, novels, paintings, music, and drama emerge faster than ever before in history. Yet modern society accumulates too much knowledge for persons to assimilate, and modern culture encourages superficial acquaintance with many artistic styles rather than an in-depth understanding of a few. Consequently, the modern world becomes more impersonal and fails to meet the personal and intimate needs of its inhabitants. If people benefit from more freedom and individuality, they also lose the ability to appreciate the products of this freedom and individuality.

Because of the diversity and the originality of Simmel's work, others have had difficulty fully accepting and using his perspective. Scholars have benefited greatly from particular insights Simmel had about social life and enjoy reading his original and sparkling writings. However, unlike Marx, Weber, and Durkheim, Simmel's influence has been isolated and specific rather than unified and broad-based.

DISCUSSION QUESTIONS

1. How did Simmel's attraction to city life affect his personality, interests, and style of scholarship? How did his style of scholarship and Jewish background affect his acceptance by academic colleagues?

2. What changes in Jewish life occurred in Germany and Berlin during the 1800s? Describe the special nature of anti-Semitism in the academic world.

3. How did Simmel differ from other sociologists in his answer to the question of whether scholars can study society as an object separate from individuals? How did Simmel use the concepts of social forms and contents to make sense of the diversity of individual interactions that take place in society?

4. Explain how relationships of domination and subordination involve mutual influence. Give examples of the mutual influence that exists in unequal relationships.

5. What positive consequences for group life emerge from conflict? What group characteristics increase the intensity and seriousness of social conflict, create extreme solidarity, and result in bitterness and hostility?

6. How does social interaction change with group size? Give examples of the kinds of relationships that emerge in dyads, triads, and larger groups.

7. What do people living in large cities do to screen out the overwhelming stimuli they face? Discuss both the costs and benefits of city living.

8. Discuss how reliance on the exchange of money affects individual freedom, social interaction, the importance of intellect over emotion and feeling, and the tempo of life. What attitude did Simmel and others devoted to art and culture have toward money and economics?

9. Compare objective and subjective culture. What contradiction exists between the two in modern societies? Has the contradiction worsened since Simmel's time?

10. How does the size of groups affect the willingness of people to help others in unusual situations? How does size affect performance in groups?

REFERENCES

PRIMARY SOURCES

Simmel, Georg. 1950. *The Sociology of Georg Simmel* (edited & translated by Kurt H. Wolff). Glencoe, IL: Free Press.

Simmel, Georg. 1955. *Conflict and the Web of Group-Affiliations* (edited & translated by Kurt H. Wolff & Reinhard Bendix). New York: Free Press.

Simmel, Georg. 1959. *Georg Simmel, 1858–1918: A Collection of Essays, with Translations and a Bibliography* (edited & translated by Kurt H. Wolff). Columbus: Ohio State University Press.

Simmel, Georg. 1971. *On Individuality and Social Forms* (edited by Donald N. Levine). Chicago: University of Chicago Press.

Simmel, Georg. 1978. *The Philosophy of Money* (translated by Tom Bottomore & David Frisby). London: Routledge & Kegan Paul.

Simmel, Georg. 1984. *On Women, Sexuality, and Love* (edited & translated by Guy Oakes). New Haven, CT: Yale University Press.

SECONDARY SOURCES

Abel, T. 1959. "The Contribution of Georg Simmel: A Reappraisal." *American Sociological Review* 24:473–479.

Ashley, David, & David Michael Orenstein. 1995. *Sociological Theory: Classic Statements* (3d ed.). Boston: Allyn & Bacon.

Cantor, Norman F. 1994. *The Sacred Chain: The History of the Jews.* New York: HarperCollins.

Coser, Lewis A. 1965a. "Georg Simmel." In Lewis A. Coser (Ed.), *Georg Simmel* (pp. 1–28). Englewood Cliffs, NJ: Prentice-Hall.

Coser, Lewis A. 1965b. "The Stranger in the Academy." In Lewis A. Coser (Ed.), *Georg Simmel* (pp. 29–42). Englewood Cliffs, NJ: Prentice-Hall.

Coser, Lewis A. 1977a. *Masters of Sociological Thought* (2nd ed.). San Diego: Harcourt Brace Jovanovich.

Coser, Lewis A. 1977b. "Georg Simmel's Neglected Contributions to the Sociology of Women." *Signs* 2:869–876.

Frisby, David. 1981. *Sociological Impressionism: A Reassessment of Georg Simmel's Social Theory.* London: Heinemann.

Frisby, David. 1992. *Simmel and Since: Essays on Georg Simmel's Social Theory.* London: Routledge.

Gay, Peter. 1978. *Freud, Jews and Other Germans: Masters and Victims in Modernist Culture.* New York: Oxford University Press.

Hunt, Morton. 1985. *Profiles of Social Research: The Scientific Study of Human Interaction.* New York: Russell Sage Foundation.

Latané, Bibb, & John Darley. 1970. *The Unresponsive Bystander: Why Doesn't He Help?* New York: Appleton-Century-Crofts.

Laurence, A. E. 1975. "Georg Simmel: Triumph and Tragedy." *International Journal of Contemporary Sociology* 12:28–48.

Levine, Donald N. 1971. "Introduction." In Donald N. Levine (Ed.), *Georg Simmel: On Individuality and Social Forms* (pp. ix–lxv). Chicago: University of Chicago Press.

Masur, Gerhard. 1970. *Imperial Berlin.* New York: Basic Books.

Nisbet, Robert A. 1966. *The Sociological Tradition.* New York: Basic Books.

Poggi, Gianfranco. 1993. *Money and the Modern Mind: Georg Simmel's Philosophy of Money.* Berkeley: University of California Press.

Ringer, Fritz. 1969. *The Decline of the German Mandarins.* Cambridge, MA: Harvard University Press.

Ritzer, George. 1996. *Sociological Theory* (4th ed.). New York: McGraw-Hill.

Scaff, L. A. 1988. "Weber, Simmel and the Sociology of Culture." *Sociological Review* 36:1–30.

Spykman, Nicholas J. 1964 [1925]. *The Social Theory of Georg Simmel.* New York: Russell & Russell.

Turner, Brian S. 1992. *Max Weber: From History to Modernity.* London: Routledge.

Vromen, S. 1987. "Georg Simmel and the Cultural Dilemma of Women." *History of European Ideas* 8:563–579.

Wolff, Kurt H. 1950. "Introduction." In *The Sociology of Georg Simmel* (pp. xvii–lxiv). Glencoe, IL: Free Press.

REFERENCE NOTES

Citations for quotations and special points of interest are given in the text. Listed here are citations to sources for major topics covered in each section of the chapter. "Impressions of Everyday Life" reflects Frisby's (1981) book title, *Sociological Impressionism.*

1. The Attractions of City Life: Simmel in Berlin (Coser 1965a:1–2; Coser 1977a:195; Poggi 1993:39; Scaff 1988:5); Family (Frisby 1981:14; Coser 1965a:1); Gustav Graef (Scaff 1988:4); Gertrude Kinel (Scaff 1988:5); German scholarship (Poggi 1993:15; Coser 1965a:3); Simmel's studies (Scaff 1988:4); Dissertation (Levine 1971:xi); Paternal grandfather (Laurence 1975:33); Father (Laurence 1975:32); Baptism (Wolff 1950:xlii); Simmel's religious ties (Wolff 1950:xlii); Anti-Semitism (Gay 1978:98, 114; Poggi 1993:42); Simmel's job (Levine 1971:xi; Ringer 1969:37; Poggi 1993:39); Inheritance (Wolff 1950:xviii).

2. Jewish Life in Germany: Berlin (Poggi 1993:33–36; Coser 1977a: 203–204; Masur 1970:63, 73); Berlin culture (Poggi 1993:35); Berlin Jewish life (Gay 1978:172; Masur 1970:110); Jewish mobility (Cantor 1994:232, 234, 237, 241, 244; Masur 1970:117); Labor union movements (Cantor 1994:273); Jewish loyalty (Cantor 1994:241, 248); Religious tensions (Cantor 1994:310–311); Fluctuations in interest rates (Masur 1970:75); Jewish migration (Gay 1978:187); German academic traditionalism (Ringer 1969:1–3, 9); Extreme anti-Semitism (Masur 1970:112; Gay 1978:101,106; Poggi 1993:43); Later genocide (Gay 1978:162).

3. Sociology and Social Forms: Early career (Coser 1965a:2–3; Laurence 1975:35; Levine 1971:xiii); Teaching (Coser 1965b:33; Laurence 1975:34–36; Coser 1965a:2; Coser 1977a:196); Critics (Coser 1965b:32); "The Problem of Sociology" (Simmel 1971:23–35; Poggi 1993:48); Simmel on Comte and Spencer (Abel 1959:474); Define society (Frisby 1981:40; Abel 1959:474); Social interaction (Frisby 1981:14, 40, 95; Spykman 1964:27; Coser 1965a:5; Nisbet 1966:97; Levine 1971:xxvii, xxxvii); Unity of society (Frisby 1981:96; Turner 1992:165); Actively interpret reality (Coser 1977a:202; Levine 1971:xxxii); Social forms (Poggi 1993:49; Levine 1971:xxiv; Spykman 1964:32; Frisby 1981:52; Coser 1965a:7).

4. Forms of Domination and Conflict: Professional rejection (Coser 1965a:3; Coser 1965b:30); Strong recommendations (Ashley & Orenstein 1995:306); Academic anti-Semitism (Poggi 1993:41; Gay 1978:122); Threat to other scholars (Coser 1977a:195; Poggi 1993:44–45; Ashley & Orenstein 1995:307); Unconventional style (Poggi 1993:44; Frisby 1981:69; Coser 1965b:31–32); Domination and submission (Simmel 1971:96–120); Conflict (Simmel 1955:13–123).

5. The Consequences of Group Size: Response to failures (Laurence 1975:45; Frisby 1981:30; Coser 1965b:35; Coser 1977a:207); Art and culture (Frisby 1981:27); Support for women (Frisby 1981:28; Coser 1977b:872; Vromen 1987; Simmel 1984:65–101); Refused presidency (Frisby 1981:26); Stopped attending (Frisby 1981:27); Dyads, triads, and group size (Simmel 1950:118–180); "Metropolis and Mental Life" (Simmel 1971:324–339).

6. Money in Modern Social Life: Cultural elite (Poggi 1993:17, 53; Ashley & Orenstein 1995:309; Coser 1977a:206–208); Simmel's home (Laurence 1975:37; Frisby 1981:20; Vromen 1987:572); Discussion groups (Coser 1977a:196–197); *Philosophy of Money* (Frisby 1981:106; Poggi 1993:132–212; Spykman 1964:219–256; Simmel 1978).

7. Simmel's Legacy: New job (Frisby 1981:29; Laurence 1975:34, 41; Ashley & Orenstein 1995:307; Frisby 1981:31); Gertrude Kantorowicz (Laurence 1975:40); War (Ashley & Orenstein 1995:307); Disillusion (Wolff 1950:xxii); Cancer (Wolff 1950:xxiii); Widow and son (Laurence 1975:46); Preceded Weber in his interest (Ashley & Orenstein 1995:307); Modern culture (Poggi 1993:164, 195; Nisbet 1966:217; Ritzer 1996:278); Subjective culture (Levine 1971:xix); Contradiction (Simmel 1971:338; Poggi 1993:53); Helping behavior (Latané & Darley 1970); Group size and human performance (Hunt 1985;155–199).

chapter 5

Uniting Self and Society:
George Herbert Mead
and Symbolic Interaction

In everyday life, people tend to take an individualist or psychological view of the causes of social behavior. Think of your close family members or best friends. According to an individualist view, each brings a unique personality and individual set of behaviors to the family or friendship group, and the individual traits of each member combine with those of other members to create a group. Although part of a family or group, we still think of ourselves as separate from the other people that belong to it, distinguishing our own traits, selves, and beliefs from the groups and social world around us.

At the extreme, this kind of thinking—this sense of separation from others, groups, and the larger community—contributes to selfishness: each person should worry about his or her own problems, and let others worry about their own problems. People sometimes seem excessively concerned about their own ambitions, possessions, and self-esteem, seeing others as competitors or obstructions to their own goals. Individualism can thus lessen the attention we give to the social community and its needs.

In fact, our selves are merged more closely with social groups than we might think. Even when alone, our thinking often takes the form of internal conversation: "Should I study more or go out? I need to do well on this exam, but my friends are having a special party. I really like this class, but I hate to miss time with my friends." Thinking as internal conversation can similarly involve self-evaluations: "Why did I go to that party instead of studying? That was stupid"; or "I may not do well on the exam, but my friends really like me." This thinking relies on language and meanings that we learn from others. Therefore, our thinking and sense of self become possible only through interaction in social situations.

Early sociologists did not fully consider the implications of these sorts of internal conversations. They stressed the importance of social life and rejected psychological views, but they had not examined the role of language and social communication in the emergence of individual thinking and selfhood. George Herbert Mead, an American sociologist during the early twentieth century, took the next logical step of connecting society to our innermost thoughts. In so doing, he not only helped highlight the differences between psychology and sociology but also contributed to the founding of a school of sociological thought that focuses on the communication of individuals in social interaction.

Perhaps most important to Mead himself, he developed a perspective that emphasizes community action to fight social problems. Mead grew up in the late nineteenth century with a strong religious background that instilled in him a desire to improve the world. Beyond devoting his scholarly life to understanding how the individual relates to society and how society shapes individual selves and thinking, he committed much of his time to working with groups concerned with remedies for the social problems of cities.

Consistent with his goals for social reform, Mead's theories emphasize the connection between the individual and the community: the intimate ties of the individual mind and self to the larger group and community make social interaction crucial to understanding human life. We need to understand how human thinking consists of internal conversation and emerges from the use of language, words, and other symbols that we learn from interacting with others. Similarly, we need to understand how humans treat their own selves as objects in internal conversion and how human selves emerge from taking the viewpoint of others during social interaction.

Mead's attention to symbols and interaction directed sociologists to the in-depth study of the social meanings that people construct in everyday life. Building on Mead's insights, sociologists developed a particularly American theory of social life—termed *symbolic interactionism*—that emphasizes the importance of using symbols to communicate in social interaction. This theory, which has had much influence on sociology since Mead's time, offers a perspective on the social world that usefully complements the ideas of the classic European sociologists.

1. RELIGIOUS GOALS TRANSFORMED INTO SOCIAL ACTION

After graduating from college in 1883 at the young age of 20, George Herbert Mead had trouble settling on a career, feeling himself pulled in two directions. On one hand, he wanted to work with and help people. Since social work at that time involved Christian acts of goodness, a career of helping humanity seemed to require religious faith and an occupation as a minister. Indeed, Mead believed that "Christianity is the only power capable of grappling with evil as it exists now" (Shalin 1991:27). However, he also believed that he himself could not follow the Christian faith fully and that the doubts he had about God and Christianity made him unsuited for the ministry and the traditional means of helping people.

On the other hand, Mead loved ideas and philosophy. But although he might find teaching philosophy personally rewarding, it would not satisfy his desire to help others—it seemed selfish to concern himself with abstract speculation about the nature of existence and the sources of knowledge when other people faced daily problems of sickness, poverty, and misery. Besides, philosophy in the late 1800s in the United States could offer employment to only a select few: rather than philosophy, theology dominated in the many religious colleges of the United States, where most professors taught religion to future ministers.

Mead's dilemma reflected that of many other young American men and women of his generation. Because they spanned America's shift from a rural and religious nation to an industrial and increasingly secular nation, those born between 1854 and 1874 faced new and special conflicts. Raised in households dominated by the strict Puritanism of early America, with its strong religious and moral values, they developed a strong sense of right and wrong and a stern conscience.

As they reached adulthood, however, many members of Mead's generation experienced the declining importance of religion in a modernizing, industrializing America. In a world where the "ministry no longer seemed intellectually respectable" (Crunden 1982:ix), they resisted pressures from older generations to become ministers or missionaries; yet they lacked an outlet for the strong moral beliefs they had adopted as children, which created periods of doubt, conflict, depression, and wandering. Eventually, they found ways to channel their energy into new professions such as social work, journalism, higher education, and politics. In this way, they could apply Christian ideals to an increasingly nonreligious, or secular, world.

A Religious Childhood

Mead's life closely fit the model of his generation. Born in 1863 in Massachusetts, the center of Puritan religious life, he was descended from a long line of ministers. Seven years later, he moved with his family to Oberlin, Ohio, where his minister father had taken a job teaching at the theological seminary of Oberlin College. The family settled into a house on Elm Street that today houses local college students.

Mead impressed others as a "cautious, mild-mannered, kind-hearted, rather quiet boy. Apparently, he took life more seriously than do most children" (Miller 1973:xii). Some might have even described Mead as "painfully shy and withdrawn" (Crunden 1982:36). As he grew older, Mead's parents no doubt took pride in their serious and well-behaved son, who exhibited little in the way of teenage rebellion. They likely would have expected him to follow his father into the ministry.

Along with his good behavior and industriousness, Mead's intelligence allowed him to enter Oberlin College in 1879 at age 16, where he found the same kind of New England Puritanism and piety that he found at home. One visitor said, "If anyone walking along the sidewalks of Oberlin catches his foot and stumbles, nine chances out of ten, he stumbles into a prayer meeting" (Crunden 1982:7). Evangelism was as much a part of college life as meals and coursework.

Both the coursework and social life of Oberlin students reflected the conservative Protestant beliefs of the college's leaders. The courses on classics, rhetoric, literature, and ethics discouraged questioning and debate, instead emphasizing learning and memorizing truths consistent with Christian theology. Socially, Oberlin College did not allow dancing or drinking, and many students even joined the Anti-Saloon League—a group founded in Oberlin and dedicated to stopping the evils of alcohol. To prevent socializing between male and female students—and temptations toward dancing, drinking, and sexual intimacy—the library maintained separate hours for men and women.

Still living at home and personally straight-laced, Mead felt little attraction to these temptations. He did, however, discover a stimulating new mixture of traditional religion and progressive social ideas. At Oberlin, religious piety coexisted with a tradition of social activism and liberal politics. It had been a station on the Underground Railroad that helped escaped slaves get to freedom in Canada and was one of the first colleges to admit blacks. Similarly reflecting progressive ideas, it was the first college to grant bachelor's degrees to both men and women.

At the same time that he was encountering a version of Christianity that emphasized community service along with personal piety, Mead became acquainted with new developments in the natural sciences. In particular, Darwin's work on the evolution of species confronted Mead and others with a version of creation that challenged Christian scripture. Despite the narrow theology they had learned at home and in many classes, intelligent students like Mead found the recent discoveries of natural science exciting. This exposure to scientific knowledge led Mead and many others to reject the primarily religious fare offered in college.

The emphasis on the goal of social betterment and the findings of modern science created religious questions and doubt in Mead and his best friend in college, Henry Castle. In their discussions about life, God, poetry, and evolution, the two friends came to favor modern secular beliefs over religious doctrines, yet Mead did so with sadness rather than confidence. He felt the loss of meaning in a world that did not rely on complete acceptance of the Christian God. Without faith in the beliefs of Christianity, how could he live a moral and meaningful life? To what goals besides selfish pleasure could he devote his life?

A Secular Adulthood

As these questions occupied Mead during his college years, he faced another crisis. In 1881, about midway through his undergraduate education, his father died. Left with little in the way of savings or inheritance, his mother had to sell the house and move her family into rented rooms. To earn income, she also began to teach classes part time at Oberlin. Mead helped financially by waiting tables to help pay for college and even spent one summer as a door-to-door book salesman. For someone as painfully shy as Mead, these jobs must have been difficult. However, keeping busy with both work and studies, he no longer had time to agonize over the meaning of his life.

On graduating from college, he again had to confront his questions about religion and his dilemma about a career. Despite some hopes of starting a literary paper, he decided he had best start earning money immediately to help support his mother. He first worked for four months as a schoolteacher, but left because of the students' misbehavior and lack of interest in learning; he later worked as a surveyor for a railroad in Minnesota and Canada, augmenting this by doing private tutoring during the winter months. Although his hard work and carefulness impressed Mead's supervisors, neither surveying nor tutoring offered a satisfactory lifelong career.

During these four years of work after graduation, Mead read widely during his spare time—and worried constantly about choosing a profession. He wished fervently for some security and certainty in his life and goals, but having failed to find a meaningful substitute for his lost religious faith, he felt useless and unable to do good in the world. He also felt the lack of intellectual stimulation and an outlet for his energetic mind.

By keeping him outdoors and active, surveying somewhat lightened his worries about the future. When he had time to reflect, however, he felt empty. Writing to Henry Castle, he said, "I seem so far off from anything worth living for, and I do not see that I ... can reach anything better. My life is ... without purpose" (Crunden 1982:32). Similarly, "I see no prospect of success or pleasure in any field. I am discontented, disappointed, disgusted with myself" (Crunden 1982:32). His doubts and sadness resulted in anxieties about his health: he worried obsessively about getting kidney disease and diabetes.

Disgusted with his life, but unsure of how to improve it, Mead simply decided in 1887 to try something different. His friend Henry Castle had been admitted to the graduate program in philosophy at Harvard University. Mead still did not view philosophy as an acceptable calling—it would not satisfy his need to help others—but Castle persuaded him to give graduate school a try. They could live as roommates and continue their philosophical discussions—which certainly sounded better than continuing his depressing life as a surveyor.

Once at Harvard, Mead managed to support himself with part-time work and to do well in his courses. As expected, he found his philosophy courses stimulating but too abstract and isolated from the real world for his taste. And the exposure to advanced philosophy further eroded his remaining Christian beliefs, without offering a satisfying alternative to the Christian tradition of good works for humanity.

Perhaps surprisingly, he decided to study the physiological basis of psychology. A branch of philosophy in those days, psychology seemed more practical and scientific to Mead than the obscure thought of many of the philosophers he studied. By relying more on observation of the world than on abstract and isolated reasoning, psychology allowed him to avoid the still-painful philosophical debates about Christian beliefs. Mead thought that, as a physiological psychologist, he could continue to hold his nonreligious beliefs without becoming a threat to any church-controlled college where he might teach.

Models of Reform

For his second year of graduate study, Mead won a scholarship to study in Germany, the location of the world's most renowned specialists in physiological psychology. Finding the academic environment in Germany stimulating, he planned to write an ambitious dissertation on the concept of space that one of Georg Simmel's teachers and colleagues at the University of Berlin would supervise. However, Mead never finished the dissertation and never completed his doctorate. In 1891, he ended his graduate training early to accept a position at the University of Michigan teaching philosophy and psychology.

Two experiences in Germany affected Mead's life in more important ways than did his graduate studies. First, Henry Castle brought his sister Helene with him to Germany to visit Mead. Over several months, Helene and Mead became close, eventually marrying in October 1891, just before returning to the United States for him to begin teaching.

Second, Mead observed social reform programs in Germany that he thought could improve life in the United States. The new German social security program for disability and retirement, the fair-minded negotiations over wages between German workers and employers, and the growing power of the German Social Democratic party in representing workers all impressed Mead. He noted the contrast between these practices in Germany and the resistance to socialism, social reform, and state involvement in the economy in the United States.

Mead brimmed with enthusiasm about bringing these reforms home. He thought local efforts to devise social programs on behalf of workers and the needy could provide a nonreligious outlet for his desires to help people. Mead's enthusiasm even led him to propose a plan to Henry Castle; together, they would gain control of a newspaper in an

American city—say, Minneapolis—and use it to crusade for the kind of social reforms they had observed in Germany. Castle, however, found the plan unrealistic and refused to involve himself. Mead also dropped the plan—but not his enthusiasm for social reform.

Mead began to realize, however, that an academic career could allow him to combine his concerns with both ideas and moral reform. Although he still felt conflict between his desire to help humanity and his interest in academics, his experiences first at the University of Michigan and soon after at the University of Chicago offered a solution to his dilemma. By combining philosophical thinking with social action and reform, Mead would discover a purpose for his life. In so doing, he would also contribute to the growth of sociology and its intellectual respectability in the United States.

2. THREATS TO AMERICAN VALUES: CHICAGO AND THE GROWTH OF CITIES

Given his American background, Mead's experiences as a young man differed greatly from those of the Europeans who helped found sociology. From its beginnings as an independent nation, the United States had differed from European nations in its principles and institutions. Unlike Europe, America had no history of feudal structures with a monarchy, an aristocracy, and serfdom. Indeed, suspicious of the potential for the abuse of power by monarchs, the founding fathers had devised a new system of government that provided constitutional checks and balances on the use of power by its leaders; the Bill of Rights especially aimed to protect individual rights against the force of the government.

Consistent with the founding principles to limit state power, Americans strongly adhered to the values of liberty, equality, and individualism, and they showed less obedience to political authority and less respect to their social superiors than Europeans. Combined with the availability of vast natural resources, these values of freedom and individual effort contributed to the development of a form of market capitalism relatively free from government control.

Consequences of American Values

American values had other consequences beyond contributing to the economic growth of the new nation. Whereas socialist movements had gained sufficient influence in Europe to promote social welfare programs targeted to deprived workers, the American worker movement did not. After periods of struggle, European nations had come to accept the responsibility of the government to provide work, food, housing, and financial aid. In contrast, all male citizens in the United States, including the poor and the propertyless, had received the vote without the kind of class struggle that occurred in England, France, and Germany. Partly as a result, American policy during the nineteenth century promoted individual accomplishment through education rather than class equality through government social protection.

Along with its unusually democratic and egalitarian politics, America differed from European nations in the devotion of its citizens to Christianity. Alexis de Tocqueville, the famous French observer of early nineteenth-century America, wrote, "There is no country in the world where the Christian religion retains a greater influence over the souls of men than in America" (in Lipset 1996:62). Because America had no official state religion, as in England and France, many settlers came to the United States to practice their religion in freedom. The devotion to religious freedom and the variety of religious denominations to choose from made for high levels of church attendance and daily concern with following the Bible.

Because of their religious devotion, Americans seemed moralistic to many European observers. Moralists tend to view differences and conflict in terms of principles of right and wrong rather than in terms of economic interests; in political debates, therefore, Americans tended to treat their opponents as immoral and evil and their own side as virtuous and moral. For example, "A key element in the conflicts that culminated in the Civil War was the tendency of both sides to view the other as essentially sinful, as an agent of the Devil" (Lipset 1996:65). During the decades after the Civil War, the period when Mead grew up, religion may have lost some of its influence, but American moralism remained strong.

In important ways, the nation responded to problems brought on by the fast growth of industry, immigration, and cities as threats to its traditional values. Industrialization made some segments of the population enormously wealthy but also heightened inequality between workers and employers. High rates of immigration, initially from Germany and Ireland and later from Eastern and Southern Europe, created new cultural diversity and conflict. Sudden urbanization produced overcrowded and filthy slums, without running water and bathing facilities; the poor and immigrant residents of growing cities faced smallpox, cholera, tuberculosis, and scarlet fever because of the unsanitary living conditions.

These problems and changes disturbed American political and religious leaders. In political terms, these changes widened the gap between democratic ideals and American reality. American values of equality required participation of all citizens in the civic life of the community and its democratic activities, yet poorly educated workers and illiterate immigrants threatened the ideal of popular democracy. Rather than advocating socialism as in Europe, however, Americans suggested that a solution to these problems would come from social reform and greater democratic participation: regulation rather than replacement of capitalism, and improvement rather than rejection of democracy, would make the country better.

The Growth of Chicago

Perhaps no city typified the changes occurring in the United States during the last half of the nineteenth century more than Chicago—soon to become Mead's home for the rest of his life. Although never as large or important as New York City, Chicago grew faster and became modern more quickly than any other city in the United States. Consisting of only a single log fort in 1833, Chicago had a population of 300,000 by 1871.

Even greater growth would come in the next several decades. In 1871, the famous Chicago fire destroyed the center of the city, left 90,000 people homeless, and killed 300. It was "the greatest natural disaster up to that time in American history" (Miller 1996:15). Yet within two decades, Chicago's inhabitants had rebuilt the city. It had the busiest and most carefully planned downtown in the country, the nation's tallest building (12 stories), and dozens of other modern structures. Chicagoans took civic pride in the amazing accomplishments that had emerged from the destruction of the fire, believing that the growth of their city revealed the benefits of focusing on the future rather than the past.

Chicagoans also exhibited a confidence that hard work and ingenuity would allow them to overcome and control nature. "Built on a windswept prairie marsh—a place so forbidding the Miami Indians refused to settle on it—modern Chicago was a triumph of engineering over nature's constraints" (Miller 1996:18). Chicagoans, like Americans more generally, believed that they could surmount any obstacle nature or humanity could put in its way. Employing new technologies, engineers managed to create drainage systems for the marsh, pump in fresh water, pump out sewage, and build shipping canals, while architects developed innovative new designs for buildings that would house the growing population and business activity.

Chicago soon became a center of commerce and moneymaking. Wealth came initially from the city's links to the rich resources of the agricultural Midwest. Rivers and canals connected Chicago to the vast forests, farmland, and grazing prairies to the west, and its Lake Michigan harbor connected the city to ports on the East Coast and mineral-rich areas to the north. It became the world's biggest livestock and grain market as well as railroad center. Capitalists made millions as the owners of meat stockyards and packing plants (Philip Armour), railroad cars used for sleeping and dining (George Pullman), and department stores (Marshall Field).

The fast-growing city also attracted immigrants to fill the many unskilled and low-paying jobs available in the factories and stockyards. By 1890, 70 percent of the Chicago population had two foreign-born parents. Brawls occurred between Irish, Italian, and Polish Catholic immigrants and resentful Protestants who distrusted the newcomers. Similarly, Russian and Polish Jewish immigrants, who still wore the long beards, long black coats, and broad-brimmed hats of their homeland, faced beatings and harassment by local street toughs.

With all its accomplishments and growth, however, came chaos: Chicago was "a sprawling spectacle of smoke and disorder" (Miller 1996:19). With wealth came poverty, with modern downtown buildings came nearby slums, with beautiful parks and streets came ugly factories, with commerce came greed and selfishness among business leaders, and with power came corruption among politicians. "Chicago was the site of some of the greatest achievements and failures of American urban life" (Miller 1996:19).

Vice, Corruption, and Violence

Problems of vice appeared in the widespread and open practice of prostitution in certain parts of the city. One reporter visiting from London wrote, "Chicago makes a more amazingly open display of evil than any other city known to me" (Miller 1996:508). In one section, called Hell's Half Acre, almost every building was a saloon, bordello, or dice parlor. Many young single women who came to Chicago from rural areas and small towns to look for work and a more exciting life found that selling sex was not illegal and was viewed by many as a necessary evil. Not until 1900 did reformers mount a campaign to outlaw prostitution.

In politics, a spoils system developed, whereby the victorious mayor and members of the city council would reward supporters with government jobs. Owing their job to politicians, government employees worked harder for their candidates than for the community as a whole. They ignored conditions of the slums and factory sweatshops but would take bribes to help local businessmen and to further improve the already-impressive downtown.

Given this corruption, election day always brought excitement to the city. With about half of the city's polling places in saloons, men could win free drinks with their vote. Both Republicans and Democrats rounded up drifters, drunks, and flophouse residents, then gave them lists of false names and addresses to use while voting throughout the city. The next day they paid them 50 cents for each vote. With many residents voting early and often, it was not unusual to find ballots from George Washington, Thomas Jefferson, and Abraham Lincoln. Further, gangs representing each party would threaten opposition voters with violence; riots, stabbings, shootings, and fights occurred often, with one politician saying that "you had to have a fist like a ham in those days" (Miller 1996:467).

Conflict and struggle also existed between employers and a small but growing labor movement, and in 1886 the nation's most violent confrontation between workers and the police occurred in Chicago. During a strike for an eight-hour day, a scuffle between strikers and replacement workers in one Chicago factory led to the shooting deaths of two strikers by police. Labor leaders called for a demonstration the next day at Haymarket Square, where, during a confrontation between police and about 2,500 demonstrators, a bomb exploded in the front ranks of the police. The police began firing, and some demonstrators returned fire. A few minutes of wild carnage ended with 7 policemen killed and 60 injured; probably about the same number of casualties occurred among the demonstrators.

Although they could not identify or catch the bomb-thrower, police and prosecutors, supported by vengeful citizens, arrested eight leaders of the Chicago anarchist movement, who were convicted by a jury and judge already convinced of their guilt before the trail began. Four were hung, one committed suicide, and three went to prison. Both the killing of the police and the disgraceful trial generated debate and divisions throughout the country. One historian wrote, "The Haymarket tragedy was the central symbolic event for [a] generation of reformers ... convincing them that class division threatened the very fabric of the American Republic" (Miller 1996:481). Even Friedrich Engels, following the events from England, wrote, "I only wish Marx could have lived to see it! The breaking out of class war in America" (Miller 1996:481).

These problems, exemplified in Chicago but also existing in other U.S. cities, conflicted with the American values of equality and democracy. It led in the late 1800s to the early 1900s to a desire to solve the problems of American life. A new generation of reformers accepted America's traditional goals but rejected the traditional religious and conservative means of reaching them. Both sociology as a field of study and Mead as a social theorist would emerge from this environment of social reform and idealism.

3. COMBINING LEARNING AND PROBLEM-SOLVING

As a young professor at the University of Michigan, Mead began to develop the purpose in life he had been seeking. The idea that he could combine scholarship and social action, although first emerging in Germany, took concrete form in one of his colleagues at Ann Arbor. Another young philosopher, John Dewey, provided a role model for Mead by uniting the two pursuits of social involvement and academic success.

Academically, Dewey had published his first book at age 27 and his next at age 29 (Strauss 1964:ix). He would produce over his long life a large and wide-ranging set of writings and gain notable influence in the academic community with his ideas and ability to lead. At the same time, he wanted to make his opinions known to the general public and convince them to adopt his liberal goals of social reform. Through a series of popular books, he became the country's most well-known philosopher, tirelessly advocating for citizen participation in democratic affairs, creative efforts to solve social problems, and the use of modern educational methods to prepare young people to become intelligent, imaginative, and active citizens.

Mead and Dewey immediately recognized their close interests and became lifelong friends. In long discussions, they found that they possessed complementary skills. Dewey had a broad vision of how to apply his ideas to a wide range of topics, as well as a facility for quick writing to publicize these ideas. More careful and less prone to publish quickly, Mead offered greater depth and precision in his ideas than Dewey. Together, they reinforced each other's desire to combine the two pursuits of political action and academic research.

In 1893, one year after Mead had joined Dewey at the University of Michigan, Dewey received an offer to become the chair of the department of philosophy at the University of Chicago; he accepted under the condition that he could hire Mead. Although Mead had never finished his doctoral dissertation and had yet to publish anything of significance, Dewey's influence and high regard for his colleague also helped Mead get a promotion from lecturer to assistant professor at Chicago.

A New University

The University of Chicago offered an exciting intellectual environment for the two young philosophers. Using some of the millions earned from his oil company, John D. Rockefeller, along with several rich Chicago industrialists, had contributed funds to the founding of a new university, one they hoped could compete with older eastern universities such as Harvard, Yale, and Princeton. Convinced that the university would do best in a city where it could focus on both scholarship and moral reform, Rockefeller agreed to locate the new university in Hyde Park, an exclusive neighborhood near the shore of Lake Michigan and south of downtown Chicago.

To help create a great university, the founders appointed William Rainey Harper, a professor of Bible at Yale University, as the first president of the University of Chicago. A child genius who had obtained his Ph.D. at the remarkably young age of 18, Harper worked with extraordinary energy to create a world-class university almost overnight. Rising at dawn, and taking cat naps in his office chair between endless cups of coffee, he worked at a ferocious pace well past midnight.

Traveling across the country to recruit faculty members, Harper promised light teaching loads and double their current salary to those he wanted to hire. Harper's deliberate raiding of other universities for their best scholars created ill will; from their viewpoint, he swooped down like a marauding hawk to steal faculty away. Yet by 1892, the opening year of the University of Chicago, the method had already created a renowned faculty. In the following years, Harper continued in his efforts by adding Dewey, Mead, and many other superb scholars to the university.

Although devoted to teaching and scholarship, faculty at the University of Chicago involved themselves in community service more than their counterparts at most other universities. If the university could share the benefits of scholarship and culture with the less educated, it would contribute to the spread of democracy in America and serve the needs of humanity—this was the university's prevailing philosophy. The obvious problems of poverty, illiteracy, and corruption in Chicago provided the opportunity for the university to become involved with the local community. The university thus offered extension classes for community residents, many faculty studied community problems, and university leaders supported city reforms.

Influenced strongly by Dewey and the environment of the University of Chicago, Mead began to evolve a philosophy of social life that combined service and academics, thus bringing the focus and purpose to his life that he had been seeking since his college days. The philosophy aimed to combine (1) thought and action, (2) science and progress, and (3) the individual and community.

Thought and Action

In somewhat different ways, Dewey and Mead both began to draw out the implications of a strand of philosophy that had been founded in the United States. This philosophical school, called **pragmatism**, provides an intellectual justification for social action, therefore meshing nicely with the American respect for problem-solving, progress, and democracy.

In essence, pragmatism extends the scientific methods of the natural sciences to all areas of intellectual life. Science tests ideas and theories by matching the outcomes of experiments to predictions made by more general ideas and theories. The theories that best match experimental observations receive tentative support. According to pragmatism, philosophy should proceed in a similar way. All ideas and theories can be tested in the real world for their consequences; those that make society better, help solve problems, and work in real life are judged valid. In pragmatism, "the meaning of a concept resides wholly in the practical effects that might follow from holding the concept" (Levine 1995:254).

Unlike many philosophers, Mead rejected isolated thinking as a means of answering questions about life, ethics, and knowledge. Rather than settling philosophical arguments with verbal debates, book reading, or pure reason, Mead and other American philosophers thought that all ideas could be tested in the real world for their consequences; actions by people rather than thought and logic alone can identify the truth of ideas. This distinctly American philosophy thus focuses on the concrete and practical concerns of social and personal progress. Philosophy must test ideas in the real world, and truth must come through both thought and action.

For example, is the statement "God exists" true? Despite centuries of religious and philosophical debate, logic and thought alone have not been able to answer this question. Pragmatists would translate the statement into another form, asking how the belief affects our lives. Does the belief in God make for a better society, encourage moral action, or improve the adjustment and happiness of people? The real consequences of a belief in God would thus become the core of philosophical inquiry. In this way, pragmatism makes action and the consequences of action part of thought and philosophy.

Mead and other pragmatists further realized that truth can vary with the diverse circumstances of the modern world. If actions by people define the truth of ideas, this means that multiple truths exist. People in different situations view reality according to their own problems and devise their own set of actions; people facing different problems require different solutions and define different truths. The truth of the belief that God exists depends on how that belief affects the lives of individuals and groups, and this might differ for, say, small farming societies and large modern societies.

Note that pragmatism fits "the rough-and-ready ethic of American settlers who were concerned with practical problems of taming a new land" (Baldwin 1986:22). This philosophy of action involves individual and social efforts to overcome problems and address uncertainty in the world, optimistically claiming that careful attention to the practical consequences of ideas could solve the personal and social problems of the country. Pragmatism both met Mead's desire to improve the world and offered an intellectual justification for his goal of social reform.

Science and Progress

Dewey and Mead's pragmatism confidently accepted the unity of science and progress much as it accepted the unity of thought and action. They believed that science provides a clearly defined and effective way to test ideas about how to improve the future. Rather than relying on guesses or biases as guides for personal and social action, citizens in a democracy can rely on scientific evaluation of what works. Applied to education, for example, teachers can act like scientists in evaluating new learning programs, selecting the most useful ones, and continually changing them to best help their students.

Progress through the use of reason and science offered a substitute for the evangelism of Mead's youth. By themselves, Christian ideas had little meaning for him—they had to be put into action by the community to become valuable. Unreasoning faith, isolated prayer, and lonely contemplation had little value to society according to Mead; science and democratic social action, however, could give a nonreligious meaning to life. Where evangelism aims to change the heart of individuals as a means of improving society, science offers a socially based source of progress.

Darwin's theory of evolution strongly influenced Mead's thinking on science and progress. Much as it applies to species, evolution applies to social organization and societies. Mead wrote, "Evolution is the process of meeting and solving problems" (Ritzer 1996:380). At the societal level, members of groups, communities, and societies cooperating with one another can identify problems, propose and test solutions, and implement new forms of social action. Social groups can consequently enjoy steady movement toward more freedom and fewer social problems.

Evolutionary ideas also apply to individuals in Mead's thinking. Like scientists, individuals can use their intelligence to adjust to the problems they face in everyday life. In trying to deal with a poor neighborhood school, for example, parents can reflect on available choices for action, consult the scientific studies on schooling, and select what appears to be the best course of action. Having acted, they can also observe the consequences of their action and change their behavior accordingly. Although people have always changed to some degree through trial-and-error, modern methods of science allow adjustment and change to occur more quickly and efficiently.

Mead's optimistic belief in scientific rationality as a means toward progress contrasted with the ideas of those who viewed the future with pessimism and concern. Mead did not crudely equate progress with more money and greater success, but rather with greater individual freedom, more effective democracy, and better cooperation within communities. Whereas some thinkers believed modern progress destroyed many of the traditional sources of meaning in life, Mead shared the confidence of many Americans that, through the use of science and intelligence, the future would get better.

Individual and Community

Mead's emerging pragmatic philosophy took an additional step to integrate the individual with the community or society. Since he hoped for both individual freedom and community cooperation, he rejected viewpoints that treated individuals as separate and independent from society. Instead, he wanted to treat individuals as integral parts of community social life. The closer the ties between individuals and society, the greater the justification for the involvement of individuals in working toward social betterment. If we are as much members of communities as individuals, how can we reject community closeness in favor of selfish individualism?

Whereas philosophers in the past had argued about the primacy of the individual versus the primacy of society, Mead wanted to give equal importance to both. On one hand, society emerges from individuals, who use language to communicate and interact with one another. On the other hand, because individuals enter into and emerge as social adults through their experiences in society, they are social beings. Mead (1934:6) wrote, "The behavior of the individual can be understood only in terms of the behavior of the whole social group." In his work to come, he would build on the insight that the individual and society cannot be separated as competing influences on behavior.

4. A SOCIAL VERSION OF BEHAVIORISM

Mead made an immediate impression on students and faculty at the University of Chicago. He stood over 6 feet tall, weighed about 200 pounds, and sported a magnificent mustache and goatee. To keep active, he jogged around the campus and rode a bicycle to work—both eccentric behaviors at the time. On seeing Mead enter his office building in jogging clothes, a security officer once had him arrested as a suspected burglar. Despite his imposing size and eccentricities, however, he looked and acted friendly; his kind, cheerful, steady, soft-spoken, and modest manner made him well liked by both faculty and students.

He also impressed others with his encyclopedic knowledge and the enormous range of topics his classes covered. He taught courses on the history of philosophy, ethics, Hegel, physiology, biology, and logic—he even taught a course on the philosophical implications of Einstein's theory of relativity. Most important, though, soon after coming to Chicago he began teaching a course on social psychology that reflected his emerging ideas about social behavior.

Mead as a Teacher and Writer

As a teacher, Mead had many strengths that attracted students to his well-attended classes. The attraction came more from the clearly organized and stimulating ideas he discussed than from a powerful style of presentation. Not relying on written notes, he spoke softly in a monotone, seldom looked directly at the students, and discouraged questions and discussion. He never entered the classroom before the bell rang; when the bell sounded at the end of class, he would immediately stop lecturing and quickly leave before any of the students could talk to him. A basically shy person, he became a master at avoiding students and their questions. Even so, most students found him and his lectures fascinating and original.

Despite the striking originality of his ideas and lectures, Mead humbly downplayed his own contributions, presenting his thoughts merely as modifications of the work of others, and had little interest in recognition by the larger scholarly community. Unlike Dewey, he cared little about shining in the limelight. Instead, he felt most at ease in small gatherings at his home or the homes of his close friends, where he best displayed his quick wit and humor.

Mead performed better in conversation and lectures than in writing. In part because of his modesty and in part because of a perfectionism that left him dissatisfied with his writing, he never authored a full statement of his philosophy. "He would spend agonizing hours at his table, sometimes verging on tears when he despaired of giving adequate expression to the rapid flow of his thought" (Coser 1977:346). Although he wrote more than 80 articles on education, war, democracy, labor, immigration, and social work, he never published a book in his lifetime and thus did not convey his basic philosophy to the wider scholarly community.

Yet his writer's block did not harm his lectures. One student wrote, "His thought was too rich in internal development to allow him to set his ideas down in an ordered array. His genius expressed itself best in the lecture room ... [His lectures were] suggestive, penetrating, incomplete, conversational in tone, [and] the most fitting form for his thoughts" (Morris 1934:vii). Eventually, students who recognized the brilliance of his lectures as well as his failure to publish them hired a stenographer to record verbatim the lectures in his course on social psychology and later published them.

Although listed in the philosophy department, Mead's classes attracted many sociology students. He did not belong to the sociology department and in general had only a modest influence on its faculty, but several famous sociologists at the University of Chicago sent their graduate students to his classes. Mead would greatly influence sociology through these students.

Why would sociology students find his ideas attractive? Mead provided an original justification for the new field that meshed nicely with American values and concerns. Given the differences in social life in

America and Europe, American and European sociology had different aims and methods. American sociologists did not simply adopt the theories of Durkheim, Weber, or Simmel, but instead searched for their own perspective. Mead would contribute to this search.

Sociology in America

Like Mead himself, many early sociologists had trained for the ministry, or came from a family of ministers, but found themselves restless and dissatisfied with traditional religion. Most were from rural, small-town backgrounds and wanted to help people, and some wanted to bring Christian ethics to the new field. "The first generation of sociologists with official positions in the field resembled nothing so much as a private club for Protestant clergy interested in mitigating the impact of industrialism on America" (Crunden 1982:81). Many had studied sociology in Germany but wanted to give sociology an American emphasis that was more humanitarian and oriented toward reform. They paid less attention to the restraints of traditional patterns of social life, instead giving more attention to the ability of individuals to improve the world. Their goals matched the special American emphasis on freedom and progress.

Toward that end, American sociology specialized in observation of the social world. Disease, poverty, crowded housing, and illiteracy led to special efforts to measure the extent of these problems and devise solutions. Sociologists at the University of Chicago did this type of research better than in any other sociology program in the nation—they effectively used Chicago as a laboratory for in-depth studies of the social life and problems of city residents. As a result, they received national prestige and recognition for their work.

The sociology department at the University of Chicago had another advantage that helped make it the preeminent location of social research in the nation. At a new university, sociology did not have to compete against long-established departments in more traditional fields. Whereas philosophers, economists, and psychologists opposed the establishment of sociology in many other universities, sociology had respect from the very founding of the University of Chicago. As a result, Chicago sociology dominated the field for the first decades of the twentieth century.

Despite its reputation, sociology at Chicago (like American sociology more generally) lacked a broad theory to justify its special perspective on social problems and its practical research concerns. Although influenced by Simmel and aware of Durkheim and Weber, American sociologists had not yet developed their own theory of the nature of society, the relationship between the individual and society, and the basis of social cooperation. Mead's ideas helped provide such a theory. In his social psychology class, he made the case for a sociological conception of the world that sociology students found particularly attractive.

Psychology and Behaviorism

In contrast to popular psychological conceptions of human behavior, Mead's social psychology treated individual experience and behavior as stemming from communication and interaction within social groups. In arguing for his sociological view of the individual, Mead began with a popular branch of psychology called behaviorism. Strongly influenced by the evolutionary study of animal species, behaviorism initially concentrated on animal psychology; and because scientists cannot examine the inner thoughts of animals, behaviorists advocated the study of outward animal behavior, such as how different species respond to external rewards and punishments.

Taking the next logical step, behaviorists applied the same perspective to humans, arguing that the scientific study of humans must focus on observable behavior rather than on unobservable thoughts. Ignoring inner experiences, mental images, and subjective consciousness as unscientific and unimportant, they charted the connections between external stimuli and outward human responses. For example, one famous behaviorist, John B. Watson, illustrated how a young child can become fearful. At the exact moment he would show the child a harmless white mouse, he would also have a painfully loud and sudden sound come from behind the child. After a few repetitions of the experience, the child exhibited physical symptoms of fright and nervousness whenever the mouse appeared—even if the loud sound no longer occurred. Watson then explained the internal emotional state of fear in terms of an unpleasant external stimulus and a physical response.

In their explanations, behaviorists eliminated any reference to mental processes that might come between the stimulus and the response. In their view, thinking was merely silent speech and differed not at all from outward speech observable by others. So why not simply ignore unobservable thoughts and study observable speech and behavior directly? That would make psychology as objective as the other natural sciences and eliminate the unscientific concern with personal thoughts and feelings.

Criticisms of Behaviorism

Although Mead saw the advantages of the scientific study of observable behavior, he rejected simple behaviorism because it made no distinction between humans and other animals. Humans differ from other animals in their ability to think about themselves, foresee the possible consequences of future actions, and communicate with others through language. Since these abilities separate humans from other animals, it seemed crucial to include them in the study of human behavior.

In criticizing behaviorism, Mead raised a point about human abilities first argued in an influential paper by his friend John Dewey: humans respond to stimuli by actively making choices rather than by passively or automatically exhibiting reflexes. Because many situations involve ambiguous stimuli and uncertain responses, humans must select and interpret stimuli from the infinite complexity of the outside world before they choose a response. On entering a room filled with strangers, for example, a person might see the situation as threatening, harmless, or enjoyable. The interpretation a person gives to the situation will depend on his or her social experiences and group membership. Having interpreted the situation, a person will then imaginatively rehearse possible actions and their consequences before responding to the strangers. The simple model of stimulus and response hardly captures the complexity of human behavior.

Given the special human capacities to interpret and plan, Mead wanted to develop a social behaviorism that would improve on psychological behaviorism, one that would link the internal thoughts of humans with their external actions. He suggested that external, observable behavior belongs to a larger process of social action that also includes internal thoughts and experiences. Mead called the internal parts of the act *attitudes*. Both parts—directly observable behavior and attitudes—need to be understood and studied.

How could one study attitudes? Mead's answer revealed the sociological nature of individual behavior: he argued that individual attitudes, personal thoughts, and inner experiences stem from membership in social groups. Thinking, for example, represents an internal form of conversation, but conversation relies on language and language comes from interaction in social groups. Therefore, mental processes emerge in interaction with others, and interaction with others can be studied scientifically. Where behaviorist psychologists viewed the emergence of language as subjective and hidden, Mead saw language as primarily social rather than personal. He simply treated inner experience as a part of the social act. By studying external social behavior, then, one could understand internal thoughts and attitudes.

Mead's argument contained a broader criticism of psychology. Psychologists might account for the actions of a social group in terms of the conduct of the separate individuals who make up the group. Mead argued the opposite: the behavior of the individual, including inner attitudes and outward behavior, stems from the organized behavior of the social group. Mead (1934:7) wrote, "The whole (society) is prior to the part (the individual) ... and the part is explained in terms of the whole." Without society and social communication, then, humans as actors with thoughts, attitudes, and consciousness could not exist. By incorporating thinking into the social act, Mead's argument rejected the distinction between individual thinking and social behavior.

Mead did not dismiss the importance of humans' biological and psychological characteristics; on the contrary, his background in physiolog-ical psychology led him to recognize the special human capacity for lan-guage and thinking. The neurons of the brain and the shape of the vocal cords give humans the potential to interact with others in ways other an-imals cannot; nonetheless, learning language through interacting with others transforms a biological and psychological individual into a social person, and this requires the study of social psychology.

5. HUMAN THINKING COMES FROM SOCIAL INTERACTION

During his time at the University of Chicago, Mead progressed steadily up the academic ladder, moving from assistant professor to associate professor in 1902, to full professor in 1907, and eventually to chair of the department of philosophy—all without having received a Ph.D. or pub-lished a major book. If Mead's work gained little national recognition during his lifetime, his promotions demonstrated the substantial influ-ence he had among students and faculty at the University of Chicago.

In 1904, John Dewey left the University of Chicago to become the chair of the philosophy department at Columbia University in New York City. Mead and Dewey remained close, sharing ideas as they had in the past whenever Dewey's travels brought him to Chicago. However, Dewey's exit cleared the way for Mead to make contributions beyond those of his older and more famous colleague.

Mead's Community Involvement

Mead's growing prestige at the University of Chicago came in part from his involvement as a community leader. Like several members of the so-ciology department, he devoted himself to solving the social problems so common in Chicago neighborhoods near the university. As always, prac-tical action proved as important as philosophy and theory to him. Con-sider some of his activities.

1. *He worked to implement methods of progressive education in Chicago schools.* In terms of theory, Mead wrote many articles on educational matters and edited a journal for elementary school teachers. In terms of practice, he participated in an experimental elementary school founded at the University of Chicago, belonged to several local educational com-mittees, and helped support a school for hearing- and sight-impaired children.

The agenda of educational change fit naturally with Mead's goals for social reform. He gave great importance in his writings to the socializa-tion of children into the larger social community. Because education con-tributes to socialization, it helps shape the social values of community members. Properly done, education would neither indoctrinate nor oppress students, but would help blend their individuality with community needs. Education would, in other words, become an essential part of a strong democracy.

2. *He involved himself with problems of immigrants in Chicago.* Consistent with his goals of community involvement, he hoped to help integrate new immigrant groups into the democratic life of America. "Mead believed there would be greater social harmony if the various members of the diverse ethnic groups could, through their own action, create a single community" (Barry 1968:182). To help integrate diverse ethnic groups, he advocated better education for the children of immigrants and the poor, believing that schools concentrated too much on the needs of middle- and upper-class children to the neglect of other children. Proper education would help those from less advantaged families find good jobs after leaving school, bargain for better wages with employers, and join fully in American democracy.

Mead's commitment to helping immigrants also appeared in his service for a number of years as vice-president of the Immigrants Protective League. In one case, he worked hard to prevent the extradition to Russia of a Chicago immigrant unfairly accused of crimes against the czar. He also helped organize a conference with other prominent academics and civic leaders to protect immigrants who had come to the United States to avoid political persecution.

3. *He belonged to a civic group called the City Club that devised and publicized ideas to solve the problems of Chicago.* They advocated policies to improve housing, transportation, sanitation, and health in the city. As chair of the City Club's Committee on Public Education, Mead presented statistics on the high dropout rate of young teenagers and helped raise the mandatory age of schooling to 16.

4. *He acted to improve the working and living conditions of unskilled employees.* For example, he helped sponsor a five-year survey of stockyard workers in the meat-packing industry. One part of the study found that the typical wages paid by employers to many workers did not cover the cost of minimal needs for rent, food, clothing, and living expenses. Mead used this finding to urge employers to improve working conditions. He perhaps naively hoped that once the employers understood the problems of the workers, they would agree to act for the good of the community rather than for their own economic interest.

In another instance, he took a more active role in aiding garment workers striking against Hart, Schaffner, and Marx clothiers. As the head of a fact-finding committee on the garment industry, he condemned the employer's treatment of workers. Although community leaders viewed criticism of business and the free market as radical and dangerous, he nonetheless spoke out on behalf of the strikers. Without advocating socialism, which no American university would have tolerated, Mead nonetheless worked for peaceful change in industrial relations. His efforts eventually helped establish an arbitration board to settle worker grievances.

In summary, Mead's efforts at social reform remained central to his career and helped overcome the tension between his desires to serve people and to enjoy academic pursuits. His involvement with progressive causes and efforts toward a peaceful reform of American society reflected an American optimism about the potential for social betterment. Even World War I, which European sociologists found deeply distressing, did not dampen Mead's hopes. Despite the horrors of war, he saw an American victory as necessary to create democracy in Europe and peace throughout the world. He also saw the war effort as a model for the kind of cooperation needed to solve social problems at home.

Despite his support for America's participation in World War I, Mead committed himself most strongly to change through peaceful, democratic means. He favored legislation that helped the needy, but he wanted legislators to respond to demands for change from the larger public: real democracy would come when the press, unions, businesses, teachers, politicians, workers, and the needy could join together to act for the common good. Once people and groups understood the interests of the community as a whole, Mead believed they would discard their special interests. In this way, democracy would resolve social conflict amicably and allow each new generation to cooperate in acting for the good of the larger community.

Thinking and Communication

Not surprisingly, Mead's social philosophy of behavior overlapped with his goal of peaceful change. For social change to come from individual action, close ties must exist between the individual and society. If, as Mead claimed, human thinking emerges from social communication and interaction, the ties of individuals to the community could not be closer. His theory advocated the involvement and cooperation of individuals in public discussion, community activities, and political democracy.

To further demonstrate the relationship between human thinking and social communication, Mead first compared humans to other animals. Although animals perceive external stimuli through their senses, they cannot assign meaning to their perceptions; in contrast, human consciousness or awareness involves the use of language and symbols. A hungry dog that spots food will race to eat it, but a hungry human will wonder where the food comes from, who the food belongs to, and whether more food lies nearby. The human may also ask someone else about the food before eating it. In Mead's terms, then, the human mind has the ability to deal with meaning.

Since newborn infants do not understand the meanings of symbols, words, and language, they must learn them through dealings with other humans. Learning shared meanings thus transforms the biological human organism into a social being with a mind and special capacity for thinking. In tracing the emergence of the human mind through the use of language, Mead described the development of simple gestures into a complex system of symbols. In general terms, **gestures** involve movements of one organism that call forth responses of another organism. However, simple gestures involving the automatic reactions to stimuli common among animals differ from complex systems of gestures common among humans.

At the simplest level, communication involves a conversation of gestures. Animals respond automatically or instinctively to gestures without deliberation or planning. When one dog growls, the other dog responds quickly by growling, attacking, submitting, or fleeing. Gestures communicate the likely future action of each dog—baring teeth suggests an attack will follow, while wagging a tail suggests play will follow. However, animals lack conscious awareness of the meaning of their gestures. On occasion, humans respond automatically and instinctively, such as when attacked, startled, or surprised; more generally, however, humans rely on meaningful communication and complex gestures.

Vocal gestures, especially in the form of language, have more potential than body movements to create shared meaning among those involved in communication. Mead noted that the vocal gesture has a special quality: although we cannot see our facial gestures, we can hear our voice. Because we can hear ourselves just as others hear us, vocal gestures similarly affect both the speaker and listener. Because they have the potential to carry the same meaning to both persons, they give people the capacity to answer themselves as another person would answer.

Although animals can make sounds, they lack the human abilities to observe their own vocal gestures, understand how others observe their vocal gestures, and become aware of the shared meanings of the vocal gestures. Even parrots, which can sound just like humans, have no sense of the meaning of the sounds they make. Given their special capacity for understanding, humans can use vocal gestures in a unique form of communication.

Shared Meanings and Human Thinking

Simple vocal gestures such as grunts, screams, or whistles represent symbols that can produce the same meaning in speaker and listener. More important, however, the use of language increases the potential for shared meanings. Symbols stand for something else, as the word *dog* stands for a certain type of animal, and summon a similar mental image. **Significant symbols**, in Mead's scheme, call up the same meaning in the speaker and listener; that is, they have the same significance to both people. Language, then, consists of spoken and written significant symbols.

When a vocal gesture does not have the same meaning to speaker and listener, the symbol is nonsignificant. Someone speaking Arabic to an American likely uses nonsignificant symbols that the listener does not understand. Similarly, young people using slang in the presence of older persons will have to explain the meaning of their words. In nonhuman animals, communication involves nonsignificant symbols, since the sounds of a bird or dog do not have the same meaning to the animal making the sound as to the one hearing it. The growl of a dog does not frighten the dog making the sound. Similarly, babies make sounds, but they do not understand the meaning of the sounds in the same way as the adults who hear them.

But just because significant symbols call out the same meaning in two people, it does not mean that the speaker and listener necessarily respond identically to the symbols. A bully's threat to someone weaker, although understood as a threat by both, produces anger in the bully and fear in the victim. Understanding the meaning of the threat can lead the victim to act friendly and confident so as to avoid a beating, possibly leading the bully to calm down. The two actors use shared meaning to adjust their behavior to one another.

According to Mead, thinking also takes place through the use of significant symbols. He treated thinking as a kind of inner conversation: much as we talk to others using significant symbols, we can silently or mentally talk to ourselves. All of us have asked ourselves "What should I do next?" as if we were talking to another person. These conversations and the decisions that emerge from them involve the use of symbols. What we call intelligence actually involves the use of significant symbols in an inner conversation to solve a problem.

To return to the original goal of explaining the close ties between individuals and society, consider the significance of Mead's reasoning. Rather than assuming the existence of the mind *before* communication, Mead showed how it emerges *during* communication. Since symbols come out of social interaction with others, the individual mind emerges from social experience and communication through significant symbols. Children slowly progress from displaying their feelings with simple physical and vocal gestures to communicating shared meanings to others with significant symbols. They therefore become fully human in their thinking through social communication with others who share the same meanings of symbols. By beginning with social groups and working inward to the mind, Mead helped unite the individual with society and make social psychology a valuable and separate field from psychology.

6. THE EMERGENCE OF THE SOCIAL SELF

While at the University of Chicago, Mead met Jane Addams, the city's (and one of the world's) most famous woman. Before becoming renowned as one of the nation's first social workers, Addams had struggled—much like Mead—with how to give meaning to her life. Raised in a religious household in the Midwest, she lost her faith as a young woman, but not her Christian-based desire to help others. She found an outlet for her charitable goals by founding one of the nation's first settlement houses. In 1889 she turned a run-down mansion called Hull House in a poor section of Chicago populated by immigrants into a neighborhood center.

Hull House and Social Reform

Devoted primarily to helping less privileged women, Hull House offered day nurseries, college courses, social activities, and guidance in dealing with problems of daily life. Addams hoped to help women cope with their difficulties through education and knowledge, believing that social workers could help remake the character and better the lives of immigrant women by introducing them to art, literature, and higher culture. Accordingly, Hull House became a kind of intellectual center, with Addams and her co-workers holding reading groups, lecture series, art classes, and art exhibits that attracted many visitors.

Sharing similar ideas and goals about creating a better world, Addams and Mead became close friends. Both had suffered through a period of depression as they searched for meaning in a life that rejected traditional religion, and both had also found purpose in combining learning with helping the disadvantaged. Along with her social work, Addams wrote 11 books and hundreds of articles, won the Nobel Peace Prize in 1931, and made Hull House a center for research and social thought (Deegan 1988:6). Not surprisingly, her accomplishments much impressed Mead.

Until women gained the vote in 1920, Mead worked with Addams and others to support women's suffrage, speaking at local meetings and hosting visiting suffragettes from England in his home. He even participated in one demonstration by marching down Michigan Avenue with others in support of women's right to vote. Viewing gender differences in social terms, Mead rejected the biological determinism used by some to claim women's inferiority to men. Well ahead of his time, he supported advanced education for women, opposed segregation of the sexes at the University of Chicago, and thought women should have the right to a career and access to nursery school care to make it possible to work without causing harm to children.

Mead joined Addams in her efforts to make Hull House a center for progressive social action and learning, seeing the potential for Hull House to foster equality and opportunity through peaceful means. By building community ties and bringing the disadvantaged into Chicago's civic life, Hull House could help remake the larger society. In his scholarly work during these years, Mead would further explain how free and open social communication, such as occurred in Hull House or larger communities, formed the basis of the individual self. Much as it did for the human mind, Mead's theory of social relations traced the emergence of something as personal as the human self to social communication.

The Self as Object

Unlike other animals, humans have the ability to see themselves as objects. In a sense, people can step outside their bodies and view themselves as something separate. People tell themselves—as if talking to another person—that they behaved stupidly after making a mistake or that they behaved impressively after doing something well. We refer to our self in these one-person conversations as more than our body; it includes the whole of our behavior, thoughts, feelings, accomplishments, failures, and general sense of well-being when viewed from the outside.

Viewing oneself as an object, however, involves interpretation and meaning. Just as individuals use socially learned symbols and meanings to converse or interact with others, they use socially learned symbols and meanings to interpret their own feelings and actions. When speaking of self-love, self-esteem, self-hate, shame, or guilt, people apply to their own selves the meanings they have learned during interaction with others. For example, someone told often enough that he is a failure will come to view himself in these terms. Persons generally act toward themselves as others act toward them.

Mead was not the first to identify the social nature of the self. Charles Horton Cooley, a sociologist at the University of Michigan, had used the term "looking-glass self" to indicate that we see ourselves in the mirror of other people. Our self becomes an object when we can take the point of view of another, when we see our self as others see us. However, whereas Cooley assumed an already developed self, Mead went further to show how the self emerges from communication and social interaction.

Development of the Self

To understand the formation of the self, Mead examined the activities and socialization of children. Newborn babies do not have a sense of themselves as objects, instead responding automatically and selfishly to hunger, discomfort, and the world around them. As infants grow older, however, they come to distinguish between themselves and others. Eventually, they learn to identify with or take the role of other persons, which means they can see their own actions from the point of view of other persons. As children further mature, their self expands to identify with larger and more complex social roles.

In his theory, Mead traced the patterns of interaction that contribute to the emergence of the social self during childhood. To take the point of view of other persons, children must learn the meanings of symbols and language. Much of this learning comes from various forms of play, which Mead described with unusual insight.

1. *Imitation.* The initial play of infants involves the emerging awareness of other people and physical objects. Babies learn to grasp, hold, and use simple objects like spoons, bottles, or toys. When their physical skills develop further, they learn to play with objects by observing and imitating their parents; for example, a parent might pick up and roll a ball, then try to help the baby do the same thing. Until they learn to speak, babies can do little more than imitate the external actions of other people. Still, imitation involves learning: babies discover that some behaviors bring punishment and others bring rewards.

2. *Role play.* While the initial imitation of babies differs little from the play of puppies or kittens, who also learn from older dogs and cats, human language allows for more complex play. Rather than simply imitating the outward actions of their parents and others, children gradually learn through the use of language and shared meanings to adopt the role or attitude of other persons. They not only *act out* the roles of others— they *assume* them in their imagination. In play, they adopt the point of view of mothers, fathers, and siblings, and later teachers, relatives, friends, and others in society; they even assume the roles of toys, animals, and cartoon characters. Children imagine themselves as mommy or daddy, Superman, Tiger Woods, or their pet dog. In this way, children develop a better sense of the meanings and attitudes held by other people.

3. *Games.* Role playing involves putting oneself in the place of others one person at time. The next level of social maturity requires children to take the roles of several other persons and to understand the relationship between these roles. In organized games, participants need to understand the possible actions of teammates and opponents. Baseball and football not only define a different role for each player but also require each player to understand the complex rules and roles that guide the behavior of all the other players. A good quarterback must foresee how the receivers, blockers, and defenders will act and react to one another and respond on the basis of these expectations. Learning the diverse roles in organized games helps children understand the more general workings of social life.

4. *The generalized other.* Eventually, children and adults learn to do something more than take the role of concrete people: they come to take the attitude of the whole community, which Mead called the **generalized other**. Adopting as one's own the attitude of a social group or organized society allows diverse individuals to share values, norms, and beliefs and therefore cooperate with one another. By taking the attitude of the generalized other, for example, a teenager may decide not to join friends in stealing. The generalized other becomes part of the teenager's own attitudes and values, serving as a socially created conscience.

In summary, by learning social attitudes, a baby acting out of selfish needs eventually becomes a moral member of a community and society. Developing a social self and a moral conscience does not, however, eliminate our individuality. Each individual identifies with a different mix of other people, social attitudes, and generalized others; in turn, each unique individual makes a special contribution to group social life. The individual self in social interaction thus undergoes constant change that makes for both uniqueness and shared meanings.

Implications of the Social Self

Mead distinguished components of the social self corresponding to the influence of the social group and the unique individual. He referred to the **me** as the judgmental and controlling side of the self that reflects the attitudes of other members of the larger community and society while the **I** is the creative and imaginative side of the self. Because of its impulsive, unpredictable, and surprising nature, the I helps change rather than simply reflect society. The two components of the self thus have two benefits: they both control the individual and provide the creative means for change. The I counteracts the socially constraining force of the me, and the me counteracts the individuality of the I.

The emergence of the self in interaction demonstrates that individuals and society do not exist separately from each other. Individuals carry society around within them in the form of a social self, and society depends on the functioning of the I and me components of the self. Although Mead gave less attention to large social organizations than did European sociologists, he nonetheless attributed much importance to social influences on individual behavior.

Indeed, Mead's treatment of the self reversed other perspectives used to explain individual behavior. Individuals, according to psychological views, have their own needs, drives, and interests that lead them to act in certain ways. Mead's theory of the self, however, notes that people interpret their wants, needs, motives, and interests—as if they stood separate from them—before acting on them. Given the social interpretation of the meaning of our own feelings, Mead rejected the idea that individual drives, needs, feelings, and unconscious motives directly determine our behavior.

Psychologists argue that people act to avoid pain and to gain pleasure. Although Mead would not disagree, he claimed that people interpret the meaning of both pain and pleasure based on social communication and interaction. Even something as individual as our own physical pain involves interpretation. Because of their different social experiences and circumstances, a football player may gain satisfaction from overcoming pain, a pianist may suffer immensely from a small finger cut, and a doctor may view pain objectively in order to diagnose a problem. Each interprets the meaning of the same kind of pain quite differently.

If Mead rejected psychological views, he also rejected sociological views that ignore social meanings and interpretation. Some sociological theories treat individuals as passively accepting and responding to social norms and values. Yet, like theories of psychological characteristics, theories of social pressures fail to capture the active interpretations people give to the social world around them. Since the self includes an I as well as a me, social life allows for novelty and freedom. Since constant change characterizes both individuals and society, Mead rejected strict social determinism.

Mead's arguments about the dependence of the self on society related to his activities on behalf of Hull House and other progressive causes. The close ties between society and the individual self imply that personal interests need not compete with community interests. The unique individuals who came together as part of Hull House, for example, could build a sense of community from their social interaction. Through open and equal communication, they could reject individual solutions to problems in favor of democratic solutions based on the union between the individual self and society.

7. SYMBOLIC INTERACTIONISM

In 1931, 37 years after he had first came to the University of Chicago, Mead decided to leave. A new university president forced the department of philosophy to hire a Catholic philosopher whose religious views contrasted with the pragmatic, secular views of Mead and others in the department. Offended by the unwillingness of the new president to consult with him, Mead accepted a job at Columbia University in New York City for the next fall. Before he could take up his new post, however, he fell ill. Having given his last lecture for a course on Problems of Philosophy on January 28, 1931, Mead died at the age of 68 on April 26.

Through his courses, Mead had informed an entire generation of

Chicago sociologists of his theories. In 1934, three years after his death, students edited the lectures they had transcribed and published them as *Mind, Self, and Society*. This book found a large audience among sociologists outside of Chicago, and Mead's sociological reputation spread to other universities. In addition, Mead's ideas gained enormous influence through the theories and studies of a new generation of sociologists at the University of Chicago during the 1940s and 1950s.

Blumer Interprets Mead

After Mead's unexpected death, one of his former students, a young man named Herbert Blumer, taught Mead's courses. Blumer had received his Ph.D. in sociology from the University of Chicago in 1928 and would stay on as a professor of sociology until he moved to the University of California at Berkeley in 1952. During his long career, Blumer became the major teacher and advocate of Mead's theory, introducing a new generation of students at the University of Chicago to Mead's ideas. He did more than anyone else to make Mead a central figure in the founding of modern sociology.

As a sociologist rather than a philosopher, Blumer publicized the sociological implications of Mead's social philosophy. He not only presented in clear and readable language the relevance of Mead's ideas to sociologists but also bluntly criticized other sociological approaches that he thought inconsistent with Mead's arguments. Blumer used the term **symbolic interactionism** to describe Mead's perspective, and the term and perspective came to define America's most original school of social theory.

Symbolic interactionism shifts the focus of social theory from social structure to social interaction. Following Mead, it consists of a microsociology of the interaction of individuals rather than a macrosociology of the structures of capitalism, the state, religion, and morality. Interaction within society occurs as actors influence one another and take the roles and attitudes of others into account. Interaction is symbolic since it relies on the use of symbols to communicate shared meanings. Like Mead, Blumer claimed that neither society nor the individual precedes the other: persons create society through interaction, but symbolic interaction creates persons as social beings.

More than Mead, Blumer stressed the fluidity and change of social life. Rather than being based on a set of rigid and fixed rules, interaction requires social actors to constantly clarify their meanings and adjust their behaviors. To illustrate, a student who asks to meet with his professor usually tries to explain and justify his purposes in wanting to meet, and will carefully consider the possible responses of the professor to the request. The way he asks questions will, in turn, influence the professor's sense of the situation and affect whether she responds with friendliness, defensiveness, abruptness, or helpfulness. Continuing on, the professor's interpretation and response shape the student's interpretation and response. Negotiation of meanings in situations like this requires people to constantly create and readjust their orientations, attitudes, and behaviors. Routine behavior comes from accepting common interpretations, but problems and changes continually require new behaviors and new negotiations.

Blumer's attention to change in social life matched Mead's concern with social reform. Since definitions of and meanings ascribed to the situation shape behavior, changing social definitions and meanings can change behavior. Consistent with Mead's optimism, the potential for social and political change remains great in symbolic interactionism. Whereas other theories see social inequality, domination, conflict, coercion, and power as obstacles to change, symbolic interactionism remains more optimistic about social improvement.

To investigate social life, symbolic interactionism tries to understand the meanings and interpretations of the participants in interaction. In Blumer's (1969:16) words, "One has to get inside the defining process of the actor in order to understand his action." Rather than impose their own views on the world, sociologists need to understand the actor's own views. This type of understanding requires investigators to observe social behavior in its natural settings and to take the role of the actors they study. Real knowledge comes from staying close to the real world rather than from solitary contemplation or book learning.

In criticizing methods and theories that ignore the importance of socially created meanings in interaction, Blumer spoke for a minority of dissidents who criticized mainstream sociology. He and others rejected the attempt of sociologists to imitate the methods and objectivity of the hard sciences with statistical studies. Answers to a questionnaire, for example, may tell us how people talk to an interviewer, but not how they really behave in other situations. Social scientists need instead to understand the situation as the actors do.

Despite some controversy about whether Blumer's methods conflicted with Mead's more favorable views on objective science, graduate students under the influence of Blumer and like-minded faculty at the University of Chicago used symbolic interactionism as the framework for many famous studies. Relying on participant-observation, in-depth interviews, and other naturalistic methods, these studies aimed to understand the social world of particular groups and how they construct meanings.

Constructing Social Problems

Constructed meanings, for example, prove crucial to defining "social problems." We tend to think of social problems as troublesome situations that need changing. However, the public must define a situation as troublesome to make it a social problem. And given the innumerable troubles of the world, defining a social problem inevitably involves interpretation and selection. As Mead argued, people actively create and impose meaning in symbolic interaction to give themselves some certainty in a confusing and complex world.

Given the importance of interpretation, social problems can change without any clear relation to objective circumstances. Child abuse and sexual harassment have always created personal problems for individuals, but only relatively recently have they been defined as social problems requiring public action and new laws; racism was once a normal part of life in America, but now it constitutes a serious social problem. Conversely, some social problems of the past have become accepted parts of social life: once outlawed, abortion and homosexuality have gained substantial (although not universal) legal and social acceptance.

The discussion these days about the abuse of alcohol by college students and the danger of drunk driving provides a good example of how the meanings of behavior change over time to define new forms of deviance and new social problems. Joseph Gusfield (1996), a product of the sociology department at the University of Chicago, has studied drinking patterns in the United States over the last century. He notes that while drinking behavior has changed little since Prohibition, the views on and explanations of alcohol use and abuse have changed decisively. The changing meaning of alcoholism sheds light on the nature of modern society.

During the nineteenth and early part of the twentieth century, most people treated drinking as sinful and dangerous. Viewed from a religious perspective, drinking attracted those too morally weak to control their desires. One dated image of alcohol abuse in rural areas reflects this perspective—the weak and easily tempted but good-natured and fun-loving Otis in reruns of "The Andy Griffith Show" would let himself into jail after having gotten drunk on illegal moonshine. Another dated image, more applicable to alcohol abuse in cities, characterizes the alcoholic as a skid-row bum who gives up his family, job, self-respect, and decent life to drink.

Given the interpretation of drinking as sinful behavior, the solution to the problem required government action to prevent and punish the sinners. At one time, police routinely arrested and jailed people for public intoxication. Going further to prevent drunkenness by removing the temptation, some counties and states outlawed alcohol altogether early in the century. From 1920 to 1933—the period known as Prohibition—the sale and use of alcohol was illegal throughout the United States. Many rural areas and some states remained dry for decades after Prohibition.

Over the past several decades, a view of alcoholism as a disease that needs medical treatment replaced the view of alcoholism as a moral weakness. As a disease rather than a sinful failure of self-control, alcoholism lost much of its stigma. Alcoholics require treatment from doctors, social workers, and scientists rather than moral disapproval; unless it leads to dangerous driving, violence, or disruption, drunkenness no longer leads to arrest. As a result, many people today, including celebrities, politicians, and athletes, publicly admit their abuse of alcohol without shame. Alcoholic behavior may not have changed, but its interpretation has.

Re-Creating the Social Self

For those undergoing treatment for alcoholism, social interpretations and meanings again are crucial. Employing symbolic interactionism theory, Norman Denzin (1987) argues that Alcoholics Anonymous (AA) attempts to socialize the alcoholic to move toward a new sense of selfhood. In AA meetings (as in any of the popular 12-step groups), participants tell stories and listen to others tell stories about their lives as alcoholics. The stories contrast the misery of their alcoholic life with their difficult, but still much better, life after they stopped drinking and followed the AA creed. The treatment thus takes the form of a collective rather than individual effort.

Re-creating a new, nonalcoholic self in AA, according to Denzin, mirrors the emergence of the social self described by Mead. Despite entering as strangers, members of AA treatment groups mesh into a small community that shares similar identities. Bonds develop from interpreting past experiences in terms of the wreckage caused by alcoholism. Slowly, members internalize the perspective of the AA group, learn a new interpretation of life, and develop a new sense of self that no longer depends on alcohol. In Mead's terms, recovery requires that new participants learn to take the attitude of specific others in the group and then adopt the generalized other of the treatment group. As in social life more generally, symbolic communication and interaction in AA create the conditions for the emergence of a new self.

Consider the comments of some participants in AA reported by Denzin (1987:122, 158, 166). They reveal the changes in self during recovery that stem from the AA group experience.

◆ A 47-year-old male: "I lost everything. Family home, wives, kids, job, everything. Even my parents turned against me. I fought like hell to get it all back and it didn't work. They went off to be who they were and left me to find myself. I think they hated me. Lot of self-pity on my part. I finally found you people. Now you're my family. Wherever I go, you're there. ... [The group] gives me everything I ever wanted and ever looked for. I feel like I'm needed again."

+ A 48-year-old male: "I'm nothing without AA—nothing. Without the Steps, the higher power, my sobriety which is given on a daily basis, my sponsor, these meetings, my new friends—without all this I'd be nothing and nothing was just what I was when I got here."

+ A 32-year-old female: "When I first got here I couldn't talk. I was shaking and crying. I sat in the corner. When it came my turn to talk I mumbled something, I don't even remember what. I felt like I had just crawled out of a hole. ... I couldn't look people in the eye. I was like this for months. Finally I started to be able to talk. I started to get some self-confidence back. It used to be that I couldn't go into a room with more than two people in it without being high on drugs and alcohol. I was afraid of people. Today I feel comfortable here. I can actually talk. That's quite an accomplishment for me. It helps me remember who I was and what I used to be like. I've come a long way."

As illustrated by studies of alcohol problems and treatment, Mead's ideas remain current. The connections he demonstrated between the individual and society help us understand social change and modern society in original and insightful ways. Mead's hopes that social communication and democratic discussion would make for a better world may not have been realized, but his explanation of the potential to overcome the opposition between personal and social needs remains a central part of sociological thought today. The importance Mead attached to the human ability to understand the point of view of others in their group and community unites individuals' selves and society and makes sociology central to understanding human behavior.

SUMMARY

Unlike many philosophers, Mead rejected isolated thinking as a means of answering questions about life, ethics, and knowledge. Rather than settling philosophical arguments with verbal debates, book reading, or pure reason, he and other American philosophers thought that all ideas could be tested in the real world for their consequences. Those ideas that make society better, have positive consequences, and work in real life can be considered valid. Actions by people thus define the truth of ideas.

Along with stressing the need to test ideas through action, Mead stressed the need to understand the close ties between the individual and community or society. To effectively improve their communities and societies, individuals must view themselves as essential parts of the larger group rather than as separate and independent beings. The closer the ties between individuals and society, the greater the justification for individuals' involvement in attempts at social betterment. Mead therefore gave importance to both individual and group aspects of social life.

Social communication plays a central role in Mead's efforts to connect the individual and social community. Humans differ from animals in their ability to use symbols and language; the meanings humans share in speaking and writing make a special form of social interaction possible. Even something as personal and individual as our own inner thoughts depends on symbols and social interaction. Since silent or internal conversations occur as if we were talking to another person, our innermost thoughts stem ultimately from what we learn from others.

Humans differ from animals in another way—they have the ability to view themselves as objects. In a sense, people can step outside their bodies and view themselves as something separate. They not only talk to themselves but often judge themselves in doing so. We refer to our self in these one-person conversations not simply as a body, but almost as another person. The ability to treat our selves as separate objects again comes from social interaction: we learn in social interaction to view ourselves as others view us. Indeed, people develop an image of themselves based on how others treat them in social interaction.

Mead described how the social self emerges during childhood and youth. Newborn babies do not have a sense of themselves as objects, instead responding automatically and selfishly to hunger, discomfort, and the world around them. As infants grow older, however, they come to distinguish between themselves and others—that is, they develop an early sense of selfhood. At very young ages, children merely imitate the outward behavior of other people: they smile back when others smile at them, play simple games their parents teach them, and try to repeat words they hear their parents say.

As they get older and learn to use language from interacting with their parents, young children do more than imitate the outward behavior of others—they adopt the roles, attitudes, and points of view of other persons. By imagining themselves to be a mommy or daddy, children learn the meanings and attitudes held by other people. As they grow yet older, children develop more advanced social skills. In games such as baseball or football, they learn to understand the roles of several other people and how they relate to one another. Learning the diverse roles that exist in organized games helps children understand the more general workings of social life.

Eventually, children and adults come to take the attitude of the whole community—what Mead called the generalized other. In adopting the attitude of a social group or society as one's own, adults and children come to develop a socially created conscience. Over the years, then, a baby acting on selfish needs eventually becomes a moral member of a community and society by learning social attitudes.

In explaining how the individual mind and self emerge from social interaction, Mead did not deny our individuality. Rather, he noted that a uniquely individual part of each person exists along with the socially determined part. The two components of our selves both influence behavior, with one providing for creative change and the other constraining individuals in accordance with the values of the larger community. Still, the social part of the self that comes from social experience and communication with symbols remains crucially important in our lives.

Although he never identified himself as a sociologist, Mead's ideas came to have enormous influence on the field through the sociology students who took his classes. Herbert Blumer, one of Mead's students, publicized the sociological implications of Mead's social philosophy. Coining the term *symbolic interactionism* to describe the key points of Mead's perspective, Blumer emphasized the use of symbols by individuals in social interaction. Like Mead, he noted that persons create society through interaction but that symbolic interaction also creates persons as social beings. Others adopted the viewpoint, establishing symbolic interactionism as one of the major theoretical and empirical perspectives in sociology and highlighting Mead's intellectual contributions to the field.

DISCUSSION QUESTIONS

1. Why did careers in religion and philosophy both seem unsatisfactory to Mead? How did his experiences at Oberlin College contribute to Mead's dilemma?

2. Compare American and European values toward equality and authority. Using examples from the history of Chicago, identify the changes brought on by industrialization that threatened American values. Do these threats remain today?

3. How did pragmatists propose to evaluate philosophical ideas and theories? Give examples of how truth can come from the study of human action rather than from thought and logic alone and how science can bring about progress.

4. What special interests did sociologists in the United States have? How did the faculty at the University of Chicago in particular combine their concerns with intellect and activism?

5. What objections did Mead have to the tenets of behaviorism? How did Mead propose to study internal attitudes ignored by behaviorists? What implications did Mead's proposed study have for psychological views of social behavior?

6. Give examples of Mead's community activities in Chicago. What do these activities show about Mead's beliefs concerning the potential for democratic social change?

7. How do humans differ from animals in the use of symbols? How does the use of significant symbols demonstrate that the human mind and thinking emerge from social interaction?

8. Give examples of how humans treat themselves as objects. Describe how this ability emerges from social interaction, making reference to imitation, role play, games, and the generalized other.

9 Give examples of how, according to symbolic interactionism, social life is fluid and changeable. What methods can symbolic interactionists use to investigate the fluidity of social life?

10. How have the interpretations of drinking changed over the last century according to Gusfield? Based on Denzin's study, how do the strong group ties in Alcoholics Anonymous help re-create the social self?

REFERENCES

PRIMARY SOURCES

Mead, George Herbert. 1934. *Mind, Self, and Society* (edited by Charles W. Morris). Chicago: University of Chicago Press.

Mead, George Herbert. 1964. *On Social Psychology* (selected and edited by Anselm Strauss). Chicago: University of Chicago Press.

Mead, George Herbert. 1982. *The Individual and the Social Self: Unpublished Work of George Herbert Mead* (edited by David L. Miller). Chicago: University of Chicago Press.

SECONDARY SOURCES

Ashley, David, & David Michael Orenstein. 1995. *Sociological Theory: Classic Statements* (3rd ed.). Boston: Allyn & Bacon.

Baldwin, John D. 1986. *George Herbert Mead: A Unifying Theory for Sociology.* Beverly Hills, CA: Sage.

Barry, Robert M. 1968. "A Man and a City: George Herbert Mead in Chicago." In Michael Novak (Ed.), *American Philosophy and the Future: Essays for a New Generation* (pp. 173–192). New York: Charles Scribner's Sons.

Blumer, Herbert. 1969. *Symbolic Interactionism: Perspective and Method.* Berkeley: University of California Press.

Collins, Randall. 1985. *Three Sociological Traditions.* New York: Oxford University Press.

Collins, Randall, & Michael Makowsky. 1989. *The Discovery of Society* (4th ed.). New York: Random House.

Colomy, Paul, & J. David Brown. 1995. "Elaboration, Revision, Polemic, and Progress in the Second Chicago School." In Gary Alan Fine (Ed.), *A Second Chicago School? The Development of a Postwar American Sociology* (pp. 17–81). Chicago: University of Chicago Press.

Coser, Lewis A. 1977. *Masters of Sociological Thought* (2nd ed.). San Diego: Harcourt Brace Jovanovich.

Crunden, Robert M. 1982. *Ministers of Reform: The Progressives' Achievement in American Civilization 1889–1920.* New York: Basic Books.

Deegan, Mary Jo. 1988. *Jane Addams and the Men of the Chicago School, 1892–1918.* New Brunswick, NJ: Transaction Books.

Denzin, Norman K. 1987. *The Recovering Alcoholic.* Newbury Park, CA: Sage.

Faris, Robert E. L. 1967. *Chicago Sociology 1920–1932.* San Francisco: Chandler.

Fine, Gary Alan. 1995. "Introduction." In Gary Alan Fine (Ed.), *A Second Chicago School? The Development of a Postwar American Sociology* (pp. 1–16). Chicago: University of Chicago Press.

Gusfield, Joseph R. 1996. *Contested Meanings: The Construction of Alcohol Problems.* Madison: University of Wisconsin Press.

Hawthorne, Geoffrey. 1976. *Enlightenment and Despair: A History of Sociology.* London: Cambridge University Press.

Joas, Hans. 1985. *G. H. Mead: A Contemporary Re-Examination of His Thought* (translated by Raymond Meyer). Cambridge, MA: MIT Press.

Levine, Donald L. 1995. *Visions of the Sociological Tradition.* Chicago: University of Chicago Press.

Lewis, J. David, & Richard L. Smith. 1980. *American Sociology and Pragmatism: Mead, Chicago Sociology, and Symbolic Interaction.* Chicago: University of Chicago Press.

Lipset, Seymour Martin. 1996. *American Exceptionalism: A Double-Edged Sword.* New York: Norton.

Maines, David R. 1992. "Pragmatism." In Edgar F. Borgatta & Marie L. Borgatta (Eds.), *Encyclopedia of Sociology* (pp. 1531–1536). New York: Macmillan.

Miller, David L. 1973. *George Herbert Mead: Self, Language, and the World.* Austin: University of Texas Press.

Miller, Donald L. 1996. *City of the Century: The Epic of Chicago and the Making of America.* New York: Simon & Schuster.

Morris, Charles W. 1934. "Introduction: George H. Mead as Social Psychologist and Social Philosopher." In Charles W. Morris (Ed.), *Mind, Self, and Society* (pp. x–xxxv). Chicago: University of Chicago Press.

Natanson, Maurice. 1956. *The Social Dynamics of George H. Mead.* Washington, DC: Public Affairs Press.

Ritzer, George. 1996. *Sociological Theory* (4th ed.). New York: McGraw-Hill.

Shalin, Dmitri N. 1991. "G. H. Mead, Socialism, and the Progressive Agenda." In Mitchell Aboulafia (Ed.), *Philosophy, Social Theory, and the Thought of George Herbert Mead* (pp. 21–56). Albany: State University of New York Press.

Strauss, Anselm. 1964. "Introduction." In Anselm Strauss (Ed.), *On Social Psychology* (pp. vii–xxv). Chicago: University of Chicago Press.

Stryker, Sheldon. 1992. "Symbolic Interaction Theory." In Edgar F. Borgatta & Marie L. Borgatta (Eds.), *Encyclopedia of Sociology* (pp. 2127–2134). New York: Macmillan.

REFERENCE NOTES

Citations for quotations and special points of interest are given in the text. Listed here are citations to sources for major topics covered in each section of the chapter.

1. Religious Goals Transformed into Social Action: Mead's Christian views (Shalin 1991:27–28); Religious colleges (Collins 1985:183); Mead's generation (Crunden 1982:ix, 15–16); Birth (Coser 1977:341); Move (Ashley & Orenstein 1995:446); Personality (Miller 1973:xii; Crunden 1982:36; Shalin 1991:27); Oberlin College (Miller 1973:xii; Shalin 1991:27; Crunden 1982:7; Coser 1977:342); Social activism (Ashley & Orenstein 1995:446; Coser 1977:341); Exposure to scientific knowledge (Joas 1985:15; Coser 1977:342; Ashley & Orenstein 1995:447); Loss of meaning (Miller 1973:xii; Joas 1985:16); Father died (Coser 1977:342); Mead's jobs (Coser 1977:342; Ashley & Orenstein 1995:447; Crunden 1982:27; Miller 1973:xiii); Worries (Ashley & Orenstein 1995:447–448; Joas 1985:17; Miller 1973:xix; Shalin 1991:29); Germany (Joas 1985:19; Baldwin 1986:9; Ashley & Orenstein 1995:448; Shalin 1991:29); Reformism (Ashley & Orenstein 1995:448; Joas 1985:20; Shalin 1991:30; Crunden 1982:16, 37).

2. Threats to American Values: Chicago and the Growth of Cities: American exceptionalism (Lipset 1996:13, 18–23, 63, 154); Gap between ideal and reality (Shalin 1991:35, 38, 51); Chicago (Miller 1996:15–18, 24); Chicago's growth (Miller 1996:17); Economic growth (Miller 1996:24–25); Immigration (Barry 1968:176; Miller 1996:442, 461); Social problems (Miller 1996:18–19, 508–513); Politics (Miller 1996:465–467); Haymarket riot (Miller 1996:473–481).

3. Combining Learning and Problem Solving: John Dewey (Ashley & Orenstein 1995:448; Shalin 1991:31; Strauss 1964:ix); Mead and Dewey (Coser 1977:351; Shalin 1991:31); Mead and Dewey at Chicago (Joas 1985:21–22; Shalin 1991:32); University of Chicago (Faris 1967:23; Miller 1996:395); Harper (Miller 1996:393–401; Faris 1967:23); Chicago faculty (Strauss 1964:viii; Miller 1996:400); Pragmatism (Baldwin 1986:14–22; Levine 1995:254; Maines 1992:1532); Individual and social efforts (Strauss 1964:xx); Unity of science and progress (Shalin 1991:54–55); Substitute for evangelism (Crunden 1982:57; Miller 1973:xxiii); Evolution (Strauss 1964:xix; Ritzer 1996:380; Joas 1985:33–35; Baldwin 1986:84); Individual and society (Mead 1934:6; Levine 1995:262).

4. A Social Version of Behaviorism: Mead (Ritzer 1996:367; Miller 1973:xxxii–xxxiii; Baldwin 1986:12); Teaching (Baldwin 1986:10; Miller 1973:xxxiii; Crunden 1982:27); Modesty (Ashley & Orenstein 1995:449; Strauss 1964:x; Coser 1977:347; Miller 1973:xxxv); Writing problems (Collins & Makowsky 1989:178; Coser 1977:346; Deegan 1988:106; Morris 1934:vii–viii); Mead and sociology (Strauss 1964:xi; Coser 1977:345); American sociology (Hawthorne 1976:191–192; Crunden 1982:68, 81; Faris 1967:8; Levine 1995:251); Sociology at Chicago (Hawthorne 1976:210; Faris 1967:12, 128; Deegan 1988:1; Collins 1985:199); Mead on behaviorism

(Mead 1934:1–8); One famous behaviorist (Mead 1934:101); Respond to stimuli (Strauss 1964:xxi; Levine 1995:259; Mead 1934:1–41); Mental processes (Baldwin 1986:50, 63; Morris 1934:xvi; Ritzer 1996:363; Coser 1877:339).

5. Human Thinking Comes from Social Interaction: Promotions (Miller 1973:xxii); John Dewey leaves (Baldwin 1986:10); Community involvement (Coser 1977:344–345; Deegan 1988:111); Progressive education (Deegan 1988:108–111; Ritzer 1996:379–380); Immigrants (Barry 1968:178, 182; Deegan 1988:109, 117; Shalin 1991:36); Civic groups (Barry 1968:176–177; Deegan 1988:115); Labor issues (Deegan 1988:112–116; Shalin 1991:33–35; War (Ashley & Orenstein 1995:452); Democracy (Shalin 1991:39, 53); Mead's social philosophy (Shalin 1991:51); Animal perception (Baldwin 1986:83); Gestures (Mead 1934:14; Baldwin 1986:70–72); Vocal gestures (Mead 1934:43, 61–68; Natanson 1956:9); Significant symbols (Mead 1934:68–75; Baldwin 1986:77–78); A bully's threat (Mead 1934:147); Intelligence (Baldwin 1986:84); Mind (Mead 1934:49; Strauss 1964:xxii; Morris 1934:xxii).

6. The Emergence of the Social Self: Jane Addams (Miller 1996:419–422; Crunden 1982:24); Hull House (Deegan 1988:5; Miller 1996:421); Addams and Mead (Ashley & Orenstein 1995:449; Deegan 1988:4–5); Work for women's rights (Deegan 1988:116, 209; Crunden 1982:65); Mead and Hull House (Deegan 1988:107); Mead's theory of social relations (Joas 1985:35; Morris, 1934:xxiii; Strauss 1964:xxii); Cooley (Miller 1973:xx); Social self (Mead 1934:134–135, 140, 152–164); Socialization (Baldwin 1986:92–93; Coser 1977:335); Role play (Mead 1934:150; Morris 1934:xxiv); Games (Mead 1934:151); Generalized other (Mead 1934:154–155); Implications of social self (Mead 1934:173–178; Morris 1934:xxv–xxvi); Contrast with other perspectives (Blumer 1969:61–64; Ashley & Orenstein 1995:458; Deegan 1988:107).

7. Symbolic Interactionism: Decides to leave (Miller 1973:xxxvii); Blumer (Strauss 1964:x; Lewis & Smith 1980:170; Colomy & Brown 1995:20; Fine 1995:x); Blumer's interpretations (Colomy & Brown 1995:23; Blumer 1969:70); Symbolic interactionism (Stryker 1992:2127–2131; Blumer 1969:66); Objectivity (Colomy & Brown 1995:23–25, 58–59; Blumer 1969:73; Stryker 1992:2132; Ashley & Orenstein 1995:480; Lewis & Smith 1980); Constructing social problems (Gusfield 1996:4–5, 17); Drinking behavior (Gusfield 1996:36, 181–182, 195); Alcoholics Anonymous (Denzin 1987).

chapter 6

W. E. B. Du Bois and the Tragedy of Race in America

Over one hundred years ago, W. E. B. Du Bois (1993 [1903]:5) wrote, "The problem of the twentieth century is the problem of the color-line." Despite enormous change since then, the same might be said about the twenty-first century. A title of a best-selling book by political scientist Andrew Hacker (1995) summarizes race relations today: *Two Nations: Black and White, Separate, Hostile, and Unequal.* Although slavery, legal segregation, and the most blatant forms of racism have ended and race relations have improved immeasurably, economic inequality and new forms of discrimination continue. Tensions between black and white Americans underlie debates over affirmative action, poverty, and even the response to Hurricane Katrina in New Orleans, while marriages, close friendships, and leisure activities all too rarely cross racial lines.

Although racial conflict is a problem all over the world, it takes a special form in the United States for a simple reason. The country was founded on the premise that all citizens in a democracy should have equal rights. Yet slavery, segregation, and inequality have since the nation's founding violated that premise. Through most of our nation's history, legislators, leaders, judges, and police have ignored the Constitution and the democratic ideals of the new nation. The contradiction between the stated goal of equal rights and actual practice of racial discrimination has created a dilemma that is uniquely American.

European sociologists at the turn of the twentieth century recognized the special issues raised by race but gave it little attention in their writings. American scholars around the same time gave it more attention but sometimes in ways that worsened rather than improved the problem. Some used genetic and evolutionary theories to justify the subordinate position of nonwhites. Others recognized the evil of racism and supported reform, but few made it central to their work.

One African-American sociologist stands out in both his studies of race and his efforts to extend the democratic rights that whites enjoyed to black Americans. W. E. B. Du Bois was the first sociologist to provide scientific evidence on the plight of black men and women and develop the foundation for a social theory of race inequality. He never presented a system of theoretical ideas, as Marx, Durkheim, and Weber did. More like Simmel and Mead, he offered insights on specific issues and problems—in this case, race relations in the United States. More than a hundred years ago, he described better than anyone the contradiction between the ideals of America and the reality of race.

In the words of Manning Marable (1986:viii), a contemporary African-American social scientist, "Few intellectuals have done more to shape the twentieth century than W. E. B. Du Bois." An editor of the work of Du Bois on social theory (Zuckerman 2004:3) declares that "he is arguably one of the most brilliant social theorists this country has ever produced." The praise reflects not only the sociological and intellectual contributions Du Bois made but also his political influence. As a founding member of the highly influential National Association for the Advancement of Colored People and a writer widely known to the public and political activists, he helped direct the civil rights movement during the first half of the twentieth century. Not until Martin Luther King, Jr., did another African-American civil rights leader gain the prominence of Du Bois (Lemert 2000:347).

In describing the life and sociological work of Du Bois, this chapter extends sociological theory to the topic of race. It highlights the tragic nature of the treatment of blacks in America and gives attention to an African-American scholar who was central to the development of sociology—even if it has taken a long time for sociologists to recognize his contribution. Despite the passage of more than a century since his first publications, Du Bois' work continues to offer insights into race relations, the experiences of African Americans, and the persistence of inequality in modern society.

1. PREPARING FOR HIS LIFE'S WORK

By the age of 26, W. E. B. Du Bois had become one of the best educated men in the country. As an African American, he faced more obstacles than most people in getting this education, yet his sheer intelligence and hard work took him to the top of the academic world. After attending historically black Fisk University in Nashville, Tennessee, he received undergraduate and graduate training at Harvard University and extended his education by studying in Germany—the intellectual center of the world at the time. With his dissertation and a Ph.D. nearly in hand, he had obtained an education that only a tiny fraction of Americans—white or otherwise—could claim.

Yet, as he began to search for a job in 1894, he felt the pain of racial discrimination. No prospects or invitations came from the top universities in the North that, based on his qualifications alone, should have enthusiastically recruited him. In desperate need of money, he wrote letters to black colleges for a job and accepted the first offer that came through. Wilberforce University in Xenia, Ohio, a respected if poorly funded Methodist school for blacks, hired him to teach Greek and Latin.

It turned out that Du Bois' training and personality did not fit the university. He soon offended his colleagues with strong opinions about the flaws of the college and the narrow religious outlook of many of the faculty. Wilberforce had no funds to support a library and often was late in paying its teachers. Du Bois made his criticisms public, often alienating others and appearing arrogant and conceited.

Something more important upset Du Bois about the job. Teaching Greek and Latin did little to meet his desire to help improve the circumstances of blacks in America. Du Bois wanted instead to apply his education to understanding social life and even volunteered to teach a sociology course on his own time—an offer that would have led to the first sociology course in the nation. The college president, however, refused to allow students to take such a class. Du Bois felt intellectually isolated, unhappy with Wilberforce University, and disillusioned with traditional scholarship.

The unpleasant experience nonetheless had a benefit. His time at Wilberforce helped clarify his life's work: to use history and other social sciences as a weapon that, sharpened by research and writing, would lead to the emancipation of the American Negro. He would soon have his chance to do so and would embark on a career as a sociologist, researcher, theorist, scholar, and activist. Du Bois (1968:192) writes in his autobiography that his life until then had, at least in hindsight, moved in a coherent direction toward his goal. Indeed, his life until then was unusual in many ways for a black American in the nineteenth century.

A Sheltered and Happy Youth

William Edward Burghardt Du Bois was born in 1868 in Great Barrington, Massachusetts, a small farming community in an area of hills and forests in the western part of the state. The town of about 4,000 people was largely white, but several black families, including the Burghardts, relatives on the side of Du Bois' mother, had settled there several generations earlier. A largely middle-class town, Great Barrington had only modest inequality, and the races got along well compared to the south and larger cities. The great problems of the world, including the racial conflict after the Civil War and the end of slavery only a few years before, did not reach into Great Barrington.

Du Bois' great-great grandfather had been taken from West Africa by Dutch slave traders to the Hudson Valley in New York, where he became a servant for a white Dutch family and adopted their last name of Burghardt. After serving in the American Revolutionary War, he was given his freedom and eventually moved to the Great Barrington area. The family prospered modestly there; most family members farmed or worked in town as servants, laborers, and barbers.

Du Bois' mother, one of the youngest of 10 children of Othello Burghardt, worked as a housemaid, and in her 30s met Alfred Du Bois, who had recently moved to the town. Alfred had a French grandfather and a black grandmother, and his father lived over the years in the Bahamas, Haiti, Connecticut, and Massachusetts. Born in Haiti, Alfred wandered much himself, not settling down until 1867 when he arrived in Great Barrington at around age 35. Rather than adopting the French pronunciation of his last name (due bwah), Alfred pronounced his name as due boyss, with the accent on the last syllable. His son would insist on the same pronunciation.

Du Bois (1968:72) describes his father as a handsome, adventuresome dreamer, who was distrusted by the Burghardt family because "he was too good-looking, too white . . . [with] no property or job." Despite feuding with the Burghardt family, Alfred married Mary, and Willie, as he was known as a child, was born soon afterward. However, following his desire to travel, Alfred soon moved to Connecticut to build a house for his family and presumably get away from the influence of the Burghardts. Probably at the urging of her relatives, Mary decided she did not want to move, and Alfred did not go back to Great Barrington.

After the age of two, Du Bois would never see his father again. Du Bois' mother and relatives seldom spoke about his father, but the split left Mary Du Bois depressed and quiet. By his own account, Willie Du Bois led a happy, sheltered life, thanks in part to the aid and support of many in the community. He experienced little in the way of discrimination from white classmates, joined in activities with friends, and enjoyed life in the small town. Above all, he excelled in school, which made him a favorite of his teachers and gave him self-confidence in dealing with others. At least as he described himself in his autobiography, written many decades later, Du Bois felt happy, confident, and well-liked rather than resentful, mistreated, and inferior.

His small-town upbringing instilled many values that stayed with him throughout his life. Of most importance, he developed expectations of equality. Blacks did not do as well as whites in the town, but the wealth gap was not great in largely middle-class Great Barrington. Prejudice against Irish immigrants who were new to town seemed stronger than prejudice against black residents who had been a presence for decades. Du Bois believed as a youth that wealth came from talent and hard work and poverty from poor training and laziness.

Like others in small New England towns, he was quiet, soft-spoken, and formal in addressing others. Over the years, he would act reserved and proper and dress formally rather than act warm, easy-going, and casual. These personality characteristics served him well as a youth in school, at odds jobs, and in church and Sunday school but would make it hard to deal with his more outgoing acquaintances later in life. Some would view him as an overdressed snob. His success in school and confidence in his abilities made him certain of his opinions, sometimes even cocky and arrogant. Throughout his life, Du Bois would strongly express and doggedly defend his beliefs. He also developed habits of hard work that served him well in his career but also led him to criticize others who did not work as hard.

Du Bois himself said that, given his intelligence and school performance, he developed a sense of disdain for anyone who did not like him or treated him poorly. That his principal, teachers, and some of the wealthier town residents helped purchase his school books and raised money to help pay for his college made him feel closer to the white elite of the city than to the poor. He believed that character was far more important than race, but that belief would soon change.

New Worlds

Given a sheltered life generally unharmed by the disease of racism, Du Bois was stunned when he moved at age 17 to Nashville to attend Fisk University. He saw for the first time the huge diversity of African Americans and the treatment they received in the segregated South. He saw that whites treated him not as part of the educated elite but as part of a group defined by skin color, even though he had little in common with poor and uneducated southern blacks. Worse, the scorn, hate, and violence directed against blacks appalled him. He would write, "No one but a Negro going into the South without previous experience of color caste can have any conception of its barbarism" (Du Bois 1968:121).

Despite his unpleasant introduction to racism in the South, Du Bois enjoyed his college experience. His education in Great Barrington had been so good that he was placed in sophomore classes his first year, and he graduated in 1888 after only three years at Fisk. He also enjoyed the companionship he found in the black community. On graduation, he worked to realize his desire to attend Harvard University. With the support of his Fisk professors, he was accepted at the prestigious university and, although he had already received a degree from Fisk, entered Harvard as a junior. Aided by a grant from an educational foundation, he planned to study philosophy.

While at Harvard, he had few dealings with white students and their clubs and fraternities. After living in the South for several years, he accepted the more informal nature of segregation in the North and avoided intruding on situations where he was not wanted (although his independence may have struck students as standoffishness and conceit). Concentrating more on his studies than on social activities, he enjoyed the support and encouragement of his professors. Taking courses in philosophy from William James and many other notables, he also began to learn a bit about sociology.

After receiving another undergraduate degree, his academic success continued. He followed the encouragement of his professors by enrolling in graduate studies at Harvard. During these years, Du Bois first began to apply philosophy to the historical interpretation of race and to take first steps toward viewing sociology as a science of human action. Toward that end, he planned a dissertation on the topic of the suppression of the American slave trade. He wanted still more—to study in Germany, which had the world's best universities at the time—and was confident that he would continue his steady trajectory of academic success. Although he had some difficulty getting financial support for international study, the funds came through and he left America in 1892.

Just as the South had been an eye-opening experience for Du Bois on the evils of the color line, Europe was equally awakening in a more positive sense. He interacted with whites who showed no prejudice and treated him more as a privileged American student more than as a member of an inferior race. He realized that the ways of living and dealing with race in America could be radically different. While studying in Berlin, he furthered confirmed his desire to use the new methods of social science to study race. Social science during the time of Max Weber in Germany offered the kind of method and perspective that Du Bois thought could be applied to understand racial problems.

After taking courses for three semesters in Berlin, Du Bois returned to Harvard to finish his dissertation and Ph.D. The foundation supporting his European coursework had decided that it would prefer him to receive a degree from an American university and declined to renew funding just a few months short of receiving his degree from the University of Berlin. Still, a degree from Harvard was plenty satisfying, and Du Bois became the first African American to earn a doctorate there. From our perspective today, when the Ph.D. has become common, it may be hard to grasp the special accomplishment this degree signified. He had moved steadily and without fanfare to become one of the nation's best educated men of any race.

In 1894, then, Du Bois began his new job at Wilberforce University; one year later he completed his Harvard Ph.D.; two years later he published his dissertation, *The Suppression of the African Slave Trade*. He spent two years at Wilberforce, from 1894 to 1896, teaching Latin and Greek, all the while hoping for something more. He married a student at Wilberforce, Nina Gomer, in 1896 and began a family in the next few years. Otherwise, however, the time spent there represented a prelude to a career as a researcher, writer, and political activist.

2. THE FAILURE OF RECONSTRUCTION

Du Bois was born only five years after the Emancipation Proclamation of President Abraham Lincoln started the process of freeing the slaves and only three years after the bloody Civil War between the North and South had ended. During Du Bois' youth, great hopes for the advancement of the freed slaves were dashed by the eventual establishment of segregation laws in the South known as the Jim Crow system. Many people interpreted this failure of former slaves to advance as a sign of their inferiority and viewed the system of segregation as necessary given this inferiority. Du Bois would devote much of his work to refuting this claim.

The victory of the North over the South in the Civil War—formalized when General Robert E. Lee surrendered to General Ulysses S. Grant at Appomattox, Virginia, in 1865—created for the nation new political and economic struggles. What conditions would be placed on the South in rejoining the Union? What controls would be required to guarantee the fair treatment of the newly freed slaves? How much freedom should the southern states have in rebuilding their governments and economies?

Initial Progress

President Abraham Lincoln and President Andrew Johnson, who became president on Lincoln's assassination, did not favor imposing harsh conditions on the South. They hoped that generosity rather than punishment would speed the process of reintegration. The process would begin with the Thirteenth Amendment to the Constitution, which had been ratified in 1865. In stating that "neither slavery nor involuntary servitude . . . shall exist within the United States," the amendment represented a start in dealing with the treatment of southern blacks. The optimistic hope was that, with their defeat, Southerners would give black citizens the freedom and opportunity of white citizens.

However, soon after the end of the Civil War and slavery, some southern cities and states passed a series of laws known as **black codes**—laws that restricted the jobs, movement, and ownership of land of blacks. Some of these codes outlawed use of insulting gestures and language and made it illegal to assemble. Others prevented blacks from serving on juries, owning weapons, marrying whites, and attending schools with whites. Some southern towns had curfews for blacks and required all blacks entering the city to have their papers checked; others required blacks to register so authorities could check their papers on demand.

Many congressmen who wanted to treat the South as a conquered enemy responded to the black codes with new legislation and demands for federal control in the South. Over the opposition of President Johnson, Congress passed a Civil Rights Act in 1866 that outlawed discrimination by race and a Reconstruction Act in 1867 that put the South under military occupation. So began the period of **Reconstruction,** a process that aimed to rehabilitate the ex-Confederate states and readmit them to the union.

Two important constitutional amendments followed to counteract black codes in the South. In 1868 the Fourteenth Amendment was ratified. It reads: "No State shall make or enforce any law which shall abridge the privileges or immunities of citizens of the United States; nor shall any State deprive any person of life, liberty, or property, without due process of law; nor deny to any person within its jurisdiction the equal protection of the laws." In 1870, the Fifteenth Amendment was ratified: "The rights of citizens of the United States to vote shall not be denied or abridged by the United States or by any State on account of race, color, or previous condition of servitude."

With the U.S. military present to enforce the new laws, blacks in the South made some political progress. By 1870, Hiram Revels of Mississippi became the first African American elected to the U.S. Senate, and during the 1870s there were 22 blacks from eight states elected to Congress. Many others were elected to state legislatures and local boards during the 1870s. Representing a majority in some areas of the South, blacks could play a leadership role. In addition, the federal government established the Freedman's Bureau to furnish supplies, set up schools, and resettle newly freed slaves. These changes did not translate into real power or major economic progress among ex-slaves, but they certainly represented movement in that direction.

The South Responds

Resistance among southern whites to this threat to their power formed immediately. Many claimed that the newly elected politicians fostered mob rule and rewarded the corrupt actions of carpetbaggers—Northerners who came south to gain power and wealth from the defeated states. In December 1867, some ex-Confederate soldiers formed the Ku Klux Klan, a secret society of white men with the goal of using violence and intimidation to resist giving blacks the same rights as whites.

New ways of preventing blacks from voting emerged. Poll taxes that required payment to vote, property requirements that required ownership of land to vote, and literacy tests that required education to vote all would come to disenfranchise the largely poor and uneducated black population. So-called grandfather clauses did much the same. They required voters to prove that their grandfather had been eligible to vote, when nearly all blacks in the South had grandfathers who, as slaves, had not been allowed to vote. Mob violence and lynchings would prevent still others from voting. By the mid-1870s, white Democrats with Confederate sympathies were increasingly elected to office and replaced blacks and Republicans more supportive of equality.

New forms of economic control emerged as well. Unable to afford to buy their own land, many former slaves began to farm as sharecroppers. They worked land owned by whites and turned over a share of the crops to the owners. Seldom more than a way to barely survive, the system kept agricultural wealth in the hands of whites and prevented economic progress among the rural black population.

In 1876, a close and disputed national election led to the selection of Rutherford Hayes as president, but he took office in 1877 only after agreeing to a compromise that would end the military occupation of the South. Northern liberals devoted to the rights of all races had tired of the battle and southern whites wanted full control of their state governments. That year, having realized few of the goals to improve the lot of ex-slaves, the last of the federal troops left the Confederate states. The South had reentered the union but not with equal rights guaranteed for all.

New Forms of Segregation

With the end of northern control, new and even more blatant forms of legal segregation steadily emerged in the South. Some of the changes had already begun—white and black children never attended the same schools—but other forms of segregation in public transportation, facilities, and hotels developed anew. Historically, physical segregation of the races had been more common in the North, where white and black residents lived in separate areas of cities and worked at different kinds of jobs. Contact between the races in the South had been too close under the slave system to enforce most kinds of segregation. Yet this too changed.

In 1890, Louisiana passed a law that required blacks to ride in separate railroad cars. Other laws in states throughout the South would restrict access of blacks to schools, restaurants, hospitals, and public places. Signs indicated separate entrances, exits, restrooms, park space, and water fountains for whites and coloreds. These laws mandating segregation became known as the **Jim Crow system,** for a character in entertainment skits that depicted blacks in racist terms as poor and uneducated.

With the federal government having abandoned nearly all efforts to protect the rights of blacks, the new laws gained strength. Enforcement was severe; southern prisons and chain gangs were used to punish violators. Suits were filed claiming that segregation laws violated constitutional rights. Yet the courts consistently sided with the states. The Supreme Court had overturned the Civil Rights Act of 1875, an effort to ensure equal rights for all races, as unconstitutional. It would also rule that the Fourteenth Amendment, which guaranteed equal protection of the law, did not prohibit individuals and private organizations from discriminating.

The most important confirmation of the legal acceptance of segregation laws came from an 1896 Supreme Court decision, *Plessy v. Ferguson.* A man of mixed race, Homer Plessy, sat in a Louisiana train car reserved for whites, was arrested for refusing to move, and sued to end the law as unconstitutional. Affirming a lower court decision, the Supreme Court ruled that separate but equal accommodations did not violate the constitutional rights of blacks or treat the "colored race with a badge of inferiority." Later decisions extended the doctrine of separate but equal to schools and led to Jim Crow laws throughout all the ex-Confederate states. Not until the 1960s would the system disappear.

Along with legalized means of segregation, illegal means flourished. Mob violence and lynching of blacks became common in the South. Two experts summarize the extent of lynching: "The scale of this carnage means that, on the average, a black man, woman, or child was murdered nearly once a week, every week, between 1882 and 1930 by a hate-driven white mob" (Tolnay and Beck 1995:ix). Seemingly minor infractions such as gambling and being disrespectful toward whites, more serious crimes such as rape and murder, and legal behaviors such as trying to vote or voting for the wrong party could incite mob violence. The crime itself had little importance; rather, lynching was a form of social control that helped maintain the system of segregation and racial inequality.

The circumstances of blacks in the North differed from those of the South but also contributed to racial inequality. Free blacks remained disadvantaged relative to whites and through discrimination and prejudice had little access to quality education, good jobs, and houses in white parts of the city. Difficulties of the black population in the North worsened with the initial movement of southern blacks to large cities in the hope of finding work. Racial inequality of one form or another remained throughout the country.

Explaining the Failure

Historians writing in the late nineteenth and early twentieth centuries labeled Reconstruction as a failure—it in fact did not meet the goal of bringing blacks into society as equal members. However, their explanation of the failure blamed those who tried to bring about change. One of the most well-known historians writing about Reconstruction, William Archibald Dunning of Columbia University, argued that carpetbaggers (Northerners who migrated to the South after the Civil War) and scalawags (southern Republicans who cooperated with Northerners) who were at first elected to office were corrupt and incompetent. He further argued that the freed slaves who voted for carpetbaggers, scalawags, or other blacks lacked the skills, experience, and intelligence to make wise choices in voting or to take advantage of the new economic opportunities that freedom brought them.

Racial inequality and segregation were, as a result, necessary to bring about social and economic order in the face of the chaos left over from the war and freeing of the slaves. Reconstruction had failed, according to Dunning, and the desire to maintain peace and order justified the compromise that removed troops from the South.

Du Bois had little personal experience with these problems until he went to college in Nashville, Tennessee, but he nonetheless recognized the problem of race in the decades after the Civil War. He could see the gap between the principles of democracy that should guide the nation and the treatment of black Americans. As a highly educated African American, he could also see, more than most, that existing social science and scholarship helped maintain the color line. The scholarship on Reconstruction seemed to blame freed slaves for their failure to progress and to justify the emergence of segregation. Du Bois offered a powerful alternative perspective on the problems of blacks in American society.

3. THE PHILADELPHIA NEGRO

A Welcome Opportunity

In 1896, Du Bois gained the opportunity to realize his goal of using scientific methods to counteract both the existing intellectual scholarship on blacks and the system of inequality. Out of the blue, he received an invitation to become an assistant instructor of sociology at the University of Pennsylvania for the purpose of completing a study of the social life of blacks in Philadelphia. The title meant little because the university would contribute nothing to the study other than the payment of his salary. The opportunity—Du Bois called it salvation—to realize his career goals meant much more.

In Du Bois' view, Philadelphia was one of the most corrupt cities in the nation, but every so often it went through a spasm of reform. In this particular case, the black community of Philadelphia, the largest in the North, supported a crooked political machine that reformers wanted to end. A few idealistic leaders thought that documenting the terrible conditions of the black community would help discredit and replace dishonest city leaders. The effort was likely to have more credibility if it came from the University of Pennsylvania, a respected Ivy League school in Philadelphia. In fact, the study would not lead to the long-term goal of a change in leadership that its backers wanted, but it would have considerable intellectual influence.

Du Bois happily accepted the salary of $900 for a period of one year to complete the study. Samuel McCune Lindsay of the department of sociology, no doubt aware of Du Bois' Harvard degree and published book on the slave trade, had recommended him for the job. Du Bois praised Lindsay for handing over full responsibility for the study—others might have hired a black man as a clerk and taken credit for the study themselves. Lindsay would return the praise, noting that Du Bois' fine work exceeded their expectations.

Others in the sociology department and the university were less supportive. Given the resistance of white faculty, Du Bois was not offered an instructorship, office, or chance to teach. On the advice of the president, the catalogue initially neglected to list Du Bois as a member of the university. Even the title of assistant instructor was a snub to someone as accomplished as Du Bois, but race trumped qualifications. Although he was thrilled to have the job and leave Wilberforce, Du Bois remained bitter about the snub years later. Even after he had proven his skills by successfully completing the study, he still did not receive an offer of an instructorship.

Du Bois and his wife, Nina, married only a short time, moved into a one-room apartment in the center of the black area he would study. The Seventh Ward of Philadelphia was a densely populated 18-block area with nearly 10,000 black residents. The area is now populated largely by affluent whites, but at the time it presented the worst the city could offer. Du Bois described his apartment as located in the midst of dirt, drunkenness, poverty, and crime. Despite the meager living conditions, husband and wife seemed happy, and a son was born the next year.

Goals and Methods

Du Bois set to work with characteristic industriousness. He would conduct and write the study himself, having no funds for assistants to help with the enormous task. Toward that end, he started knocking on the door of every black household in the area to request an interview. He must have been an unusual sight, moving through the noisy, dirty, and poor neighborhood dressed in a formal suit, usually with gloves and a cane. Despite his formality, he overcame the suspicions that residents had of outsiders who wanted to study them. Over a three-month period, Du Bois spent 835 hours interviewing people in 2,500 households.

Du Bois' method of investigation reflected larger theoretical preferences. He distrusted grand theories common in the nineteenth century that used principles like natural selection or "survival of the fittest" to make broad generalizations about the evolution of societies. Such efforts, he thought, ignored or failed to establish the facts of social life, which scholars should steadily accumulate from scientific study and observations. Theory should emerge from observation and historical understanding rather than from armchair speculation. Otherwise, it would miss the important role of "human choice, wish, whim and prejudice" (Du Bois 1996 [1899]:98). Unlike many theorists, Du Bois emphasized that both freedom and constraint shape social life and must be studied in the real world.

At the same time, Du Bois wanted more than careful science and accurate theory—he wanted his fact-based understanding of the life of black men and women in Philadelphia to lead to reform. The careful, scientific study of the black community would, he hoped, convince academics of the value of his work, while at the same time his ideas about the sources of racial inequality would help lead to reform of social conditions. His forthcoming book "would speak calmly yet devastatingly of the history and logic of poverty and racism" (Lewis 1993:190). He would not make brash claims but would back up his generalizations with evidence and understanding of the social conditions he was study-ing. The goal would be to replace ignorance with knowledge.

In 1899, *The Philadelphia Negro: A Social Study* was published. It con-tained some 520 pages of text and references, innumerable tables and fig-ures, and an appendix written by a colleague, Isabel Eaton, on the cir-cumstances of domestic workers in the city. Any reader must be impressed by the multiple sources and thoroughness of evidence. The census figures, historical records, in-depth interviews, hundreds of tables, dozens of personal stories, and detailed maps of blocks, homes, and the location of social classes are both overwhelming and fascinating. It was not the first such statistical study, but it was probably the best until then.

At the time the book was written, *Negro* and *colored* were terms most commonly used to describe blacks or African Americans. Du Bois fol-lowed this terminology, but unlike most writers, he insisted on capital-izing *Negro* to give his race the respect he felt it deserved.

On its publication, *The Philadelphia Negro* received largely positive reviews (Katz and Sugrue 1998:26–27). Scholars praised its thorough and accurate presentation of the facts and the attention it gave to issues of validity in the data. More important, they praised its insights on how social and economic conditions and race prejudice, rather than racial abil-ity, affected social behavior. This breakthrough work made Du Bois one of the most promising young sociologists in the country. Over the next century, the book's themes would show up in major works on race (An-derson 1996:xxiv), and its perspective on the sources of minority group problems would become fully accepted by sociologists.

Race and Social Conditions

Throughout his book, Du Bois sought to refute an underlying theory about the source of problems among blacks in Philadelphia and America more generally. The theory emerged in the work of Reconstruction his-torians, social theories of survival of the fittest, and the preaching of white supremacists. More central to Du Bois' study, it emerged among the public and leaders in Philadelphia. "There is a widespread feeling that something is wrong with a race that is responsible for so much crime" (Du Bois 1996 [1899]:241). The feeling led to claims that their great city "was going to the dogs because of the crime and venality of its Negro cit-izens" (Du Bois 1940:58).

Early in the book Du Bois presented historical evidence that such claims were wrong. He noted that blacks in Philadelphia had steadily im-proved their lives after emancipation occurred there in the late 1700s. They started new churches, schools, small businesses; they entered the trades and professions; by 1810, they had grown to 10 percent of the city population. Such progress contradicted claims of inferiority and the in-ability to advance. After 1820, however, conditions for the city's racial minority worsened. The growing number of free blacks competed for jobs with white immigrants, which heightened race tensions and led to discrimination. In 1834, for example, rioting whites destroyed 31 houses and two black churches and killed one black resident, and in 1838 new laws ended the right of blacks to vote.

In another period of prosperity, from 1840 to 1870, new black leadership and the success of blacks in the restaurant and catering business moved the community forward. The wealth of the city grew, offering more job opportunities to blacks and increasing the value of their property. Then changes yet again caused by the influx of freed slaves from the South led to new restrictions on personal liberty and greater segregation. Twice in the history of Philadelphia, the black minority made substantial economic progress only to have the progress checked by immigration—once by whites from Europe and once by former slaves from the South. These changes, both the improvement and the deterioration, reflected social forces rather than innate inferiority.

At the time of the study in 1896, the Philadelphia black community certainly suffered from many problems that Du Bois described fully. He found rundown houses, high crime, broken families, excess alcohol use, bad health, early death, poverty, illiteracy, unemployment, low pay, gambling, and vote-buying. The images and stereotypes of whites often exaggerated the problems, and Du Bois noted that only a small part of the black community suffered most from these troubles. At the same time, however, he did not minimize their seriousness and tried to understand their causes.

Causes of Social Problems

The key theme of Du Bois' book was that black problems were a symptom of problems with the organization of social life rather than a result of racial inferiority. Given the same social circumstances, any other race would respond in much the same way and experience the same difficulties. One contemporary expert summarizes the theme: "The problems of black Philadelphians stemmed largely from their past condition of servitude as they tried to negotiate an effective place in a highly competitive industrial urban setting," while at the same time "the legacy of white supremacy was strong and their competitors were favored because of their white skin" (Anderson 1996:xix). Slavery, competition for work, and white supremacy each played a role.

First, the legacy of slavery limited the opportunities of many blacks in Philadelphia. Their former treatment as slaves did not prepare them well for work in the industrial North, and the sudden movement of many from the South to the North made adjustment difficult. The stream of black migrants thus contributed to many of the problems of the black community, such as the difficulty in sustaining stable marriages and families, trouble competing in the labor market, and rising rates of crime. As Du Bois (1996 [1899]:269) stated, "When a group of persons have been for generations prohibited from self-support, and self-initiative in any line, there is bound to be a larger number of them who, when thrown upon their own resources, will be found incapable of competing in the race of life."

Second, the intense competition with white immigrants over jobs limited the work opportunities for blacks, even those who had been free for generations and were well-prepared for the demands of employment. Given the choice between white and black workers, employers favored the white immigrants. Yet competition for jobs created antagonism among white workers, who viewed blacks as a threat and refused to work with them. As a result, blacks were forced by lack of other opportunities to take jobs most closely associated with slavery—jobs as servants and maids. Many had difficulty finding any work at all, and the surplus of unemployed blacks kept wages low for those who could find jobs.

Third and most important, race discrimination and prejudice limited opportunities. Du Bois disputed claims that prejudice did not exist in Philadelphia because the city did not have Jim Crow laws as did the South. He cited instance after instance of blocked opportunities, exclusion from good jobs, and mistreatment in daily life. Blacks must, he wrote, continually deal with the feeling that in the eyes of whites that they are something less than Americans. Du Bois further disputed claims that such prejudice was merely the natural reaction of whites to the poverty, unemployment, crime, and illiteracy they saw among blacks. On the contrary, color prejudice to a large extent caused these problems in the first place. It made little sense to blame the poor when whites had been actively engaged in keeping them poor through racial discrimination.

The threat to ambition and self-respect faced by blacks in Philadelphia because of color prejudice often led to hopelessness. With few opportunities to do better in life, many turned to crime, gambling, prostitution, alcohol, and corruption, and many had trouble developing stable family relationships. In Du Bois' (1996 [1899]:241) words, "He had lately been freed from serfdom, he was the object of stinging oppression and ridicule, and paths of advancement open to many were closed to him." No wonder discouragement, idleness, and poverty had become common. In many ways, blacks in Philadelphia had done well given the impossibly difficult circumstances they faced.

At the same time, Du Bois emphasized that the majority of the black community endured this mistreatment with continued work and effort. That most blacks did not fit stereotyped images as poor, unemployed, and prone to crime came from the clear evidence of class distinctions within their community. In terms of social classes identified by Du Bois, Grade 1 consisted of those earning enough to live well, Grade 2 consisted of the respectable working class living in comfortable conditions, Grade 3 consisted of the poor who struggle to make an honest living, and Grade 4 consisted of "the lowest class of criminals, prostitutes, and loafers; the submerged tenth." Most grades in fact did well, yet whites discriminated similarly against all blacks regardless of their social class or accomplishments.

Based on the ideas and data he presented, Du Bois called for change. He called for blacks to protest against prejudice, injustice, and mistreatment and also to devote greater efforts to bettering themselves and doing more to educate their children. He called for whites to recognize how their treatment of blacks had in fact led to the conditions that whites then used as an excuse for further mistreatment. "Such discrimination is morally wrong, politically dangerous, industrially wasteful, and socially silly. It is the duty of whites to stop it, and to do so primarily for their own sakes" (Du Bois 1996 [1899]:394).

Many years after the publication of *The Philadelphia Negro*, Du Bois expressed pride in the effort and the praise it received. However, he also recognized that his early work sometimes had an unnecessarily moralistic and judgmental tone (Zamir 1995:94; Zuberi 2004). His blunt criticism of laziness, loafing, shiftlessness, sexual looseness, and ignorance reflected his New England religious upbringing. Still, this tone does not detract from an idea that has become well accepted today but was radical at the time the book was written: racial discrimination, lack of decent work opportunities, and social mistreatment had devastating consequences for the lives of African Americans.

4. *THE SOULS OF BLACK FOLK*

With his first-rate education, research accomplishments, and contributions to the new field of sociology, top universities throughout the nation should have been competing to hire Du Bois. Yet again that did not happen. Du Bois did, however, receive an offer from Atlanta University to teach sociology and carry out research plans to study African Americans throughout the country. Although small and poorly funded, this black university had leaders with vision. They hoped to develop sociology as a field of study that would help to understand—and reform—the conditions and problems of blacks. Du Bois was well suited to lead in this task.

In 1897, still not yet 30 years old, Du Bois began at Atlanta University, where he spent the next 13 years teaching, doing research, and participating in a variety of civil rights activities. He became known as an excellent though demanding teacher, and his reputation as an African-American scholar and sociologist spread. These years were also touched with frustration and tragedy. The frustration came from living in segregated Atlanta. To avoid having to put up with the indignity of Jim Crow laws, he stayed on campus as much as possible. Still, he could not avoid seeing firsthand the abuse of blacks and facing mistreatment himself. The tragedy was the death of his 18-month-old son, Burghardt Gomer Du Bois, from sewage pollution in the city water system (and, in Du Bois' view, the difficulty of finding medical care for blacks in segregated Atlanta). The couple would have a baby girl a few years later, but they had difficulty coming to terms with the death of their firstborn.

Direction of the Civil Rights Movement

While at Atlanta University, Du Bois hosted a series of annual conferences that helped establish the foundation of the sociology of race. He had grandiose plans for setting up a research program to last for the next hundred years. Even in the 13 years he spent at the university, he accomplished much. The annual conference produced a series of books on topics such as Negro businesses, college graduates, schools, churches, artisans, mortality, crime, family, and morals and manners. Under Du Bois' direction, the publication of the equivalent of an encyclopedia of Negro social life made Atlanta University the only institution in the nation studying social life of black Americans.

Despite his own success and the recognition the annual conferences received, Du Bois began to question the value of his work. He began his academic career with the belief that the discovery of the truth through scientific methods would convince white America of the injustice and stupidity of prejudice and discrimination. It became apparent over the years, however, that knowledge did not translate into reform and uplift of blacks. During the time he spent at Atlanta University, circumstances worsened rather than improved: segregation grew stronger, voting rights were lost, and violence against blacks intensified. The interest of southern whites in maintaining Jim Crow laws seemed too entrenched to be changed by new knowledge.

The public lynching of blacks by violent mobs of whites particularly distressed him. In one such lynching outside Atlanta, the victim was torn apart, his body barbequed, and his burnt hands displayed in a city shop window. Disgusted by the lynching, murder, and starvation of blacks, Du Bois (1968:222) said that he "could not be a calm, cool, and detached scientist."

Given his doubts about the influence of his academic studies, Du Bois began to become involved in political activities. The best-known black leader at the time, Booker T. Washington, urged blacks to focus on vocational training and jobs in skilled trades, industry, and laboring. Such work would lead, he argued, to the steady accumulation of property, economic stability, respect from whites, and, in generations to come, equality between the races. Washington favored practical training over higher education, minimized the importance of gaining the vote, and seemed to tolerate the existence of segregation as he focused on other ways to develop black economic self-sufficiency. Du Bois saw things differently, and with full self-confidence in his opinions and the willingness to make his disagreements known, he created much controversy in the black community by bluntly criticizing Washington.

Du Bois disagreed with Washington on two counts: (1) he highly valued education even if it failed to bring material gain, and (2) he wanted to take action to end segregation and voting restrictions immediately rather than to wait for economic improvement first. Washington (in Marable 1986:42) once said, "The wisest among my race understand that the agitation of questions of social equality is the extremest folly." While recognizing the many contributions Washington made to black progress, Du Bois could not accept the kind of compromise with white supremacy that Washington seemed to suggest. He thought that the most educated of blacks—the talented tenth, he called them—could provide political leadership to help the black masses reject compromise and mobilize in opposition to their treatment. And they needed to do so right away rather than wait.

Leaving the Ivory Tower

In one of the many political activities in which he began to participate, Du Bois helped organized a small group of men opposed to the Washington strategy. Termed the Niagara Movement because it first met in Canada near the falls, the group aimed to take a more militant approach to gaining freedom and equality. It demanded full voting rights for blacks and equal opportunity for education and employment, and it rejected the accommodations supported by Washington and favored by whites. The movement consisted largely of highly educated black men and never gained mass support, but it had two important outcomes: it identified Du Bois as an able civil rights leader, and it would become part of a famous and highly effective civil rights organization, the National Association for the Advanced of Colored People (NAACP), that would soon be established.

Du Bois had other reasons to reevaluate his commitment to research and his position at Atlanta University. Funding for his research remained inadequate, and charitable organizations seldom provided support for the conferences he organized. In fact, many whites seemed to want to punish Du Bois and Atlanta University for the controversial stands on equality he had taken. He wrote (Du Bois 1968:252) "That on account of my attitude toward Mr. Washington, I had become a *persona non grata* to powerful interests, and that Atlanta University would not be able to get support for its general work or for its study of the Negro problem so long as I remained at the institution."

Du Bois resigned from Atlanta in 1910 to take a job with the NAACP in New York City, where he edited the organization's magazine. Du Bois did not have the personality of most national leaders—he was too intellectual in his orientation, too quiet and formal in his interaction, and too combative and arrogant in his views. Still, in his new position he became the voice of the civil rights movement over the next several decades.

Well before leaving Atlanta, however, Du Bois published one of the most important books in American intellectual history. Based on the compilation of previously published articles, *The Souls of Black Folk* came out in 1903. Its impact on blacks may have been greater than any book since the antislavery novel *Uncle Tom's Cabin* (Aptheker 1989:71), and its ideas still resonate with readers today (Hubbard 2003:1). Many scholars were equally impressed; Max Weber, for example, wanted to translate it into German and offered to write an introduction.

American sociologists paid little attention to the book, however. It differed in style from most efforts at sociological theorizing. Rather than aiming to dissect, qualify, expand, and test its concepts, *The Souls of Black Folk* was poetic and literary in style. It referred to the Bible and classical literature more than sociological studies, it relied on personal stories more than general laws, and it offered brief statements of ideas rather than in-depth analysis. Its strength is as a work of black literature as much as a work of social theory. Still, the sociological insight it contains foreshadowed work to come several decades later and remains fresh today.

Double Consciousness

In the book's first chapter, Du Bois introduced a theme that helped make sense of the special experiences of blacks. He noted that blacks have the peculiar sensation of looking at themselves through the eyes of a white world that treats them with contempt or ignores them altogether. George Herbert Mead, who also studied at Harvard under William James, developed general arguments about how people develop a sense of self through social interaction; Du Bois emphasized the impact of this process on blacks. He said that black Americans develop a **double consciousness** by virtue of their dual social positions. As both blacks and Americans, they have two souls (hence the title of Du Bois' refers to *Souls* rather than *Soul*) and two warring ideals that create inner conflict.

With double consciousness, the external conflict between the races becomes internalized in the lives and feelings of blacks. Du Bois explained that the mistreatment of blacks involved more than economic inequality and outer accomplishments—it also shaped their inner life. In slavery, blacks looked to resolve the inner conflicts by obtaining freedom. After emancipation, however, the failure to gain equality led blacks not just to feel bitter disappointment and despair but also to worsen their sense of twoness. The false hopes of emancipation and false promises that things would get much better contributed both externally and internally to the tragedy of race in America.

Blacks responded to this double consciousness by striving for wholeness by overcoming the sense of twoness. Some wanted to do so through the complete integration of blacks in white America, while others wanted complete separation of blacks from the white world. Du Bois argued that merging both the black world and the American world while maintaining the strengths of both would be the best direction to take. Foreshadowing modern ideas of multiculturalism and pluralism, Du Bois saw that blacks had much to offer America—if only whites would recognize it.

For example, the development of Negro spirituals (what Du Bois called sorrow songs) and new forms of Christian worship offered something valuable to white America. In expressing sorrow, injustice, and hope in rhythmic melody, the music of black religion "remains the most original and beautiful expression of human life and longing yet born on American soil" (Du Bois 1993 [1903]:151). The vigor of black religious worship, with stamping, shrieking, waving, weeping, and laughing made God visible in daily life and expressed the pent-up energy of blacks (who in dealing with whites were expected to behave quietly, humbly, and unemotionally even when facing insult and abuse). Noting these gifts of story, song, and spirit, Du Bois (1993 [1903]:207) asks, "Would America have been America without her Negro people?"

In addition, blacks had a special gift to offer Americans by virtue of their social position and double consciousness—a gift Du Bois called second sight. While whites suffered from ignorance of the black world and its strengths—as if they were hidden behind a veil—blacks could see more. As strangers in their own society, blacks gained a special perspective on the world. This gift didn't make up for mistreatment, but it did reflect the pride blacks could take in dealing with impossible circumstances. Du Bois suggested that blacks use their own standards rather than those of whites in measuring their accomplishments and reject the feelings of shame that come with white supremacy.

Du Bois emphasized in his essays that these gifts shouldn't be lost in the search for material gain. Unlike Booker T. Washington's focus on economic progress and ownership, Du Bois stressed the importance of education, culture, and character along with breadwinning. Self-respect could emerge from knowledge and learning even when race prejudice limited economic opportunities. In this way, blacks could move toward a harmonious identity, overcome the harm of double consciousness, and enjoy their special gifts.

A crucial implication followed from Du Bois' arguments about self and identity. Race is not determined by biological characteristics, although skin color becomes a marker that is used in social life to judge people and guide behavior. Rather than biological makeup, race comes from shared identity, common experiences, and social position. Blacks have experienced the terrible history of slavery and the false hope of freedom, but these experiences have also made them special. Spiritual ideals and cultural gifts have emerged from suffering and should be honored and maintained while working for equality. Blacks have souls, humanity, and inner lives that whites who judge on the basis of skin color never see.

In discussing double consciousness, Du Bois built on ideas that defined his work from the start. In *The Philadelphia Negro,* he used facts and statistics of the outward circumstances of blacks in a large city to back up his arguments about the social nature of race. In *The Souls of Black Folk,* he used poetry and stories about the meaning of being black in America to do the same. However different from the usual form of social theorizing, the stories Du Bois presented about blacks he knew in the hills of Tennessee, those barely able to survive in the black belt of Georgia, other black intellectuals, and his own experience losing a child had power that endures today.

5. RACE, CLASS, AND AFRICA

NAACP: 1910–1934

In 1910, Du Bois began a new career and life in New York City. He helped found the NAACP and was appointed as its director of publications and research. He began editing a journal called *The Crisis* that would turn into the intellectual voice of the organization and the civil rights movement more generally. The NAACP would concentrate on legal challenges to segregation and voting restrictions, while Du Bois would concentrate on promoting ideas, policies, and literature. He insisted on total control of the journal, which offended some other founding members and board members of the NAACP, but he put his imprint on everything that appeared in the journal.

The journal and the organization enjoyed phenomenal success. *The Crisis* grew to a circulation of 100,000 by 1919. It published work of the country's most famous black authors, debated ideas about the directions the civil rights movement should take, and demanded an end to lynching, segregation, and voting restrictions. Du Bois continued to criticize the contradiction between American democratic ideals and the existence of racism, but he also covered in the journal the artistic and social life of the black community. He helped advance the period of black artistic accomplishment during the 1920s known as the Harlem Renaissance.

At the same time, the NAACP made legal strides to go along with the success of its journal. By 1919, the NAACP would have 300 branches and 88,448 members—remarkable progress given the obstacles blacks faced in the United States. Suits against governments in the South led to the end of the infamous "grandfather" requirement for voting, and campaigns to mobilize blacks politically and stop lynchings had some success. However, progress in overcoming deeply entrenched racism came slowly. An effort to end segregation in the armed forces during World War I failed, and lynchings, Jim Crow laws, and restrictions on black voting continued.

Through both his writing and his extensive travels on the lecture trail, Du Bois attained a degree of fame among both blacks and whites. After the death of Booker T. Washington in 1915, blacks viewed Du Bois as the country's best known civil rights advocate. White Americans had views that ranged, given their disagreement about racial equality, from respect to hatred, but they recognized his leadership. That Du Bois appeared stiff, cold, and even conceited to many rather than charismatic and outgoing made his fame all the more remarkable. Rather than his personality, his powerful intellect, skilled writing, and unbending devotion to equality led to greatness.

Criticism of both the NAACP and Du Bois came with fame, however. More radical groups criticized the organization as too focused on the middle-class and elite black community. In its advocacy of legal change and the right to vote, the NAACP in fact did little to offer a broad program of economic improvement for the masses. Large parts of the black population that worried more about getting work and food than about culture and voting had little interest in the organization. Marcus Garvey, a popular black leader in the 1920s who advocated black separatism and migration to Africa, criticized Du Bois and the organization as elitist and out of touch.

Throughout the years at the NAACP, Du Bois' pride in his ideas and attention to possible slight made conflict common. His well-known feuds with Booker T. Washington and Marcus Garvey helped set the directions the movement for racial equality would take in the twentieth century. Within the NAACP, his combativeness made work with the board of directors difficult. Du Bois felt that some white board members treated him with condescension rather than respect, and he fought vigorously to defend his principles and ideas against their criticisms. He often offended powerful board members, but the success and importance of the journal made him indispensable to the organization.

By 1934, after 24 years editing *The Crisis,* Du Bois resigned from his position with the NAACP. At age 66, he decided to return to the University of Atlanta and serve as the chairman of the sociology department. The financial problems brought on by a drop in circulation during the Great Depression of the 1930s had made Du Bois dependent on the NAACP board for funds and reduced his independence. Changes in leadership of the organization had created friction, jealousy, and disagreement over the direction of the journal that made continued work there intolerable for him. Du Bois left a lasting legacy and would return later to the organization, but he now planned to return to rejoin academia.

In summarizing his contributions to the organization, the NAACP (Du Bois 1968:299) would write: "The Board has not always seen eye to eye with him in regard to various matters, and cannot subscribe to some of his criticisms of the Association and its officials. But such differences in the past have in no way interfered with his usefulness, but rather on the contrary. For he had been selected because of his independence of judgment, his fearlessness in expressing his convictions, and his acute and wide reaching intelligence."

Global Exploitation

During his long years at the NAACP, Du Bois' political views shifted. The failure of both the Republican and Democratic parties to fight against segregation and racism left him dissatisfied with politics-as-usual and more attracted to socialism. During the early decades of the twentieth century, the labor movement pressed for better pay, more worker rights, and redistribution of wealth—goals that attracted Du Bois. Despite his hopes for socialism and the labor movement, however, he also saw its limitations: white workers refused to offer to blacks the same rights they themselves wanted. Du Bois likewise supported the women's suffrage movement but was angered by the refusal of many of its members to support the same voting rights for blacks.

The financial devastation experienced by large parts of the population, particularly blacks, during the Great Depression sent Du Bois still further to the left and closer to communism. Although impressed on a visit to the Soviet Union in 1926 by the efforts he saw to end poverty, he remained skeptical of the system and did not join the Communist party. However, he did find the ideas of Marx to be increasingly useful for his own writings. During the years 1910–1934 when he worked for the NAACP and 1934–1944 when he returned to Atlanta University, two themes emerged in his work, both relating to issues of economic exploitation highlighted by Marx. One theme focused on the global exploitation of blacks through colonialism, and the other focused on the importance of social class to race relations in the United States after the Civil War.

Du Bois' growing concern with global exploitation followed from the interest he took in Africa. Beginning in 1919, he helped organize a series of Pan-African conferences that highlighted the ties between blacks in America and Africa. The conferences aimed to help improve the economic conditions of Africans around the world and link the struggles of blacks in the United States to the struggles of African peoples elsewhere. Along with demanding racial freedom and equality in the United States, Du Bois demanded that European nations give conquered African nations the same freedom and opportunity to grow economically.

In an article on the causes of World War I, Du Bois (1995:642–651) argued that Britain, France, and Germany went to war over control of colonies in Africa. Britain and France had through military force already turned many African territories into colonies, which provided raw materials, sources of trade, markets for industrial goods, places for settlers to move, and local populations forced to work for low wages. The newly unified German nation wanted a share of this new source of wealth but had entered the race to colonize Africa well after its neighboring powers. The result was military buildup and war—the killing of whites in Europe to ultimately control people of color in Africa and elsewhere.

Although European exploitation occurred worldwide, Africa had particular importance to Europe and special interest to American blacks given their heritage. The continent had abundant raw materials, such as ivory, coffee, cocoa, diamonds, rubber, gold, and copper, which the industrializing nations needed, and it had a population that the industrializing nations could exploit as cheap labor to grow, harvest, and mine these materials. In Du Bois' view, much of the wealth of European countries came from exploiting the natural resources and the labor of darker peoples of the world. European nations had in essence divided up Africa to use for their own benefit and wealth.

With colonial exploitation, a new form of slavery replaced the old form of slavery, one that paid black workers a pittance for the raw materials they produced. Economic control of the continent by white foreign powers had much the same effect of enslaving blacks; the foreign powers conquered the land and people rather than capturing the people and sending them elsewhere. As Du Bois (1969 [1920]:64) said, "If the slave cannot be taken from Africa, slavery can be taken to Africa." The misery of blacks in Africa caused by colonialism thus had similar causes to the misery of blacks in America. Both suffered under the domination of whites. Du Bois argued that common interests made it crucial for races worldwide to collaborate with one another in the fight against white oppression.

How did the most powerful nations of the world justify this oppression? As it had during periods of slavery, the different race of the peoples of Africa offered an excuse for mistreatment. Beliefs about white superiority that had emerged over previous centuries justified commercial exploitation of blacks for profit. Whites believed that payment of low wages in exchange for growing, harvesting, and mining raw materials was all the peoples of Africa could expect or handle. Du Bois argued to the contrary that the greatness and world dominance of Europe came not from any inherent superiority—African and Asian civilizations had at one time accomplished as much or more. Rather, the greater wealth and power gained by the white European nations allowed them to define terms of racial superiority and inferiority in ways to serve their interest.

That whites benefited materially from the exploitation of the nonwhite world made change difficult. Although lower-class whites had more in common economically with blacks than with upper-class whites, racism and exploitation of blacks linked white capital and labor in a common goal—to use other races to improve their economic well-being.

Du Bois (2004:137) wrote, "Every civilized man is part and parcel of the colonial system and is depending for his welfare and convenience, not to mention his luxury, upon the degradation of the majority of men."

Class and Race

As in Africa, a process of reenslavement also occurred in the American South during the period of Reconstruction. In his 1934 book *Black Reconstruction,* Du Bois applied his insight and skills as an historian to understanding how changes after the Civil War created new ways to control free blacks. Du Bois and many other black intellectuals had long felt that someone needed to counter the dominant views of historians on the topic. Most histories accepted notions of racial inferiority, arguing that Reconstruction failed because newly freed blacks were unprepared to vote, work, and run the government. *Black Reconstruction* explained the failure by revising Marxist concepts to emphasize the connections between class and race.

Making sense of Reconstruction required, according to Du Bois, a clear view of the nature of economic interests in the North and South before and after the Civil War. Before the war, industrial growth in the North created a strong class of capitalists and an emerging labor movement wanting higher wages for workers. The South, in contrast, had remained feudal in nature. A small planter class with economic and political power owned land and slaves but at the same time had difficulty maintaining its position. With prices for cotton and other crops set by a world market, profits often had to come from reducing the costs of production. That meant more ruthlessly exploiting slaves—the major economic resource of the planters.

The South did not have an industrial working class as did the North, but two subordinate groups made up the large part of the population: whites who did not own slaves (about 5 million in number) and black slaves (about 4 million in number). The poverty and powerlessness of most white Southerners put their interests closer to the interests of blacks. After all, the ability of planters to use slave labor limited opportunities for white workers. Beliefs about racial inferiority and superiority, however, created antagonism rather than cooperation between poor whites and blacks.

With these interests in place, the end of the Civil War brought demands from the North for the South to accept democracy. Full voting rights and equality before the law of all citizens would, in principle, restructure the nature of class relations. Freed blacks would have opportunities to attend schools, own land, work for wages, and vote for parties of their choice. Their position and class interests would be similar to those of poor whites in the South, creating a potentially large voting bloc in favor of economic equality. Combined with the desire of Northerners to punish the South and abolitionists to help freed slaves, the potential for real change existed.

Early on, Reconstruction indeed had some success. Du Bois argued that blacks made considerable advances in education once they had the opportunity. New elementary schools and colleges that arose throughout the South revealed the desire of blacks for knowledge and skills. Blacks also wanted jobs, land, and a stable community life. Claims to the contrary, that corruption, crime, and inactivity among blacks required that whites retake control, were exaggerated according to Du Bois. The evidence indicated that such claims offered convenient excuses to renew older forms of class inequality.

Despite some initial success, however, democratization of the South ultimately failed. As Du Bois (1975 [1935]:670) stated, it was blocked by a "determined effort to reduce black labor as nearly as possible to a condition of unlimited exploitation and build a new class of capitalists on this foundation." A small and newly emerging class of new white landowners, professionals, and merchants who wanted economic dominance similar to the past managed to overcome the interests of large numbers of poor blacks and whites. As described by Du Bois, the class struggle that led to this outcome involved the interests of the North and South, whites and blacks, and capital and labor.

One key to understanding the failure came from the willingness of poor southern whites to align their interests with those of white business and landowners. In economic terms alone, this alliance made little sense. Poor whites and blacks could have combined to take political control of the South and redistribute wealth. Despite economic differences that should have made them enemies, whites of all classes were joined together in one crucial way—they opposed giving social equality to blacks. Even at their own economic cost, poorer whites accepted this appeal to race hatred rather than class solidarity. They ended up choosing poverty—the outcome of leaving economic relations in place—over racial equality.

Another key to understanding the failure came from taking account of the interests of northern capitalists. Like the white elite in the South, this class benefited from racial conflict. Business leaders in the North hoped to prevent the formation of a united labor movement that could demand higher wages and a socialist government. Hostility between races would drive a wedge between workers in both the North and South. With blacks treated as second-class citizens, they would have to accept low wages and, given the threat that blacks would take their jobs, white workers would also be forced to accept low wages.

In this way, race and class combined to replace a revolution of democratic freedom with a counterrevolution of property ownership. According to DuBois, reconstruction ended with a bargain involving the government, northern business, and southern elite to end the experiment in democracy. The government would remove troops from the South, allowing whites to run their own governments, deny voting rights to blacks, and continue economic exploitation of the poor. In return, businesses in the North could maintain their power against a labor movement divided by North and South and white and black. Economic power became increasingly concentrated in the United States, and blacks were increasingly blocked from equality.

The process of change in the South during reconstruction had certain similarities with the process of colonization taking place in Africa and other parts of the world during the nineteenth century. Du Bois noted that when ended, new forms of control surfaced through racial domination. In both America and Africa, beliefs about racial inferiority led to exploitation of blacks. In both places, democracy was subordinated to profits. And in both places, the slave system continued to influence race relations long after slavery had ended.

Du Bois used the insights of Marx on class interests to help understand Reconstruction, but he revised them to make sense of the outcome. While Marx made it seem that the nature of their real interests would become obvious to workers, Du Bois saw that racial conflict among workers would hide and obstruct their common class interests. This insight offered an alternative to historians who believed that newly-freed slaves were incapable of advancement and that white domination was natural and inevitable. To the contrary, the attention Du Bois gave to the special combination of race and class in America highlighted the importance of economic realities and racial domination to the failure of Reconstruction.

6. LEGACY AS A SOCIAL THEORIST

After a series of disputes with the leaders and board of directors of Atlanta University, Du Bois was forced to retire in 1944 at age 76. He would live another 19 years, working for a variety of causes and writing on new and old topics. He first returned for a short and unsuccessful stay at the NAACP, and then he served as vice chairman of the Council on African Affairs, led the Peace Information Center, ran for the Senate in New York as a candidate of the Progressive party, and helped organize international peace conferences. His wife of 53 years, Nina, died in 1950, and Du Bois married activist Shirley Graham in 1951.

During these years, Du Bois moved closer to communism. Although he never joined the party and made his criticisms of Marxist hopes for revolution well known, his frustration and disappointment with the lack of reform in the United States altered his views. Du Bois was born soon after the end of slavery, witnessed the failure of the nation to extend democracy to blacks in the late nineteenth century, and experienced the continued racist discrimination against blacks in the early twentieth century. The 1954 Supreme Court decision in *Brown v. Board of Education*—a suit sponsored by the NAACP—at last made segregation in schools unconstitutional but offered too little, too late. Du Bois eventually gave up hope in the United States.

His growing attraction to communism and visits to the Soviet Union got the attention of the federal government in the 1950s—a period of intense anticommunism. Government officials accused him of taking orders from the Kremlin, demanded that he register as a foreign agent, and brought charges against him in 1950 when he refused to do so. Although acquitted, Du Bois became embittered at the government's treatment of him as a criminal and its later refusal to let him leave the country. Only in 1958 was his passport returned, allowing him to travel to the Soviet Union and the newly created communist People's Republic of China.

In 1961, Du Bois severed his ties with the United States. He officially joined the Communist party, in part as a protest for his treatment at the hands of the anticommunist U.S. government (Lewis 2000:567). Having hoped for decades that reform would bring racial fairness, he became resigned to the view that private ownership of capital and free enterprise would block that goal in the United States. He also decided that he could no longer live in the country of his birth. He moved that year to the newly independent West African nation of Ghana, where he lived as a citizen and special guest of the country.

Du Bois died on August 27, 1963, at the age of 95. That date has special importance, not only because it marks a near century of living during a turbulent period of race relations. It also marks the start of a new period in racial progress. The next day, August 28, 1963, Martin Luther King, Jr., gave his famous "I have a dream speech" to hundreds of thousands who had come to Washington DC to protest racial segregation and discrimination. As protestors gathered to hear King speak, word spread of the death of one of black America's great leaders.

A Life of Ideas

Having lived a long and productive life, Du Bois left the world more than 60 years worth of writing. He began with faith in the ability of science to destroy the ignorance on which racism was built and proposed that the black cultural elite take a leading role in bringing about change. He later recognized more fully that underlying economic interests shaped class and race relations in the United States, Africa, and other parts of the world. These interests were too strong to overcome with knowledge alone. After working for economic reform to deal with the problems, he still saw little progress and eventually joined the Communist party. Through all these changes, however, certain themes appear consistently in his work (Marable 1986:ix). He supported democratic rights and cultural pluralism and fought segregation and discrimination—all goals widely accepted today.

Du Bois never received much in the way of the recognition from mainstream sociology. As Charles Lemert (1994) suggests, his work has many of the same qualities of more famous theorists: prolific output, innovative ideas, great literary power, academic standing, publication in leading journals, and considerable political influence. Yet the first African-American sociologist was largely ignored by his field. The neglect may have resulted from the nonwhite view of the world offered by Du Bois and his unique and elegant style of writing. Unlike Marx, Durkheim, and Weber, Du Bois did not develop a theoretical system or draw out the implications of his ideas in full detail. Perhaps as a result, most of today's scholarship on Du Bois comes from historians who have come to appreciate the revisionist perspective of *Black Reconstruction* (Foner 1988), humanists who have come to recognize the literary power of *The Souls of Black Folk* (Hubbard 2003), and African-American scholars debating Du Bois' ideas about cultural leadership of the black elite (Gates and West 1997). The push to rectify the neglect in the area of social theory has only recently made some progress.

Du Bois did maintain ties to one group of sociologists—white women who worked with the poor in neighborhoods near the University of Chicago and elsewhere. He found their work helpful in researching and writing *The Philadelphia Negro* and shared with them the goals of documenting and eliminating inequality (Deegan 2002). But white male sociologists paid little attention to his work.

Although Du Bois' works never became sociological classics, his insights are widely accepted. To offer just one example, consider the work of William Julius Wilson, perhaps the country's most influential African-American sociologist. Wilson has offered arguments to explain the stubborn persistence of segregation and inequality in the United States that in certain ways extend the work of Du Bois on race and class. Both recognize that race doesn't stand on its own but intersects with class (Lemert 2000). As described in several books (Wilson 1980, 1987, 1996), this intersection has taken new forms in recent decades.

Race and Class Inequality

Wilson seeks to reorient debates over whether blacks have made economic progress or not by comparing trends among middle-class and poor blacks. He argues that changing race relations have benefited some but not all blacks. Middle-class blacks with education and white-collar jobs in government, schools, and booming areas of the South have done fairly well. They have made economic strides and moved to nicer area neighborhoods in cities and suburbs once restricted to whites. The end of Jim Crow laws and government pursuit of equal opportunity have brought them benefits. In contrast, poor blacks located in high crime areas of inner cities have not done well; their problems seem to have worsened rather than improved.

The diverging trajectories of classes within the black community have created a new form of inequality, according to Wilson. As Du Bois described in *The Philadelphia Negro,* class differences have always existed among blacks. Yet during periods of Jim Crow laws and extreme racial antagonism, all blacks from the wealthiest and most educated to the poorest and least educated were barred from white sections of restaurants, hotels, buses, trains, parks, stores, and neighborhoods. Because discrimination limited opportunity for all blacks, most attention went to inequality between whites and blacks rather than to inequality within races. Such attention is still justified given the continued advantages enjoyed by whites, but something new has occurred. Wilson argues that in recent decades the gap between middle-class blacks and those in poverty has widened.

The most serious problems today occur among lower-class blacks. *The Truly Disadvantaged,* both the name of one of Wilson's books (1987) and a descriptive term he applies to blacks living in extreme urban poverty, face two major problems. First, they lack job opportunities. Manufacturing jobs once located in city centers have moved to the suburbs or foreign countries, leaving inner-city black residents with few legitimate work opportunities. Antidiscrimination and affirmative action policies make little difference when few jobs exist. Second, they have become socially isolated. As working and middle-class black families move to higher-status neighborhoods, it leaves larger proportions of poor and jobless persons in traditional black communities. Out-migration also removes leaders, resources, and activities that once helped protect the communities from neglect, hopelessness, and crime. Together, joblessness and social isolation in urban ghettos make the problems of one class of black Americans both new and severe.

Much as Du Bois did, Wilson rejects claims that the problems of poor blacks stem from inherent traits or cultural values passed on from generation to generation. Tendencies for young people to avoid work, schooling, and social responsibility and become involved in crime are the result of—rather than the cause of—the loss of job opportunities. As Wilson (1996:xiii) summarizes, "A neighborhood in which people are poor but employed is very different from a neighborhood in which people are poor and jobless. Many of today's problems in the inner-city ghetto neighborhoods—crime, family dissolution, welfare, low levels of social organization, and so on—are fundamentally a consequence of the disappearance of work."

To illustrate, Wilson cites statistics about three historically black neighborhoods in south Chicago. In 1950, 69 percent of males age 14 and over worked in a typical week, but by 1990 only 37 percent of males age 16 and over had jobs. Other changes followed. Major streets in the neighborhoods around the 1950s contained businesses, restaurants, stores, shops, crowded sidewalks, and lively parks. The same streets today appear dark and deserted—with the exceptions of fast-food restaurants and liquor stores, the jobs and businesses have left. Poverty and associated problems of crime, family breakup, and drug use in turn worsen with the disappearance of work.

The widening inequality among blacks led Wilson to talk about the declining significance of race. Although vigorously criticized for that claim, Wilson does not deny the importance of race—even highly educated and wealthy blacks face discrimination and segregation in their lives. Rather, he emphasizes that polarization among blacks demonstrates the growing importance of class in understanding white and black differences. As Wilson (1980:1) states, "The life chances of individual blacks have more to do with their economic class position than their day-to-day encounters with whites."

As segregation by class has grown in importance, the kinds of policies needed to tackle the problem must also change. Wilson calls for policies that focus on job creation for those most isolated from economic prosperity and social life. The programs should not target blacks only but should benefit the truly disadvantaged of any race. After facing decades of racial discrimination, inner-city minorities will benefit most from such programs. Even so, the problems of poor blacks reflect economic dislocations and require economic solutions that relate to class as well as race.

Wilson's arguments remain controversial. Critics claim that regardless of antidiscrimination laws, informal norms enforce continued segregation of blacks and whites in major cities (Massey and Denton 1993). That middle-class blacks looking for housing, shopping, and dealing with police face daily instances of discrimination belies claims of the declining significance of race (Feagin 1991). These debates stress the importance to sociology today of themes present early in the century in the writings of W. E. B. Du Bois.

SUMMARY

Near the beginning of the twentieth century, the nation's first African-American sociologist, W. E. B. Du Bois, began his work with the hope of understanding and improving the conditions of black Americans. His efforts had both empirical and theoretical components. Empirically, he described in remarkable detail the lives and problems of blacks in a troubled area of central Philadelphia. In *The Philadelphia Negro*, he noted problems of rundown houses, high crime, broken families, excessive alcohol use, bad health, early death, poverty, illiteracy, unemployment, low pay, gambling, and vote-buying. More important, he found that black residents faced strong race prejudice and discrimination, had few opportunities for work other than as servants and maids, and developed a sense of hopelessness about their lives and ambitions. One hundred years later, readers are struck by the wealth of fascinating detail in this book.

Interwoven with the description and statistics, Du Bois attacked widely accepted claims of racial inferiority. Both the views of the public and the theories of scholars often attributed the problems experienced in northern cities such as Philadelphia to flaws in the character of its black residents. Du Bois argued to the contrary that a few periods of city history had revealed considerable black progress, but other periods of heightened competition for jobs and discrimination held them back. The problems of the black community thus came from flaws in the organization of social life rather than racial inferiority. This reasoning reversed common thinking by treating group behavior as a result rather than a cause of social problems.

Du Bois extended his theory to consider the social psychological implications of living in a racist society. He argued that African Americans, by looking at themselves through the eyes of hostile whites, developed double consciousness and inner tension over their positions as both blacks and Americans. In double consciousness, the external conflict between the races became part of their inner lives or souls (as in the title of his famous book, *The Souls of Black Folk*). They strove to overcome the tension in their battle for freedom but could do little to change their treatment at the hands of whites. Du Bois recommended that blacks try to merge with the white world but at the same time maintain the strengths of their own culture.

Although seldom recognized by whites, these strengths were many. Du Bois spoke of the gifts of black folk with pride and poetry. He described the beauty of their music, the vigor of their religion, the insight gained from their marginal social position, and their sturdiness in the face of suffering. He believed that these gifts—and the opportunity for blacks to gain new gifts through pursuing higher education—should not be sacrificed in the chase for material goods. Blacks could define an identity in terms of their common experiences and gifts rather than in terms of their wealth alone. Even more important, they could reject characterizations based on biological traits and white supremacy.

Moving beyond the themes of his earlier work, Du Bois later incorporated elements of Marxism in his theories about race and racial conflict. Since knowledge of African-American social life and the central role of racism in shaping it did not have much effect on changing white attitudes, Du Bois began to give more weight to deep-rooted economic interests in maintaining racial inequality. These interests extended beyond the borders of the United States. He argued that profits gained by European nations from economic exploitation of blacks in Africa led to colonialism and beliefs in white superiority to justify the exploitation. He was among the first to emphasize that white exploitation of blacks occurred on a global scale, not just in the United States.

In the United States, class interests helped block democracy in the South during Reconstruction. An increasingly powerful business class in the North combined with landowners and merchants in the South to reach two goals: (1) weaken and divide the American labor movement by fostering racial hostility among workers and (2) maintain the power of traditional elites in the South by pitting poor whites against newly freed slaves. Ultimately, the class struggle produced a compromise that ended Reconstruction. The North would allow whites in the South to run their own governments, deny voting rights to blacks, and continue economic exploitation of the poor. In return, businesses in the North could maintain their power against a labor movement divided by North and South and white and black.

Du Bois' social theory never received the recognition from sociologists—his writing style and racial perspective were too unusual for the mainstream. In hindsight, however, his ideas about the social nature of race, the psychological harm of racism, the nature of global exploitation of blacks, and the crucial connections between race and class have all become widely accepted, even if his importance in developing the ideas is not always noted.

DISCUSSION QUESTIONS

1. How did Du Bois' experiences with race relations and inequality differ from the norm in the United during the late 1800s? How did his experiences living in the South during college and looking for a teaching job expose him to problems of racial inequality? How did his first teaching job change his scholarly goals?

2. What early successes occurred in the efforts to bring democracy to the South after the Civil War? How did white Southerners respond to the changes?

3. Describe the system of laws and behaviors that ended up replacing slavery in the South. How did historians writing in the late nineteenth and twentieth centuries explain the failure of Reconstruction?

4. What problems were occurring in Philadelphia that led some leaders to suggest a study of the black community? What methods did Du Bois use in his study?

5. What evidence contradicted claims that blacks in Philadelphia were incapable of economic advance? What factors instead explained problems experienced by the black community there? In

what way were these problems symptoms rather than causes of racial inequality?

6. Contrast the views of Du Bois and Booker T. Washington on the goals of the civil rights movement. How did Du Bois' attitude toward research change while he was at Atlanta University?

7. What is double consciousness and how did it affect the lives of black Americans according to Du Bois? What gifts resulted from double consciousness and what recommendations did Du Bois offer for debates over integration and segregation?

8. How did Du Bois contribute to the success of the NAACP? Contrast the goals of the NAACP with those of more radical critics. How did Du Bois' views change during his years with the NAACP?

9. What similarities exist in the treatment of blacks in African colonies and in the American South? How might class and race interests in the South before and after the Civil War explain the failure of Reconstruction?

10. Why hasn't Du Bois' work received more attention from sociologists? How do the arguments of William Julius Wilson extend the arguments of Du Bois about the importance of race and class to understanding current racial problems in the United States?

REFERENCES

PRIMARY SOURCES

Du Bois, W. E. B. 1996 [1899]. *The Philadelphia Negro: A Social Study.* Philadelphia: University of Pennsylvania Press.

Du Bois, W. E. B. 1993 [1903]. *The Souls of Black Folk.* New York: Alfred A. Knopf.

Du Bois, W. E. B. 1969 [1920]. *Darkwater: Voices from Within the Veil.* New York: AMS Press.

Du Bois, W. E. B. 1975 [1935]. *Black Reconstruction in America: An Essay Toward a History of the Part Which Black Folk Played in the Attempt to Reconstruct Democracy in America, 1860–1880.* New York: Atheneum.

Du Bois, W. E. B. 1940. *Dusk of Dawn: An Essay Toward an Autobiography of a Race Concept.* New York: Harcourt, Brace.

Du Bois, W. E. B. 1968. *The Autobiography of W. E. B. Du Bois.: A Soliloquy on Viewing My Life from the Last Decades of Its First Century.* New York: International Publishers.

Du Bois, W. E. B. 1995. *W. E. B. Du Bois: A Reader* (edited by David Levering Lewis). New York: Henry Holt.

Du Bois, W. E. B. 2004. *The Social Theory of W. E. B. Du Bois* (edited by Phil Zuckerman). Thousand Oaks, CA: Pine Forge Press.

SECONDARY SOURCES

Adams, Bert, and R. A. Sydie. 2002. *Classical Sociological Theory*. Thousand Oaks, CA: Pine Forge Press.

Anderson, Elijah. 1996. "Introduction to the 1996 Edition of *The Philadelphia Negro*." In W. E. B. Du Bois, *The Philadelphia Negro: A Social Study* (pp. ix–xxxvi). Philadelphia: University of Pennsylvania Press.

Aptheker, Herbert. 1989. *The Literary Legacy of W. E. B. Du Bois*. White Plains, NY: Kraus International.

Davis, Ronald L. F. 2005. "Creating Jim Crow: In-Depth Essay." *The History of Jim Crow*. Available at http://www.jimcrowhistory.org/history/creating2.htm. Accessed August 2005.

Deegan, Mary Jo. 2002. *Race, Hull-House, and the University of Chicago: A New Conscience Against Ancient Evils*. Westport, CT: Praeger.

DeMarco, Joseph P. 1983. *The Social Thought of W. E. B. Du Bois*. Lanham, MD: University Press of America.

Feagin, Joe. 1991. "The Continuing Significance of Race: Antiblack Discrimination in Public Places." *American Sociological Review* 56:101–116.

Foner, Eric. 1988. *Reconstruction: America's Unfinished Revolution, 1863–1877*. New York: Harper & Row.

Gates, Henry Louis, Jr., and Cornel West. 1997. *The Future of the Race*. New York: Vintage.

Hacker, Andrew. 1995. *Two Nations: Black and White, Separate, Hostile, and Unequal* (Revised and Expanded). New York: Ballantine.

Horne, Gerald, and Mary Young. 2001. *W. E. B. Du Bois: An Encyclopedia*. Westport, CT: Greenwood Press.

Hubbard, Dolan. 2003. "Introduction." In Dolan Hubbard (ed.), *The Souls of Black Folk One Hundred Years Later* (pp. 1–17). Columbia: University of Missouri Press.

Katz, Michael B., and Thomas J. Sugrue. 1998. "Introduction: The Context of *The Philadelphia Negro*." In Michael B. Katz and Thomas J. Sugrue (eds.), *W. E. B. Du Bois, Race, and the City: The Philadelphia Negro and Its Legacy* (pp. 1–37). Philadelphia: University of Pennsylvania Press.

Krout, John A., and Arnold S. Rice. 1977. *United States Since 1865*. New York: Barnes & Noble.

Lacy, Leslie Alexander. 1970. *Cheer the Lonesome Traveler: The Life of W. E. B. Du Bois*. New York: Dial Press.

Lemert, Charles. 1994. "A Classic from the Other Side of the Veil." *The Sociological Quarterly* 35:383–396.

Lemert, Charles. 2000. "W. E. B. Du Bois." In George Ritzer (ed.), *The Blackwell Companion to Major Social Theorists* (pp. 345–366). Malden, MA: Blackwell Publishers.

Lewis, David Levering. 1993. *W. E. B. Du Bois: Biography of a Race, 1868–1919*. New York: Henry Holt.

Lewis, David Levering. 2000. *W. E. B. Du Bois: The Fight for Equality and the American Century 1919–1963*. New York: Henry Holt.

Marable, Manning. 1986. *W. E. B. Du Bois: Black Radical Democrat*. Boston: Twayne Publishers.

Massey, Douglas S., and Nancy A. Denton. 1993. *American Apartheid: Segregation and the Making of the Underclass*. Cambridge, MA: Harvard University Press.

Morison, Samuel Eliot, Henry Steele Commager, and William E. Leuchtenburg. 1980. *The Growth of the American Republic*. Volume 1. New York: Oxford University Press.

Tolnay, Stewart E., and E. M. Beck. 1995. *A Festival of Violence: An Analysis of Southern Lynchings, 1882–1930*. Urbana: University of Illinois.

Wilson, William Julius. 1980. *The Declining Significance of Race: Blacks and Changing American Institutions* (2nd ed.). Chicago: University of Chicago Press.

Wilson, William Julius. 1987. *The Truly Disadvantaged: The Inner City, the Underclass, and Public Policy*. Chicago: University of Chicago Press.

Wilson, William Julius. 1996. *When Work Disappears: The World of the New Urban Poor*. New York: Knopf.

Wilson, William Julius. 1999. "When Work Disappears: New Implications for Race and Urban Poverty in the Global Economy." *Ethnic and Racial Studies* 22:479–499.

Zamir, Shamoon. 1995. *Dark Voices: W. E. B. Du Bois and American Thought, 1888–1903*. Chicago: University of Chicago Press.

Zuberi, Tukufu. 2004. "W. E. B. Du Bois's Sociology: *The Philadelphia Negro* and Social Science." *Annals, AAPSS* 595:146–156.

Zuckerman, Phil. 2004. "Introduction." In Phil Zuckerman (ed.), *The Social Theory of W. E. B. Du Bois*. Thousand Oaks, CA.: Pine Forge Press.

REFERENCE NOTES

Citations for quotations and special points of interest are given in the text. Listed here are other citations to sources on topics covered in each section of the chapter.

1. Preparing for His Life's Work: By the age of 26 (Du Bois 1968:183); Offended his colleagues (Du Bois 1968:186–189); First sociology class (Du Bois 1968:189); Great Barrington (Lewis 1993:15); Burghardt family (Du Bois 1968:62–65); In her 30s met Alfred (Lewis 1993:23); Alfred Du Bois (Du Bois 1968:72; Lewis 1993:20–21); Pronunciation (Lewis 1993:11); Mary did not move (Du Bois 1968:72); After the age of two (Du Bois 1968:73); Overdressed snob (Lemert 2000:352); Hard work (Lemert 2000:347); Closer to white elite (Anderson 1996:xii); Fisk University (Du Bois 1968:107, 121–122); Graduated in 1888 (Du Bois 1968:126); Left America in 1892 (Du Bois 1968:438); Withdrew funding (Lewis 1993:146).

2. The Failure of Reconstruction: Black codes (Foner 1988:199–203); 22 blacks from eight states (Krout and Rice 1977:8); Ku Klux Klan (Morison, Commager, and Leuchtenburg 1980:759); Compromise in 1877 (Morison, Commager, and Leuchtenburg 1980:786); 1890 Louisiana law (Davis 2005); Civil Rights Act of 1875 (Krout and Rice 1977:10); *Plessy v. Ferguson* (Davis 2005); William Archibald Dunning (Foner 1988:xix–xxii; Lewis 2000:353–356).

3. The Philadelphia Negro: Du Bois called it salvation (Du Bois 1968:193); A few idealistic leaders (Katz and Sugrue 1998:13–14); Salary of $900 (Lewis 1993:178); On advice of the President (Lews 1993:180); 18-block area (Lewis 1993:186); 835 hours (Lewis 1993:190); Not the first such statistical study (Deegan 2002:56–58); Most promising young sociologist (Lewis 1993:210); 10 percent of the city population (Du Bois 1996 [1899]:23); 1834 riot (Du Bois 1996 [1899]:27–28); 1838 new laws (Du Bois 1996 [1899]:371); Social classes (Du Bois 1996 [1899]:310–311; something less than American (Du Bois 1996 [1899]:284);

4. The Souls of Black Folk: In 1897 (Horne and Young 2001:xxv); Indignity of Jim Crow laws (Du Bois 1968:234); Sewage pollution (Marable 1986:30); Medical care for blacks (Lewis 1993:226–227); Research program (Du Bois 1968:217); Only institution in the nation (Du Bois 1968:215); In one such lynching (Lewis 1993:226); Talented Tenth (Gates and West 1997); Max Weber (Lewis 1993:277); Double consciousness (Du Bois 1993 [1903]:9–10); Sorrow songs (Du Bois 1993 [1903]:197–207); Second sight (Du Bois 1993 [1903]:9); Material gain (Du Bois 1993 [1903]:72).

5. Race, Class, and Africa: Insisted on total control (Du Bois 1968:257); Circulation of 100,000 (Lewis 2000:2); 300 branches (Marable 1986:97); End of infamous grandfather requirement (Du Bois 1968:260); Most well-known civil rights advocate (Marable 1986:97); Appeared stiff, cold, and even conceited (Marable 1986:98); Too focused on the middle class (Lacy 1970:58); Black population that worried (Lacy 1970:66); Attention to slight (Marable 1986:80); Treated him with condescension (Marable 1986:80); Chairman of Sociology (Du Bois 1968:439); Reduced his independence (Du Bois 1968:292); Supported women's suffrage (Horne and Young 2001:220); Impressed on a visit to Soviet Union (Du Bois 1968:290); Remained skeptical (DeMarco 1983:165–166); Conferences aimed to help (Horne and Young 2001:159); Military buildup and war (Adams and Sydie 2002:296); Abundant raw materials (Du Bois 2004:35); World dominance of Europe (Du Bois 1969 [1920]:39); Revising Marxist concepts (Du Bois 2004:132).

6. Legacy as a Social Theorist: Retired in 1944 (Du Bois 1968:323); Nina died (Du Bois 1968:367); Shirley Graham (Horne and Young 2001:61); Gave up hope in the United States (Lemert 2000:361); Demanded that he register as a foreign agent (Lacy 1970:107–108); Passport returned (Lacy 1970:112); Three historically black neighborhoods (Wilson 1999:480).

Index

CPSIA information can be obtained
at www.ICGtesting.com
Printed in the USA
LVHW080313310820
664616LV00017B/1558

9 780716 779155